Cyber Racism

Perspectives on a Multiracial America Series
Joe R. Feagin, Texas A&M University, series editor

The racial composition of the United States is rapidly changing. Books in the series will explore various aspects of the coming multiracial society, one in which European-Americans are no longer the majority and where issues of white-on-black racism have been joined by many other challenges to white dominance.

Titles:
Melanie Bush, *Breaking the Code of Good Intentions*
Amir Mavasti and Karyn McKinney, *Unwelcome Immigrants:*
    Middle Eastern Lives in America
Richard Rees, *Shades of Difference: A History of Ethnicity in America*
Katheryn Russell-Brown, *Protecting Our Own: Race, Crime, and*
    African Americans
Adia Harvey Wingfield, *Doing Business with Beauty: Black Women,*
    Hair Salons, and the Racial Enclave Economy
Erica Chito Childs, *Fade to Black and White: Interracial Images in*
    Popular Culture
Jessie Daniels, *Cyber Racism: White Supremacy Online and the New Attack on*
    Civil Rights

Forthcoming titles:
Elizabeth M. Aranda, *Emotional Bridges to Puerto Rico: Migration,*
    Return Migration, and the Struggles of Incorporation
Angela J. Hattery, David G. Embrick, and Earl Smith, *Globalization and*
    America: Race, Human Rights, and Inequality

Cyber Racism

White Supremacy Online
and the New Attack on Civil Rights

Jessie Daniels

ROWMAN & LITTLEFIELD PUBLISHERS, INC.
Lanham • Boulder • New York • Toronto • Plymouth, UK

ROWMAN & LITTLEFIELD PUBLISHERS, INC.

Published in the United States of America
by Rowman & Littlefield Publishers, Inc.
A wholly owned subsidiary of The Rowman & Littlefield Publishing Group, Inc.
4501 Forbes Boulevard, Suite 200, Lanham, Maryland 20706
www.rowmanlittlefield.com

Estover Road
Plymouth PL6 7PY
United Kingdom

British Library Cataloguing in Publication Information Available

Library of Congress Cataloging-in-Publication Data:

Daniels, Jessie, 1961–
  Cyber racism : white supremacy online and the new attack on civil rights / Jessie
Daniels.
     p. cm. — (Perspectives on a multiracial America series)
  Includes bibliographical references and index.
  ISBN 978-0-7425-6157-1 (cloth : alk. paper) — ISBN 978-0-7425-6158-8 (pbk. : alk.
paper) — ISBN 978-0-7425-6525-8 (electronic)
  1. White supremacy movements—United States. 2. Cyberbullying. I. Title.
  E184.A1D244 2009
  305.800973—dc22   2008049962

Printed in the United States of America

∞™ The paper used in this publication meets the minimum requirements of American
National Standard for Information Sciences—Permanence of Paper for Printed Library
Materials, ANSI/NISO Z39.48-1992.

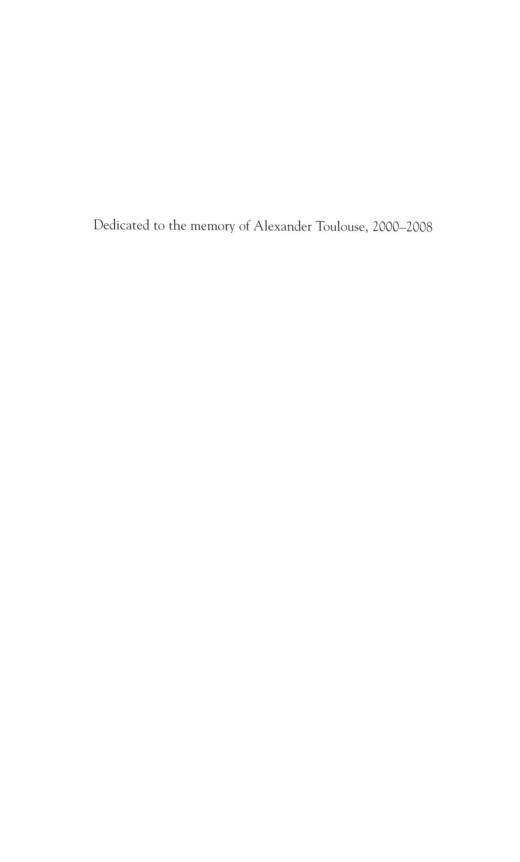

Dedicated to the memory of Alexander Toulouse, 2000–2008

Contents

List of Figures and Tables

Figures

Tables

~

Preface

I have spent almost ten years doing the research for, thinking about, and finally writing this book. In the pages that follow, I emphasize the importance of understanding standpoint when critically evaluating information on the Internet, so it seems only fitting that I should say something about my own relation to the text.

This book grows out of my experience with Internet technologies in a wide range of milieux but particularly from my time spent teaching with the aid of technology in the classroom in 1996 at a suburban, privately funded university. Students entering college for the first time in the fall of 2008 were born in 1990, about the same time the Internet began to emerge, and they have never known a time without its existence. Now I teach in a publicly funded urban university with students from a diverse range of backgrounds, most of whom have grown up digitally fluent. I wrote this book with them in mind.

My research is also informed by working in the Internet industry. For a time during what came to be known as the *dot-com boom* I left academia to serve as senior producer for Talk City, Inc., a firm that specialized in providing online community to a client list of Fortune 500 corporations. That foray provided me both insight into the culture that gave rise to the Internet industry and also some knowledge about the mechanics behind the seemingly automagical qualities of the Internet. That experience also taught me how very difficult it is to create online community in any predictable way.

Along the way I have had a great deal of fun with Internet technologies, meeting new friends, connecting with old friends, and starting (and abandoning) a number of websites, blogs, and other online spaces. Perhaps what I find most compelling about this new medium is that I have learned new things in and through Internet technologies. For someone who loves knowledge for the sake of knowledge, the Internet can seem like a paradise, and at times just wandering this vast universe has afforded me great pleasure. For almost as many years as this book has been in process, I have been involved in Brainstorms, an online community comprised of several hundred people from around the world. I have been privileged to meet many of those people in person, forming long-term friendships—and mourning the passing of one very good friend I met there. I also benefited from that community's material assistance, learning a valuable lesson about what Saskia Sassen calls the "imbrication of the digital and the material" (Sassen, 2002).

My standpoint is also informed by Internet technologies themselves and by myriad forms of activism I have participated in. I have volunteered my time in a number of Internet- and technology-related endeavors, including Computers for Youth (www.cfy.org), a New York City-based nonprofit. CFY distributes free computers equipped with educational software to low-income families in some of the city's poorest neighborhoods. I also volunteer to maintain the websites for my (queer) church and the shelter it sponsors for LGBTQ homeless youth; and these too are forms of online activism. In 2007, I (along with Joe Feagin) began Racism Review (racismreview.com), a blog by a group of scholar-activists who analyze current events through a critical-race lens.

My purpose in detailing this is to provide context for my digital-media research. For me, digital media is not merely an object of study, at some remove from the rest of my life. Rather, it permeates every aspect of my life. Yet while the Internet animates me as a source of seemingly endless fascination, most of the people who share this passion and who write the books I read about the Internet seem to regard the discussion of race and racism as irrelevant to this brave new world.

Alongside my enthusiasm for all things related to the Internet and digital media, I also have a lifelong interest, both professional and personal, in trying to understand and dismantle white supremacy. In the preface to my earlier book I wrote about my perspective as an antiracist, white lesbian growing up in a family who held decidedly racist values. After reading that preface, my father never spoke to me again and tried (unsuccessfully) to halt the book's publication. His response was a powerful reminder for me of how white supremacy, male dominance, and heteronormativity are interwoven. That experience also informs my analysis in this current book.

Upon learning that I grew up in Texas in the 1960s and 1970s and finished my graduate work at the University of Texas at Austin in the early 1990s, my academic colleagues and acquaintances often remark that, "Well, that's a good place to be from when studying white supremacy." And, indeed, it is. But Texas does not hold a monopoly on white supremacy. In fact, for more than a dozen years now I have lived and worked in New York City. For five of those years I directed a research project at Rikers Island, the city's largest jail. The fact that 95 percent of the people who are locked up at Rikers Island are African American and Latino (although black and brown folks make up only about half the city's total population), while the island of Manhattan is increasingly white and only affordable for the city's wealthiest residents, suggests to me that New York City is a very good place from which to understand how systematically white supremacy works.

Professionally, I have studied and written about racism and white supremacy in a variety of settings. Personally, I have tried in number of ways to challenge the corrosive legacy of white supremacy in my own life, through the people I choose to include in my life, through the institutions in which I choose to invest my time, through the books I decide to read, and through those that I write. Yet the people, the institutions, and the books I read concerned with *race* and dismantling systems of white supremacy are, for the most part, unconcerned with or even uninterested in the Internet.

Thus, my standpoint in this book is rooted in multiple worlds: In one the focus is on the Internet and how digital media shape life in the twenty-first century. In another the focus is on critically understanding racial inequality with an eye toward changing it. And in still another the focus is on gender, male dominance, and sexuality. In this book I aim to address these disparate conversations in ways that contribute new meaning to all of them.

As this book went into production, the United States elected Barack Obama, the first African American president. While some have speculated that this means we are entering a "postracial era," the increased popularity of white supremacy online suggests otherwise. In the days immediately following the election, so many people visited the white supremacist site Stormfront.org (discussed at length in this volume) that the increased traffic caused their servers to crash.

~

Acknowledgments

A project spanning as many years as this one has incurs a long list of debts, and I can only offer inadequate repayment.

I am grateful to two foundations that financially supported this work. The Third Millennium Foundation, a private foundation directed by Marco Stoffel, invited me to be their inaugural scholar-in-residence in 2005 and 2006 at their International Center on Tolerance Education. Marco's enthusiasm for my work, and the fellowship he awarded me, presented me with a wealth of additional opportunities, including the leisure to reflect, a beautiful space in which to do so, partial funding for my research, and a number of chances to present my work to others. In particular, as scholar-in-residence I was able to attend the Law and Cyberspace conference in Brno, Czech Republic; introducing my work to an international audience was invaluable in shaping this book. Through my role in the foundation I also met and exchanged ideas with a wide range of prominent national and international scholars, too numerous to list, who are all committed to halting the intergenerational transmission of hate and intolerance; special thanks, though, go to Dina Borzekowski at Johns Hopkins University, who visited the foundation and suggested I use the talk-aloud method, which I did. During my time with the foundation I helped develop a DIY video competition concerning tolerance that eventually became the Seeds of Tolerance competition, which aired on Current TV in the fall of 2007. The staff at the Third Millennium Foundation, including Veronique

Graham, Connie J. Kendig, and Carole Stakenas, offered tremendous enthusiasm for my scholarship as well as strategic assistance with the logistics of foundation support. And a number of incredibly bright and capable interns at the foundation, especially Nieema Galloway, Sophia Hoffman, Sana Khan, and Julia McCann, provided important research assistance. My experience as scholar-in-residence at the International Center on Tolerance Education not only advanced this project but also led to further successes, including support from another foundation.

I am indebted to the John D. and Catherine T. MacArthur Foundation for their support and for inviting me to participate in their Digital Media and Learning series, a program that should serve as a model for funders interested in cultivating new fields of study. Through the foundation I was able to publish in an edited volume, take advantage of a small financial grant, and converse, both online and in person, with similarly engaged colleagues at other institutions across a range of disciplines. The MacArthur Foundation's furtherance, and the colleagues I met as a result, profoundly shaped this work. I am particularly grateful to everyone who closely read the manuscript, commented on it, and challenged me to improve it, especially Dara Byrne, Michael Carter, Anna Everett, Raiford Guin, Frances J. Harris, Henry Jenkins, Tara McPherson, and Doug Thomas. My thanks also extend to those who generously gave of their time to participate in the online forum, including Mary Jo Deegan, Joe Feagin, Beverly Ray, Catherine Smith, and Kalí Tal.

Howard Rheingold, writer, futurist, and Internet pioneer, started and maintains the online community Brainstorms, and in 1999 he generously invited me to join. Since then that community has become an important part of my life, and the several hundred people from around the world who comprise Brainstorms create both virtual and real-life community for me. During a period of personal upheaval Brainstorm's members offered concrete support, helping me locate and secure a job and housing in a world entirely foreign to me, Silicon Valley. While I pursued projects other than this book, a number of people at Brainstorms sustained interest in the ideas that eventually became the manuscript and offered their insightful commentary; I thank Janette Agguar, Hadar Aviram, Glen Blankenship, Michael D. C. Bowen, Charles Cameron, Steve Cisler, Brad Esau, Greg Esau, Cheryl Fuller, Kate Gilpin, Karen Hanson, Kristie Helms, Jim Lai, Annette Leung, Janice MacDonald, Kellie Parker, Lester Spence, Bob Watson, Jana Wright, and Paul Younghouse.

I am most grateful to a number of individuals and organizations who refined my scholarship by engaging in clarifying dialogue or by inviting me to present my findings to an audience. In particular, Brian Marcus at the Anti-

Defamation League (ADL) conversed with me on numerous occasions about our shared interests and my work and invited me to the 2005 conference at ADL headquarters, cohosted by the International Network against Cyber Hate (INACH), which addressed international hate online. Catherine Smith and Kenneth Stern, whom I met at that conference, offered critical research assistance with the book: Kenneth is part of the American Jewish Committee and generously shared about his son's brushes with hate online, graciously allowing me to relay that story in the course of my work; meanwhile, Catherine Smith and the University of Denver law school librarians uncovered reference materials pertaining to international law and hate. Mark Weitzman, director of the New York Tolerance Center of the Simon Wiesenthal Center, shared with me his own work addressing Holocaust denial and hate online and encouraged my investigations in the area. Lynne Fallwell invited me to present my work at the City College Center for Worker Education (CWE). Kallen Tsikalas and Nicole Wierzbicki asked me to share my research with the staff at Computers for Youth in New York City and challenged me to think about its implications for teaching Internet literacy. David Machacek's enthusiasm has been heartening, and on several occasions he has welcomed me to share my work with the Humanity in Action program. Cathy Davidson and David Theo Goldberg asked me to participate in the first conference of the Humanities, Arts, Science, and Technology Advanced Collaboratory (HASTAC) at Duke University in the spring of 2007. Presenting my work, along with contemplating the other conference lectures on race and the Internet, helped me hone significant portions of my research. And, perhaps more importantly, HASTAC introduced me to a new community of scholars investigating the very questions that interest me most—those regarding the interface between the digital and the material and regarding thinking "at the interface of everything."

I owe a debt of gratitude to my colleagues and students at the City University of New York (CUNY). The departments of Urban Public Health and Sociology have offered me teaching positions through which I have met some extraordinary students who are often nothing less than heroic in their pursuit of education in the face of adversity; they inspire me anew each semester, and much of this project was developed with them in mind. My colleagues in both departments, particularly Manfred Kuechler and Lynn Roberts, have expressed interest in and support for this research. In addition, Martin Dornbaum, documentary filmmaker and activist against the intergenerational transmission of hate, was an important ally, a valuable resource, and always an encouraging colleague at the Brookdale campus of Hunter College. And colleagues at CUNY Graduate Center, including Stanley

Aronowitz, Paul Attewell, Juan Battle, Patricia Cicento Clough, Victoria Pitts, Barbara Katz Rothman, and John Torpey, have offered inspiration and guidance either in person or through their writing. Rebecca Tiger took time away from completing her dissertation at the CUNY-Graduate Center to read and review several chapters and much improved them in the process. Two former research assistants, now colleagues, Sarah Bradley and Martine Hackett, provided research in the early stages of this work. And Sophie Statzel shared with me her own research into white supremacy online and invited me to participate in a conference on the far right that she helped organize at the CUNY-Graduate Center.

A number of friends and colleagues carefully read initial drafts of this work and offered valuable commentary. Joe Feagin's early enthusiasm for the scholarship, after reading the first iterations of several chapters, provided crucial incentive for completing the project; Joe also read several complete drafts and offered invaluable suggestions that made the work more coherent. Anna Everett read and commented on early drafts of what became chapters 4, 7, and 8, doubtlessly improving them significantly. Tyson Smith-Ray generously gave of her time to read several early chapters and offered feedback on their readability. To my treatment of the virtual community at Stormfront.org Kellie Parker brought her criminal-justice background and insight from her online-community management. Nance Bell spent hours reading and commenting on two drafts late in the writing process, posing critical questions about the intended audience, epistemology, and theory that guided my final shaping of the project. Andre Oboler read drafts of several chapters and encouraged me to more fully develop my analysis of anti-Semitism.

My colleague Chris Toulouse receives thanks for sharing his infectious enthusiasm for computers in the classroom and for convincing me back in 1996 of cyberspace's importance for sociologists interested in understanding twenty-first-century society. The kernel of the idea for this book began as a conversation with Chris on a Long Island Rail Road train from Brooklyn to Nassau County, where we both taught at Hofstra University. That idea grew and matured over several years through conversations with Chris, until eventually there were actual manuscript pages. Chris then read and thoughtfully analyzed that initial draft, offering particularly insightful perspective on the segments concerning globalization. And all through this process Chris and his partner, Bonnie Steinsnyder, have opened their home to me, cooked me meals, invited me to art openings, and generally provided life-sustaining friendship at crucial times.

Julie Netherland exceeded herself and any reasonable expectations of a committed partnership by reading every draft of every chapter, despite her own rather daunting responsibilities, and continually providing the best, most-nuanced read. Over the years that this book has been in process I have learned anew the physical and psychic conditions necessary to making the production of knowledge possible. Among the two or three things I know for sure (apologies to Dorothy Allison) is the conviction that I could not have produced any of this without Julie, because she makes everything else in my life possible.

Finally, the radical hospitality; racial, economic, and gender diversity; and unwavering commitment to social justice I find at Metropolitan Community Church of New York offer me spiritual sustenance that counterbalances what can be soul-destroying work. Rev. Pat Bumgardner, Rev. Edgard Danielsen-Morales and all the people at MCCNY remind me every day that the moral arc of the universe is long but bends toward justice.

Jessie Daniels
New York
March 9, 2009

PART ONE

INTRODUCTION

CHAPTER ONE

White Supremacy in the Digital Era

The Internet gives millions access to the truth that many didn't even know existed. Never in the history of man can powerful information travel so fast and so far. I believe that the Internet will begin a chain reaction of racial enlightenment that will shake the world by the speed of its intellectual conquest.

—David Duke

White supremacy has entered the digital era. Avowed white supremacist extremists, such as David Duke, who is quoted above, were early adopters[1] of digital-media technologies. They were among the first to create, publish, and maintain Web pages on the Internet. The reality that David Duke and other white supremacists were early adopters of digital media challenges prevailing notions about who white supremacists are and about the Internet. Many assume that white supremacists are gap-toothed, ignorant, unsophisticated, and uneducated; others believe that the Internet is a place without race. In fact, neither of these notions is supported by empirical evidence. White supremacists have customized Internet technologies in ways that are innovative, sophisticated, and cunning. And the Internet is an increasingly important front on the political struggle to contest the meanings of race, racism, and civil rights. The emergence of cloaked websites illustrates a central feature of propaganda and cyber racism in the digital era: the use of difficult-to-detect authorship and hidden agendas intended to accomplish political goals, including white supremacy.

Cyber racism, a term coined by Les Back and chosen as the title of this book, refers to a range of white supremacist movements in Europe and North America and to the new horizons the Internet and digital media have opened for expression of whiteness across national boundaries.[2] The empirical investigations in this book specifically reference the paradigm shift that global, digital, and participatory white supremacy represents in the Information Age. Furthermore, this study frames white supremacy as inherent to white identity and examines how this corrodes democratic ideals of equality. The emergence of the United States as a haven for global white supremacy online makes critical the discussion of whether America was built with white supremacy as a central guiding principle and whether equality is available to all citizens, regardless of race.

By focusing on cyber racism, and specifically on white supremacy, I do not mean to diminish the important progressive rhetoric and political-organizing work that is also generated online. Democratic movements, organized at the grassroots by people of good will with Internet-enabled mobile phones, have transformed elections.[3] In 2007, using e-mail, blogs, Facebook, MySpace, and YouTube, cyberactivists organized nearly ten thousand people to the march in protest against a white supremacist judicial system in Jena, Louisiana.[4] And almost ten years earlier black women excluded by the white-dominated mainstream media and the male-dominated African American press took advantage of the participatory quality of Internet technologies to organize the Million Woman March.[5] Many take these encouraging signs about the use of the Internet to mean that the technology itself is inherently democratizing, while others see the presence of white supremacy online as clear evidence that the Internet is a source of danger, which offers little that is of value to those committed to equality. My aim here is to challenge both these assumptions and to offer a more nuanced analysis that causes readers to rethink their preconceived notions about and means of researching racial equality and civil rights in the digital era.

Why Study White Supremacy Online?

Marx wrote, "The philosophers have only interpreted the world, in various ways; the point is to change it."[6] And so the main reason to study white supremacy online is, in my view, to challenge it; thus this book is about activism that opposes white supremacy as well as scholarship that aims to understand it. Still, it is fair to question the value of such study and most scholars (and authors) are accustomed to answering it. Why, you ask, should I care? When supremacist rhetoric existed in the print-only era, it was easier to dismiss their hardly ubiquitous publications as the rants of a lunatic fringe. Now, however, with such racist vitriol easy to locate online, an important shift has occurred: anyone with an Internet connection—from a sixth-grader doing a report on Martin Luther King Jr. to a disaffected, potentially violent skinhead—can find white supremacy online. However, distinguishing between those producing white supremacy online, those seeking it out, and those stumbling upon it by chance, or ascertaining how people, especially young people, make sense of white supremacy online, is a complicated proposition, much more complicated than the mainstream media's reports about the "dangers of the Internet" would suggest. So, why should you read this book? Because, in short, the presence of white supremacy online critically informs our understanding of global society, social movements, race, the Internet, and even how young people learn in the digital era, and this book helps make sense of all this. I expand on that answer—that this study makes a number of theoretical, methodological, and empirical contributions to a range of intellectual traditions and theoretical perspectives—in the next chapter.

Estimating the Global Reach of White Supremacy Online

A majority of all websites on the Internet originate in the United States. Not surprisingly, then, according to the Council of Europe (COE) the majority of hate websites are U.S.-based, with 2,500 out of 4,000 racist sites originating in the United States.[7] However, estimates on the total number of hates sites are wildly divergent and not very reliable.

One source from the United Kingdom estimated that there were as many as ten thousand[8] such sites online in 2004, while a different source, based in France, estimated that the number was upward of sixty thousand that same year.[9] The number cited by the British source is suspect, as it comes from a software company whose marketing strategy for selling their filtering software relies on emphasizing the perceived threat from these groups. The higher number courtesy of the French is possibly more reliable, but the source fails to explain how they arrived at these numbers, and they undoubtedly have their own organizational imperative for inflating numbers.

The lowest estimates come from the U.S.-based monitoring organization Southern Poverty Law Center (SPLC), which counted 762 active hate groups in 2004. This number was compiled using hate-group publications and websites, citizen and law-enforcement reports, field sources, and news reports. Websites that appear to be merely the work of a single individual, rather than the publication of a group, are not included on the list. Interpreting the SPLC's numbers is further complicated by region. While the UK and French estimates del include all websites globally, the SPLC estimate focuses on sites based in the United States. Yet such a criterion creates ambiguity, given how difficult it can be to determine ownership, residence, and server location of a domain name—all three of which can be different.

Realistically estimating the number of white supremacist sites is complicated by the difficulties inherent in evaluating content across languages. Cloaked websites further obscure defining what constitutes white supremacy in the digital era, since they appear to be legitimate sources of civil rights information yet actually disguise—or *cloak*—white supremacist content several page-layers down. Still, despite the difficulty of culling reliable statistics, most experts agree that the prevalence of white supremacist sites online with a global reach has increased and that the majority of these are based in the United States.

What Is the Harm of White Supremacy Online?

Given the information glut generated and made available every day on the Internet,[10] one could reasonably argue that white supremacists' messages might be lost among the millions and millions of websites on the Internet.[11] Even so, white supremacy online is troubling. Consider (1) its easy access and global linkages, (2) harm it may precipitate in real life, and (3) the challenge it presents to honoring cultural values such as racial equality.

Easy Access and Global Linkages

White supremacist discourse is certainly more accessible today, thanks to the Internet. As David Duke makes plain in the epigraph at the beginning of this chapter, more so than ever before in the print-only era, the Internet facilitates publication and distribution of white supremacist discourse and ideology for those committed to producing it and increases its availability to those interested in reading it. I know this from first-hand experience researching my books. For a previous book I wrote addressing print-based white supremacist discourse, I was faced with the option of either adding my name to the mailing list of various white supremacist groups (something I was not comfortable with ethically) or visiting the Klanwatch archive of white supremacist materials housed at the Southern Poverty Law Center (which I did). My research for this book did not necessitate physical travel, since I could easily find the material I needed for a discussion of white supremacist websites merely by sitting at any computer connected to the Internet.[12] Just as using the Internet facilitated my research in some ways,[13] so too does the Internet aid those interested in reading white supremacist rhetoric for the purpose of "racial enlightenment," as Duke suggests.

The capacity of the Internet to facilitate relatively inexpensive means of communication between and among people in dispersed geographic regions of the world is certainly one of the primary benefits white supremacists see in the medium. The fact that this communication can be encrypted and anonymous is appealing for a portion of white supremacists although certainly not all.[14] While anonymity is appealing for some, networked communication simultaneously reinforces what Back has referred to as a *translocal whiteness*[15]—that is, a form of white identity not tied to a specific region or nation but reimagined as an identity that transcends geography and is linked via a global network. Recruitment is often mentioned as the chief hazard of white supremacy online.[16] Although the Internet is a *potential* site for white supremacist recruitment, the empirical evidence suggests that, thus far, such groups have failed to fully realize this potential.[17] More sinister than possible recruitment is the Internet's capacity to globally link white supremacists, regardless of national boundaries, thus affirming translocal white identity.

Harm in Real Life

White supremacy online sometimes leads to violence, harassment, intimidation, and racial terror, transcending the virtual world to damage real, live human beings. In August 1999 Buford Furrow armed himself and walked into a Jewish daycare center in Los Angeles and opened fire, wounding five people, including three small children. Furrow told authorities that the shooting was "a wake-up call to America to kill Jews." He reportedly drew some of his inspiration for this attack from white supremacist websites. Similarly, extensive Internet files concerning white supremacist Eric Rudolph were found among the possessions of David Copeland, an engineer charged with three nail-bomb attacks on ethnic minorities and homosexuals in London in April 1999. In these attacks three people were killed and more than one hundred injured. Fortunately, these types of assaults are relatively rare; that is small consolation if you or someone you love are victims of a hate crime. This book discusses a number of cases in which white supremacist rhetoric online leads to harm in real life, and the analysis aims to balance these attacks' potential versus real threat.

Cultural Values: Eroding the Ideal of Racial Equality Online

The least-recognized—and, hence, most insidious—threat posed by white supremacy online is the epistemological menace to our accumulation and production of knowledge about race, racism, and civil rights in the digital era. As David Duke suggests in the above epigraph, his goal in bringing white supremacy to the Internet is "racial enlightenment" by making "the truth" available to millions. Duke's brand of white supremacy undermines hard-won political battles for racial and ethnic equality by rearticulating an essentialist notion of white racial purity borrowing the rhetoric of civil rights. This is an example of the epistemology of white supremacy, "an inverted epistemology," as philosopher Charles W. Mills has noted, "an epistemology of ignorance," ironically resulting in whites generally being "unable to understand the world that they themselves have made."[18] The epistemology of white supremacy reinforces the white racial frame by allowing whites to retreat from pluralistic civic engagement into a whites-only digital space where they can question the cultural values of tolerance and racial equality unchallenged by anyone outside that frame.

As the lived experience of the civil rights movement fades with time, hard-won political truths about racial equality, secured at great cost, slide into mere personal opinion, open to multiple interpretations. Two cases (discussed at length in chapter 8) illustrate what is at stake here. The first presents a young woman who reads a cloaked white supremacist site that describes American slavery as a "sanitary, humane, relaxed" institution; she remarks, "Well, I guess there's two sides to everything." In another instance, yet another young woman, reading a legitimate civil rights site associated with the King Center in Atlanta, questions the site's validity because "it's created by his widow, so it could be biased." The two sites and how each is misinterpreted suggest that the very ideas of civil rights and racial equality are eroded within a digital media landscape that equalizes all websites. While each site presents information from differing points of view, merely suggesting that both are biased misunderstands the larger meaning here. It is precisely taking into account the *standpoint* of the site and the reader—whether situated in the white supremacist movement or in the struggle for civil rights and against racism—that facilitates the more accurate reading. The issue of deciding what is biased and what is not is inherently political. And on the Internet making this distinction is even more complicated.

Search engines have replaced libraries for young people in the digital age.[19] Consequently, the Internet is often the first, and sometimes *only*, source that young people consult when researching race. A random sample survey conducted in 2005 by the Pew Internet & American Life Project con-cluded that over 80 percent of teens in the United States are connected to the Web.[20] My preliminary research of a nonrandom, online sample suggests that a significant portion of teens connected to the Internet conduct online research (84 percent), and of those a large proportion (over 63 percent) have sought civil rights information online.[21] Whether it is youth of color explor-ing the history and political struggles of their own racial and ethnic heritage, white youth attempting to understand diverse "others," or youth of any given ethnicity attempting to craft a personal identity from the clues offered on-line, search engines are often the first and only information destinations for young researchers. Thus, the early emergence and persistent presence of white supremacy online calls for multiple literacies: one of digital media and one not merely of tolerance but of social justice, which offers a depth of un-derstanding about race, racism, and multiple, intersecting forms of oppres-sion and civil rights in the digital era.

Some Parameters and Definitions

This book is about white supremacy online in the context of globalization. I am primarily interested in understanding the obstacles and passageways to working toward a racially just and equitable future by articulating the con-verging relationship between the social forces of the Internet, white su-premacy, and global society. In keeping with that overall goal, I am also partly interested in organized white supremacist social movements and the way the Internet affects the discourse of those social-movement organiza-tions; however, I am less interested in exploring the supposed pathologies of individuals who possess a racist mind[22] or a racist self[23] and leave that to other scholars. Rather, I am more interested in the interplay between the ex-tremist expressions of white supremacy and broader cultural expressions of systemic racism and the white racial frame. Furthermore, rather than focus-ing on the back stories of ideologues who create white supremacy online, I am interested in how young people make sense of the white supremacist sites they encounter online. I concur with leading scholars who have long held that racialized masculinity is constitutive of white supremacy[24] and relation-ships online,[25] so a gendered analysis scaffolds much of my interrogation here. I see tremendous potential in digital media for civic engagement and a reenergized democratic future, yet my research indicates a number of ways in which this future is threatened. Therefore, this book is meant to navigate a narrow ledge between the all-too-common rhetoric of moral panic over the dangers of the Internet (especially when the subject is white supremacy) and the uncritical glee over digital media's transformative potential (especially where race and gender are concerned).

Throughout the book I use a number of specific terms that I intend to clarify with the following.

White Supremacy

White supremacy in the United States is a central organizing principle of social life rather than merely an isolated social movement.[26]

Race

Race, as I use the term, is a constructed identity and social category with boundaries that are permeable. The notion that there are distinct races of people is relatively new, historically speaking.[27] While genetic research revives the debate as to whether or not there exists a biological basis for racial categories,[28] I do not subscribe to this view.

Systemic Racism

W. E. B. Du Bois wrote that the "problem of the twentieth century is the problem of the color line."[29] Now at the beginning of a new century we continue to grapple with this problem. Du Bois, along with a number of other scholars in sociology and other disciplines, has written extensively about racism as an endemic feature of modern society.[30] The term, as I use it here, refers to the way that enduring racial stereotypes, ideas, images, emotions, proclivities, and practices have thoroughly pervaded social, cultural, and economic institutions. Though systemic racism has undergone significant changes over time, primarily through the political struggles organized by people of color, it yet remains a central feature in most major social institutions.[31] Joe R. Feagin has transformed this idea into a theory that explains the American context and argues that systemic racism is a mechanism for maintaining racial inequality that developed with European colonialism, particularly as an ideological justification for the Atlantic-basin slave trade and slavery plantations.[32] The slave-based economic systems generated the wealth on which modern Europe and the United States are based.

White Racial Frame

In his *Frame Analysis*, Erving Goffman was the first sociologist to develop the notion of frames.[33] His idea was widely adopted by sociologists interested in the study of social movements, and an important trend of identifying concepts as frames has since developed. The term *frame* refers to the set of labels that *receivers* affix to social phenomena so as to make sense of them. Building on this sociological tradition and merging it with his explanation of the systemic racism that characterizes the U.S. experience, Feagin has developed the notion of the *white racial frame* that includes the following dimensions: (1) a white racial framing of society with its racist ideology, stereotypes, and emotions; (2) whites' discriminatory actions and an enduring racial hierarchy; and (3) pervasively racist institutions maintained by discriminatory whites over centuries. The extensive rationalizing of the white racial frame began in the 1600s as a justification for the economic and racial hierarchy of colonialism and continues even today through constant reinforcement.[34]

Globalization

Globalization can be broadly defined as the movement of money (capital) and people (labor) across time, space, and national boundaries.[35] Globalization also refers to a cultural process that accompanies these flows of capital and labor.[36] Here I am primarily interested in the latter, specifically the dialectical way that white supremacy online shapes—and is shaped by—cultural values in the United States and in turn the way white supremacy online shapes a translocal white identity and a transnational white supremacist culture. Racism has always been an essential condition for capital accumulation and expansion, and that is true in the current era of globalization. Yet, globalization, in its present phase, is also producing a number of contradictions that are relevant for the analysis that follows.[37] Some scholars contend that globalization and the emergence of the Internet represent an important realignment of power away from nation-states.[38] Others scholars disagree, saying that globalization requires the existence of a strong state to (1) manage rule making and organization so that a stable environment exists to facilitate global investment and (2) maintain social order as global capitalism works against the redistribution of wealth.[39] More recently scholars have noted that rather than undermining state power, the Internet has been utilized by the joined forces of repressive governments (China) and Internet-technology firms (Google) to control and limit access to certain types of content (about democracy) within specific geographic boundaries. Later I will return to the implications globalization, the Internet, and the power of nation-states have in the fight against white supremacy.

Internet

Precisely defining *the Internet*—or *cyberspace*—can be tricky. Take, for example, the much-maligned attempt made by U.S. Senator Ted Stevens (R-Alaska), who advised his colleagues on the Senate floor that "the Internet is not something that you just dump something on. It's not a big truck. It's a series of tubes."[40] Stevens's unintentionally humorous description was mercilessly satirized in the blogosphere and by late-night comedians. It is ironic that someone empowered to legislate the Internet so profoundly misunderstands the medium. Still, Stevens's blunder is perhaps explicable, as there is no clear and consistent definition for *the Internet* or *information technology*.[41] One fairly basic definition maintains that information technology (IT) refers "only to computer-based systems" and the software and hardware that make up computer-based systems.[42] While this is a portion of what I consider to be IT, it fails to capture the current technological moment in which digital technologies are shifting away from desktop computing to mobile, wireless, and ubiquitous computing through small, handheld devices.[43] In this book, I use interchangeably the terms *Internet, information technology* (or *IT*), *Web, digital technologies*, and occasionally *cyberspace*.[44] I adopt DiMaggio and colleagues' definition of the Internet as the "electronic networks that connect people and information through computers and other digital devices allowing person-to-person communication and information retrieval."[45]

Though we have yet to define it precisely, the Internet has had an enormous impact on society, as observed by a number of sociologists and various social commentators. In his three-volume work, *The Rise of the Network Society*, Manuel Castells contends that the Internet's societal influence will ultimately be comparable to that of the invention of the alphabet.[46] Barry Wellman asserts that the Internet has contributed to a shift from a group-based society to a network-based society and that this shift is decoupling community and geography.[47] Saskia Sassen claims that the Internet is "a crucial force for new forms of civic participation"[48] and that Internet technology "brings with it a destabilizing of older hierarchies of scale and often dramatic rescalings."[49] DiMaggio and colleagues much more cautiously argue that Internet technology has transformative potential for society, noting that "the economic and psychological dynamics of Web-based human communication . . . are potentially distinct enough from those of traditional print and broadcast news media that in time we may see evidence of the Internet effect."[50] While none of the academics here posit a unidirectional relationship between Internet technology and society, their assertions about the transformational potential of the Internet are relevant to discussions of race, racism, and white supremacy in the digital era.

Globalization and the Internet are often touted as liberatory, beneficial, or even the "key to ensuring a lifetime of success," as suggested by Al Gore (among others).[51] Yet globalization—*a process*—and the Internet—*a network* of communication technologies*—come together in seemingly contradictory ways. On the one hand globalization and the Internet have combined to foster new economic growth, common cultural values, an undermining of locally driven prejudices, and greater awareness of other cultures.[52] On the other hand critics contend that this economic growth has benefited only an elite few and that globalization has led to increasing economic inequality, an intensification of racism and national chauvinism, and a willingness to restrict civil liberties and democracy.[53]

The Organization of the Book

In the chapter that follows, I take up several of the more theoretical questions concerning white supremacy online, particularly as related to epistemology, race, and the Internet within the context of globalization. Part II is an examination of white supremacy in a global context, and as such I contrast individual acts of white supremacy with white supremacist online social movements. I discuss the case of Richard Machado, a Mexican-American student at UC, Irvine, convicted of violating the civil rights of Asian students on campus when he sent them racist e-mails. I then turn to the subject of white supremacist social movements online and the distinctions between varying degrees of involvement.

In part III, I continue the empirical investigation of white supremacy online in four chapters that each address white supremacist discourse as it has moved from the print-only era to the digital era. In chapter 5, I look at gender and white supremacy online within a global context; specifically, I juxtapose a transnational "ladies only" discussion board at a white supremacist site with two case studies of virtual and actual harassment by white supremacists. In chapter 6, I follow the translation of five previously print-only white supremacist publications onto the Web to examine how social movement discourse has, or has not, changed for each. In chapter 7, I address *cloaked sites*, which at first appear to be legitimate civil rights sites but are in fact fronts for white supremacist sites. These digital forms of propaganda have significance for contested racial politics within a global context of networked information. In chapter 8, I move beyond a text-only analysis of the discourse of websites and begin to consider how their audience makes sense of them,[54] with a particular focus on young people interpreting cloaked white supremacist sites.

In the final section, part IV, I look at what is being done to combat online white supremacy in the digital era. In chapter 9, I explore the oppositional transnational efforts by individuals, organizations, and governments. Most nations in the industrialized North and West view racism on- and offline radically differently from their counterparts in the United States, who are fond of protecting even bigotry as free speech. And, finally, in chapter 10, I address racial justice and civic engagement in the digital era, arguing that while the white racial frame complicates identifying white supremacy on- and offline, the task is made clearer with critical race consciousness. I conclude this chapter and the book by calling for a complete reassessment of how we acquire and produce knowledge about race in a global networked era and how this informs social movement organizing, pedagogical practice, and engagement in civil society and life in a democracy.

Notes

David Duke 2007.

1. Rogers 1995.
2. Back 2002a.
3. Rheingold 2002.
4. Krigman 2007.
5. Everett 2004.
6. Marx 1845.
7. Council of Europe 2003.
8. This estimate is provided by SurfControl.com and was cited in an article by Rawlson O'Neil King (2004).
9. Marc Knobel, founder of *J'accuse*, a French association combating Internet racism, quoted in Julio Godoy (2004).
10. Shenk 1997.
11. Indeed, as Michael R. Best observes, "I have been online since the 1980s and have never seen such hate material on the Net. I am quite certain I can seek it out. But it does not come at the 'flick of a switch.' I would view this material only because I actively sought it" (2004).
12. Such accessibility has precipitated a notable rise in the number and range of scholars investigating white supremacy online. Visiting sites online raises its own ethical-research dilemmas, which I discuss in the methods appendix.
13. It is important to note, however, that there are some ways in which conducting online research is even *more* challenging than consulting an archive of printed materials. Consider the constantly shifting universe of the sample, the difficulty locating websites, and the fact that these sites frequently go 404 (or are no longer available). For further discussion of these issues, see the methods appendix.
14. Bostdorff 2004. See also Thiesmeyer (1999).
15. Back 2001.

16. Typical of this sort of alarm is Karen Mock's concern that "millions of people are being exposed to virulent anti-Semitism and hate propaganda at the flick of a switch on their computers." (2000). This is the statement that Best is critiquing in note 11 above. See also Lamberg (2001).

17. Ray and Marsh 2001.

18. Mills 1997.

19. Harris 2005.

20. Lenhart, Madden, and Hitlin 2005.

21. Daniels 2008b, 95–116.

22. Ezekiel 1995.

23. Blee 2003.

24. See especially Blee (2003) and Burlein (2003). See also Ferber (1998).

25. Kendall 2002.

26. Daniels 1997, 11.

27. Snowden 1983.

28. Duster 2003.

29. Du Bois 1903/1989.

30. See, for example, Cox (1948), Patricia Hill Collins (2004), Barlow (2003), Bonilla-Silva (2001), and Winant (2001).

31. Feagin 2006b, 8.

32. Personal e-mail communication with Feagin, 2006.

33. Goffman 1974.

34. Feagin 2006b, 8.

35. Sassen 1998.

36. Jameson and Miyoshi 1998.

37. Barlow 2003.

38. Sassen 1996.

39. Barlow 2003, 72.

40. Singel and Poulsen 2006.

41. Leggon 2006, 100.

42. Freeman and Aspray 1999, 25.

43. Rheingold, 2002, 26.

44. Of these terms, *cyberspace* is the most contested (see Agre 2002b), and so I use it with caution and acknowledge the discussion surrounding it.

45. DiMaggio, Hargittai, Neuman, and Robinson 2001, 307.

46. Castells 1996. See also Castells 1997, 1998.

47. Wellman, Salaff, Dimitrova, Garton, and Haythornthwaite 1996.

48. Sassen 2002, 368.

49. Sassen 2002, 371.

50. DiMaggio et al. 2001, 320.

51. Al Gore (frequently misquoted as claiming to have invented the Internet) was as vice president of the United States of America one of the chief proponents of

the new technology. In a speech in 1998 to the Democratic Leadership Conference, for example, he said that "in the Information Age, connecting all people to a universe of knowledge and learning is the key to ensuring a lifetime of success" (Gore 1998). This view of the Internet as a key to a benevolent form of globalization is pervasive beyond the realm of political speeches. See, for example, Houston (2003), in which he answers his own question in the affirmative. He writes, "Areas enmeshed in cultural traditionalism and yoked to political repression have the most to gain from the Internet's development. In those places, individuals can use the Internet to join a globalized middle class—a worldwide psychological support system. We should work to expand the Internet not merely because it expands economic activity but also because it expands individual liberty" (368).

52. Cowen 1998. Brown and Duguid 2000. Ridley 1997. Rothkopf 1997.

53. Barlow 2003, 77; Mark Abrahamson 2004, 95–120.

54. For more about the methodology used in this book, see the methods appendix.

CHAPTER TWO

Theorizing White Supremacy Online

Race is under construction in cyberspace.

—Lisa Nakamura

The Internet and the stories we tell about it have become our collective vision of the future. One of the pervasive myths about the Internet is that it allows us to escape race, racism, and racial inequality. In the late 1990s this notion was evocatively captured in a television advertisement for telecom giant MCI when the narrator assured the viewer that "Here, there is no race" and then asked rhetorically, "Utopia?" The answer: "No, Internet."[1] That the Internet might allow us to escape from embodiment, from racial and gender identity, and, indeed, from oppression and inequality altogether is a powerful idea that resonates broadly in mainstream, post–civil rights era U.S. culture, as well as in much of the social theory developed to explain the Internet. Yet the presence of white supremacy online debunks the myth and necessitates a critical inspection of race and the Internet from a sociological perspective.

Social theories about race and the Internet can help make sense of white supremacy in the digital era. Unfortunately, most theories about race do not take the Internet into account, and most theories about the social aspects of the Internet do not take race into account. Sociologists, for reasons that remain puzzling to me, have been generally slow to take up the challenge of studying the Internet,[2] particularly those interested in the intersections of race, class and, gender. Daniel Bell, writing in the 1970s, was among the earliest sociologists to study digital media.[3] Sociology's major theoretical traditions each have different insights regarding the Internet. Marxists tend to focus on elite control of production and politics through cultural hegemony and increased surveillance.[4] Weberians emphasize elements of rationalization facilitated by the Internet's capability to reduce limits of time and space, and they highlight distinctive status cultures within the digital-media landscape.[5] Durkheimians focus attention on the way digital media reinforce shared cultural values and organic solidarity.[6] Critical theorists problematize the effects of technological change on political deliberation and the integrity of civil society.[7] Notably absent from any of these mainstream analyses of the sociology of the Internet is any discussion of race. Imminent sociologist W. E. B. Du Bois is frequently left off the roster of founding sociologists, and I do not mean to repeat that mistake here. Cultural critic Kalí Tal was among the first to point out that Du Bois' work offers sophisticated tools for the analysis of cyberculture, in part because of African Americans' experience of liminality as a result of hundreds of years of racist oppression.[8]

Understanding Race in the Information Age

The Information Age is as racialized as the previous Industrial Age. In her book *Cybertypes* cultural studies scholar Lisa Nakamura criticizes the notion that the Internet is a raceless utopia and demonstrates precisely how, using interface design elements like pull-down menus with categorical lists of racial and ethnic identities, the online world reproduces racial identity constructed offline. Nakamura coined the term *identity tourism*[9] to describe "the process by which members of one group try on for size the descriptors generally applied to persons of another race or gender."[10] The link between racial oppression and visibility has been discussed eloquently by African American scholars since Du Bois[11] and emerges in discussion of race, as in this passage from Mark Hansen:

> The suspension of the social category of visibility in online environments transforms the experience of race in what is potentially a fundamental way: by suspending the automatic ascription of racial signifiers according to visible traits, online environments can, in a certain sense, be said to subject everyone to what I shall call a *zero degree* of racial difference.[12]

Yet the supposed invisibility online and the "decoupling identity from any analogical relation to the visible body" rests in part on an assumption that the Internet is an exclusively text-based medium in which racial identity is not visible.[13] While that may have been true at one point in time or may be true today in certain online contexts, it does not adequately describe the majority of life online now. Today's Internet is full of digital video, photographic technologies (such as webcams[14]), photo-sharing sites (like Flickr.com), and video-sharing sites (like YouTube.com). Most social-networking sites—such as MySpace.com and Facebook.com—prominently feature digital photos and videos that serve as important markers of digital representation and identity for the users. (Indeed, as the name *Facebook* suggests, the notion of linking visual representation of the physical body to text is the whole point.) And in the white supremacist online forum Stormfront.org, each registered user chooses a digital photo or graphic representation of their online identity. Clearly visual technologies inherently link the physical to the gendered and racialized virtual world. Furthermore, empirical research increasingly demonstrates that people go online, even to text-only online spaces, not in search of some disembodied libertarian utopia but to engage in the construction and affirmation of embodied racial identities,[15] and these identities are in turn shaped by power relations.[16] To the extent that race is ever discussed in scholarly literature about the Internet, it is usually framed around issues of racial and ethnic *identity*, with precious little discussion devoted to issues of race and epistemology as they relate to life online.

Epistemology and White Supremacy Online

The presence of white supremacy online raises some compelling questions of epistemology—the investigation of how we actually know what we claim to know. David Duke and other white supremacists like him have a vested interest in redefining truth in ways that promote their versions of racial enlightenment and that undermine racial equality. The fact that in the digital era white supremacists online have rebranded racial truths calls into question any cultural value that asserts racial equality, since the rebranding calls into question what constitutes the truth we say we know about race, racism, and racial inequality.

Traditional epistemologies tied to enlightenment notions of reason and objectivity divorced from lived experience suggest that universal Truth is knowable. Scientists committed to such an epistemology follow strict methodological rules intended to distance themselves from the values, vested interests, and emotions generated by their race, class, gender, sexuality, or unique lived experience.[17] Despite these aspirations, though, both empiricism and rationalism have facilitated racism from the seventeenth century onward, as David Theo Goldberg has thoroughly documented in his book *Racist Culture*. As a consequence, race is one of the central conceptual inventions of modernity, one that shapes our perceptions of *social subjects*, fellow human beings, in primarily racial terms.[18] As for understanding racial inequality, this sort of epistemology detached from an acknowledged awareness of race is what philosopher Charles W. Mills calls "an inverted epistemology, an epistemology of ignorance, . . . producing the ironic outcome that whites will in general be unable to understand the world that they themselves have made."[19] What follows from this epistemology is a white racial *frame*, or lens, though which the social world is interpreted and misunderstood.[20] White supremacy online is founded in an epistemology of ignorance in which whites who adopt the white racial frame are unable to see the worlds they have created and their privileged position within it but instead configure themselves as victims.

Some feminists and postmodern theorists argue that knowledge is always partial, situated, and embodied.[21] Such an epistemology renders universal Truth an impossibility, since only a relational truth between knower and known is possible. Postmodern epistemologies also call into question the notion of social justice (if not render it altogether impossible), since without Truth there is no standard from which to judge justice.[22] In many ways cyberspace is the realization of postmodern epistemologies, creating an unrestricted publication of ideas without reference to the traditional publishing gatekeepers and allowing identity formation wholly unconnected to geographically rooted identities. In this new digital era all ideas, and indeed all our identities, are up for renegotiation. White supremacy online exploits uniquely Web-based mechanisms to undermine civil rights and values of racial equality with overtly racist and anti-Semitic speech. As such, we must reexamine how we make and evaluate knowledge claims and reconceive our vision for social justice in this new digital terrain. These competing epistemologies create a theoretical impasse, with one rooted in Enlightenment ideals of objective truth, supposedly disconnected from lived experience, and the other recognizing lived experience, without any ethical ground on which to found claims of social justice.

Sociologist Patricia Hill Collins suggests a possible resolution by offering a third alternative—an epistemology in which ideas cannot be divorced from the individuals who create and share them. Instead, Collins's black, feminist epistemology establishes lived experience, ethics, and reason as interconnected, essential components for assessing knowledge claims.[23] Since values are the heart of the knowledge-validation process in this alternative epistemology, inquiry always has an ethical aim. And it is imperative that those who value racial equality not only have an apparatus for evaluating knowledge claims but also train their focus on the ethical aim of racial equality. Thus, this third, alternative epistemology of black feminist thought is crucial for evaluating the knowledge claims in white supremacy online that challenge the basis of racial equality.

This investigation into white supremacy online also raises theoretical questions about how social movement rhetoric differs online and in print. It also raises questions about how social movements with vested political interests use digital media to contest what is true and what is not. Those who produce and participate in white supremacy have not adapted uniformly to the advent of the Internet. Some white supremacists who have maintained a continuous presence in print for many years are not online today. Others that once published white supremacist newsletters have simply copied and pasted printed text onto one-way information transfer brochure-like websites. And others still have been incredibly savvy, even prescient, in understanding the potential of the Internet for furthering their ideological goals. This technologically evolved white supremacy is especially menacing when we remember that young people are increasingly much more likely to research using a search engine than consulting a traditional library collection. What is at stake for the future of political truths won in the sphere of public opinion concerning racial equality and civil rights? Sociologist Manuel Castells argues that social movements in the Information Age try to influence cultural values. I concur and argue that white supremacy online is undermining the value of racial equality. Whether or not that is a shared value (as Durkheimians might suggest) or simply reflects the systemic racism and white racial frame that sustains and reinforces an enduring racial inequality (as Feagin suggests) will be addressed at length throughout the text.

Words that Wound in the Information Age

White supremacy online is a global issue and creates new challenges for critical race theory—and specifically for the idea that words can wound (that is, that hate speech causes real harm in real life). Critical race theory places race at the center of the analysis with the stories of victims of hate speech as the starting point. Those who believe that speech can do lasting harm understand the urgency of addressing the problems posed by white supremacy online.

After the UN's 2001 World Conference on Racism in South Africa identified the Internet as a crucial mechanism for both spreading and combating "racism, racial hatred, xenophobia, racial discrimination," and related intolerance, a number of nations decided to address online racism. In 2002, for example, the Acting Race Discrimination Commissioner of Australia, Dr. William Jonas, convened a symposium on cyber racism to raise awareness and generate policy options. In 2003 the Council of Europe (COE), comprised of forty-four member states, drafted a protocol intended to shut down racist and xenophobic websites. The protocol, signed by twelve member states, reflects a strong European stance against hate speech online and stands in stark contrast to the American view that white supremacist rhetoric ought to be protected as free speech. One legal scholar refers to these divergent reactions to white supremacy online as "the U.S.–Europe cyberhate divide."[24] The cyberhate divide also means that the United States is the global destination of choice for those wishing to create and distribute white supremacy online without fear of prosecution. It is critically important that we consider white supremacy online in a global context and understand how the United States' position on "protected speech" undermines global efforts to combat this insidious racism.

Research Design and Methodological Framework

Sociology's established research design and methodologies are in a state of flux, sending scholars scrambling to determine which methods are suitable to the task of investigating society in the digital era. Faced with such a transformation in the discipline's established research design and methodologies, I chose to adapt traditional research-design frameworks and methods and improvise some new elements. The overall design of this study was inspired by Wendy Griswold's conceptualization of the *"cultural diamond."* In her conceptualization Griswold estab-lishes four connected points that are crucial to the analysis of any cultural artifact—*producer, text, social context,* and *audience*.[25] For my purposes I adapted Griswold's diamond for use with digital media. I explore a range of white supremacist websites as texts and also examine producers and texts through postings at the white supremacist discussion boards at Stormfront.org. In this, I drew on the few but important exemplars of virtual ethnographies.[26] Throughout this book I explore the social context, both North American and transnational, in which white supremacy online appears using a variety of secondary sources.

I was also interested in how young people who might be considered an audience for white supremacist sites made sense of what they inadvertently encountered while searching for information online. There is a growing and widely interdisciplinary field of digital media and learning that examines how the Internet is transforming social life and learning, particularly for young people who have grown up with digital technologies.[27] While some important work looking at race online has been undertaken in this field,[28] to date there are only a handful of studies that specifically seek to understand how young learners are affected by white supremacy online.[29] This study is intended to contribute to that emerging field of study by considering just such a link.

I employed a mixed-method study design and selected the most efficacious method for answering the theoretical questions I wanted to explore.[30] These methods include ethnographic observation of a white supremacist online forum; qualitative-discourse analysis of Web text and graphic design, layout, and images; secondary analysis of Web analytics; case studies; and autoethnography. In addition, I developed an innovative combination of experiment, usability study, and in-depth interview in which I asked young people to try and distinguish between legitimate civil rights websites and cloaked white supremacist sites (see methods appendix for further discussion).

What I found from this mixed-method analysis is that old forms of overt white supremacy (e.g., racist hate speech) have entered the digital era alongside new, emergent forms of white supremacy that include mass e-mail, user names, participatory discussion boards, overtly racist online games, and covertly racist websites with obfuscated propaganda addressing the meaning of civil rights. What I found from talking with young people is both disturbing and heartening: today's urban, multicultural, Internet-savvy youth are not likely to be recruited into white supremacist organizations merely by stumbling upon a website; that said, most of those I interviewed had difficulty distinguishing between cloaked white supremacist websites and legitimate civil rights websites.

Social-Movement Rhetoric in Print and Online: A Naturally Occurring Experiment

In his analysis of "virtual fascism in cyberculture," Les Back asserts that there is both little discussion in the literature that examines the ways in which the extreme right has utilized the medium and almost no understanding of how white supremacy online might relate to its previous media incarnations.[31] Antecedent to my study is another in which I examined white supremacist discourse in printed media; specifically, I analyzed over three hundred individual newsletters published by five different white supremacist groups, identifying themes in text and images.[32] The sample for that study spanned the years 1970 to 1993, and that arbitrary end date turned out to be significant. Shortly after 1993 white supremacists such as Don Black and David Duke began using the Internet as part of their social movement communication and media strategy. The timing of this development meant that I had a naturally occurring experiment for examining and understanding digital media and social movement discourse that would allow for prior and post-Internet comparison. As far as I know, this is the first study to date that does such a comparison, and, therefore, this research is intended to help bridge the gap in our knowledge about how social movement rhetoric is, or is not, transformed through digital media. Not all white supremacy online is part of an organized social movement, as I discuss in the following chapter with an examination of individual acts of white supremacy online.

Conclusion

Though this book is intended to make a number of theoretical and methodological contributions, it is primarily intended as an empirical work, illuminating how the discourse of one particular social movement—white supremacy—has been translated into the digital era. The methodological design, inspired by Griswold's framework, is meant to draw a fuller picture of this cultural phenomenon than would an examination that only looks at movement discourse.

To summarize this book's theoretical themes in the broadest terms, I want to understand how racism and white supremacy manifest online. The speed and ease with which hate speech travels across national boundaries and the willingness of repressive regimes to regulate Internet content that has to do with democracy and democratic ideals of equality, raises certain challenges to critical race theory, which has presented a strong case for the regulation of hate speech. Namely, it asks how free speech might be balanced with equality and human rights within a democratic society. Further, I explore the connection between extremist white supremacy and more mundane expressions of white identity and the white racial frame for defining the terms of the debate about race and controlling the production of knowledge. I assert that the threat of white supremacy online in a democratic society is less about the supposed threat of recruitment or political mobilization than it is about the real epistemological challenge it poses to undermining the very basis of racial equality. Finally, I explore the theoretical implications of white supremacy online for understanding the tension between globalization and the forces of intolerance. In the following chapter I begin the empirical investigation with a case study that illustrates many of the themes of globalization and the Internet and the way that these two forces combine to enable individual acts of white supremacy online.

Notes

Lisa Nakamura 2002, 134. *Cybertypes: Race, ethnicity, and identity on the Internet.* New York: Routledge.

1. The 1997 commercial called "Anthem," produced for MCI by ad firm Messner Vetere Berger McNamee Schemetterer, featured this voiceover: "There is no race. There is no gender. There is no age. There are no infirmities. There are only minds. Utopia? No. The Internet." Nakamura 2002, 87.

2. This is drawn from Paul DiMaggio et al. (2001), where can be found a much more extensive analysis than I can offer here in a few paragraphs.

3. Bell 1977, 34–65.

4. Schiller 1989.

5. Collins 1979.

6. Alexander 1988. See also Craig Calhoun (1998).

7. Habermas 1981. See also Calhoun 1998.

8. Tal 1996.

9. Nakamura 2002.

10. A thorough critique of Nakamura's work on race and the Internet is much needed but beyond the scope of this paper; see Kalí Tal's review available online at kalital.com/Text/Reviews/Nakamura.html.

11. Du Bois 1903. See also Kalí Tal's review referenced in the note above.

12. Hansen 2006, 141.

13. Hansen 2006, 145.

14. White 2003.

15. Byrne 2007, 15–38.

16. Pitts 2004.

17. Collins 1990, 255.

18. Goldberg 1993.

19. Mills 1997, 18.

20. Feagin 2006b.

21. Best and Kellner 1991. See also Best and Kellner (1997), Featherstone and Lash (1999), Harding (1991), and Lennon and Whitford (1994).

22. Fraser (1989). Flax (1987).

23. Collins 1990, 257–62.

24. Ramasastry 2003.

25. Griswold 1987.

26. Hine 2000. See also Kendall 2002.

27. Indeed, the prestigious MacArthur Foundation launched a five-year, $50 million initiative in 2006 to help seed the growth of this new field. I am deeply grateful for the funding from the MacArthur Foundation that supported part of my study. More information about this initiative is available at digitallearning.macfound.org. See also the consortium HASTAC (pronounced *haystack*), founded by Cathy N. Davidson and David Theo Goldberg, at hastac.org.

28. Everett 2008.

29. Lee and Leets 2002. See also Harris (2005).

30. For a thorough discussion of the methodological details, please see the methods appendix.

31. Back 2002, 631.

32. Daniels 1997.

PART TWO

WHITE SUPREMACY IN A GLOBAL CONTEXT

CHAPTER THREE

~

Individual Acts
of White Supremacy Online

The standardization of world culture, with local popular or traditional forms driven out or dumbed down to make way for American television, American music, food, clothes, and films, has been seen by many as the very heart of globalization.

—Fredric Jameson

In February 1998 Richard Machado, a twenty-one-year-old Los Angeles man, was convicted of violating the civil rights of Asian students at the University of California, Irvine, after sending them threatening e-mails. Just over a year earlier, in September of 1996, Machado had sent a nine-line, profanity-riddled e-mail message to fifty-nine students he had identified as Asian by their names. The message said, in part, "I personally will make it my life career [sic] to find and kill everyone [sic] of you personally" and was signed "Asian Hater." After being indicted in November 1996, Machado, then nineteen years old, fled to Mexico to avoid prosecution; he was subsequently apprehended and spent a year in federal custody. In addition to receiving a fine and probation, Machado was sentenced to undergo psychiatric counseling, with mandated participation in a racial tolerance program as a component of that counseling; furthermore, he was ordered to neither enter the Irvine campus nor attempt to contact any of the recipients of the threatening e-mail message.[1]

～

The case of Richard Machado illustrates a number of interesting points about globalization, individual acts of white supremacy, and the Internet. In many ways Machado's racialized crime was only possible because of globalization, both in terms of flows of people across national borders that brought him and the students he targeted together in Orange County and also in terms of the kind of Americanization of world culture to which Frederic Jameson refers in the epigraph. Clearly, Machado's e-mail crime was only possible because of the Internet. The combination of an increasingly homogenized global culture and the possibility of acts of individual white supremacy have implications for our understanding of race as well. At this point in the study I examine published accounts in mainstream news sources about Machado's story to construct a case study.[2] My two goals in this case study are (1) to offer a preliminary exploration of how an individual, quite apart from any involvement in white supremacist social movement organizations, might be involved in individual acts of white supremacy, and (2) to situate those acts within a broader social context in which globalization, the Internet, and race are imbricated. To accomplish these goals, I analyze this case thematically looking at elements of globalization, the Internet, and race. Whenever possible I also include the victims' stories, which are typically left out of the mainstream accounts; I explore this absence as well.

Globalization

In understanding globalization, and in particular global flows of people across national boundaries, we get a fuller view of what set Machado on a path toward the individual acts of online white supremacy he committed from a computer lab on the UC, Irvine, campus in the late 1990s. Globalization is always local in its consequences, and for Southern Californians one of the consequences of globalization has been a pattern of immigration and out-migration of Mexicans and Mexican Americans from Tijuana to San Diego, up through the agricultural Santa Maria Valley, and into northern California and as far north as Seattle.[3] Published reports about Richard Machado's life indicate that his family migrated along a similar path, traveling from Mexico to Los Angeles. Machado, the youngest of seven children and the first in his family to go to college, then continued this migration to Irvine, forty miles east of Los Angeles.

Globalization also facilitated the growth of the University of California system, as well as the expansion of wealthy Orange County, where UC,

Irvine, is located.[4] While the growth of Orange County originally developed in the 1960s as a suburban appendage to Los Angeles, by the 1980s it had become an economic and cultural center with its own linkages to the global economy.[5] And globalization is partly responsible for Machado's contact with Asian and Asian-American fellow students. Orange County has seen the growth of an international Asian and Pacific Islander community and a large Asian-American population. These communities were formed in the 1970s and 1980s by individuals and families with enough personal capital to pursue higher education in the United States and today are interlinked with other ethnically based communities in geographically dispersed locations within the global political economy.[6] Many in this diaspora stay digitally connected to others in dispersed, global locations via e-mail, video chat, and online communities.[7] The ethnic concentration of Asians and Pacific Islanders in Orange County is reflected in data from the U.S. Census. In 2000 approximately 29.8 percent of those living in Irvine were of Asian descent, compared to 10.9 percent for rest of the state; that same year the Latino population in Irvine was just 7.9 percent compared to 32.4 percent for California as a whole.[8] Further, the fact that Machado, who is Mexican American, adopted racist elements of the dominant culture by targeting Asians and Asian Americans is not surprising given the historical legacy of white supremacy in California with its complex interplay of economic forces and racial attitudes that simultaneously structure and allocate group position.[9] In the late 1990s the racial fault lines in California were perhaps most pronounced in higher education, as the University of California system barred the use of race and gender as admissions factors, and, as a result, the enrollment of Latino students at the university's most selective campuses plummeted; indeed, between 1997 and 1998, at one UC campus, admissions of Latinos dropped by 43 percent.[10] UC's policy shift significantly affected Machado, according to published reports, who sent threatening e-mails to the campus newspaper staff because he was upset that the paper supported the policies.[11] While globalization and state policies have worked together to provide opportunities for some, they have simultaneously excluded others, and Machado saw himself among those pushed out by such policies.

The fact that Machado and the Asian and Asian-American students were on the same campus in the UC system was, at least partially, due to globalization. What each student faced—though it is unlikely that Machado recognized his commonality with his victims' causes—was the pressure of assimilation into the dominant white, American culture. Jameson articulates the standardization of world cultures as making way for American culture (and cultural products) and standards, which gets played out on college campuses and can be agonizing for U.S.-born minority and foreign-born students who are pressured to assimilate or suffer discrimination.[12] The racial and ethnic identities of Machado (Mexican American) and the students he targeted (Asian and Asian American) were in part constructed by these global flows of people across national borders. The global trend toward creating sameness from diverse cultures has repercussions within the United States as well, as a diverse range of people with different religions, languages, and cultural histories are homogenized by the dominant culture and lumped into broad categories like *Asian*, *Asian American*, and *Mexican American*, descriptives devoid of meaning outside of an American context. However, these were not the relevant aspects of globalization that earned Richard Machado headlines.

The Internet

Machado's crime was newsworthy because he used the Internet to send threatening hate messages; as such there were unique technological features to this crime. First, Machado created an e-mail address using an alias. This is easy enough to do, and many people who are online have multiple aliases that they use for separate e-mail accounts as a way of managing different sets of relationships (e.g., a personal e-mail with the user ID hot1@myemail.com versus a work-related e-mail with the user ID jsmith@myworkplace.com). Such online aliases are easy to create, easy to discard, and, most of the time, innocuous. In Machado's case, the fact that he used an alias meant that his identity could remain anonymous (at least initially), thus allowing him to launch an attack via e-mail hidden behind a fictitious online identity.

Second, in order to locate the students he wanted to target Machado checked user names in a searchable database of enrolled students on the UC, Irvine, network and looked for names that sounded Asian to him. Here race is part of a routine technological artifact of a college database, which Machado was able to effectively use as a racial filter. While I have no doubt that the campus' cyberinfrastructure was created by well-meaning software engineers and information architects who gave no thought to race as they coded the software to run their searchable database, that race can be identified—or at least intimated—means that it is like a ghost in the machine, operating in unseen ways.[13] Machado's using the searchable database as a racial identifier is consistent with the way race is built into cyberinfrastructure in other ways; recall Nakamura's example of the drop-down menus with a list of possible racial identities from which to choose.[14]

Third, Machado used the cc[15] function of an e-mail program to send his hateful messages to multiple users; as such the Internet worked as a force multiplier of hate speech. Rather than passing a note in class to a student he identified as Asian, Machado could easily send one message to as many Asian students as he could identify at once. And because of the real-time sending and receipt of e-mail messages on the Internet, after sending the first e-mail Machado sat back and waited for a typewritten response, able to gauge the reaction to his poison-pen letter, thanks to the Internet's unique capabilities. When no reply from his victims was immediately forthcoming, Machado re-sent the original racist e-mail message to the same list of recipients.

Race and the White Racial Frame

The fact that Machado is Mexican American and the students he targeted were Asian and Asian American suggests just how race and racial identity figure into white supremacy online. Machado was not, according to pub-lished accounts, involved in an organized white supremacist group nor was he known to have visited white supremacist sites online. Yet the language of his e-mail was clearly hate speech. One explanation for Machado's action is that, no less than most other people in the United States, he had adopted the dominant white racial frame. Part of what is useful about this theoretical framework is that it situates racist actions within a larger system of racial op-pression rather than in either individual identity (not only whites adopt the white racial frame) or individual pathology of racial prejudice tied to a per-sonality disorder. Machado need not have been white to send the racist e-mails. Nor did he necessarily need to be mentally ill to have sent the e-mails, and there is no indication from the published accounts that he was. Instead, he merely needed to grow up in the United States, which he did, and adapt to the dominant culture's white racial frame. By targeting Asian and Asian-American students, Machado was simply echoing this frame.

Machado adopted this frame when he selected his targets from a list of names that sounded homogenously Asian to him. Such a strategy is ultimately a racist one that dehumanizes and deindividualizes people from a diverse range of cul-tures and ethnic backgrounds. In the United States the racial or ethnic identity *Asian* does not distinguish people from nations as diverse as China, Japan, and Korea, nations that have markedly different cultural, historical, and political viewpoints and, in each case, have engaged in protracted battles with one an-other. That Machado was unable or unwilling to differentiate between his fel-low students further evidences his adoption of the white racial frame.

While Machado, as a Mexican American, represents a somewhat anomalous case of an individual engaging in acts of cyber racism, it is also possible that he could have found a welcoming online community at Stormfront.org, the home of "white pride world wide." As I discuss at some length in chapter 5, the boundaries of whiteness are quite flexible and can expand to include individuals that might, in another context, be considered nonwhite. For example, the participant at Stormfront who goes by the name *diabloblanco14* describes himself as a Southern Italian from a "Pan Aryan neighborhood" in Brooklyn where he grew up with neighbors from a variety of white ethnic identities, including "White Hispanics." This participant describes his choice of a Spanish screen name by saying that he "wanted to use a Med language to express White Med pride," a rhetorical strategy for demarcating Mediterranean peoples as white, when historically within the United States, they have been considered nonwhite. Whether or not Machado self-consciously identified as white, or even as white Hispanic, remains an open question. What seems clear from his e-mail attack on Asian and Asian-American students is that he saw them as explicitly *nonwhite*, and in this way Machado adopted one of the more quotidian aspects of the white racial frame in identifying a racial Other.

E-mails that Wound

Placing the victims' story at the center of this analysis of hate speech, as critical race theorists suggest,[16] is difficult because of the way this story and others like it are reported in the mainstream news.[17] This is especially so in this case of hate speech via e-mail because the press accounts mainly leave out the perspective of those who are the targets of hate speech, that is, the UC Irvine students who received Machado's e-mail messages. For the most part, mainstream press accounts in this instance were written from within the white racial frame and left out the systemic pattern of virulent anti-Asian racism on the UC campus. At the time of Machado's attacks Asian students on at least four UC campuses had been the targets of virulent anti-Asian telephone calls, graffiti, and e-mail.[18]

Although many Asian-American victims of racism keep such hostility to themselves,[19] a handful of UC students organized to bring the harassment of Asian-American students to the attention of administrators.[20] Research indicates that hate crimes exact an especially heavy toll on the victims.[21] And while there is less research that examines Internet hate crimes,[22] we can infer, based on other research about the impact of hate crimes, including hate crimes that are verbal and not physical, that these crimes committed online still negatively impact people's lives. In the absence of empirical research or press accounts, we can only speculate that these hate messages, sent anonymously and multiple times via e-mail, may have created a greater sense of fear and violation for the recipients than if Machado had passed a note in class with a similar message.

The fact that Machado was convicted of a hate crime involving the Internet reveals some features of the law and the Internet in the United States. Within the States, the only time white supremacy online loses its First Amendment (speech) protection is when it is joined with conduct that threatens, harasses, or incites illegality.[23] Yet the Machado case suggests that the law is not evenly applied to all people in the United States. The fact that the only individual prosecuted so far for white supremacy online is Mexican American is consistent with the racialized bent of the American criminal justice system in which minority men are viewed as inherently suspect and differentially arrested, prosecuted, and incarcerated. The fact Machado's victims were Asian and Asian American, often stereotyped as model minorities and unlikely to name this harassment as part of systemic discrimination, made it easy for those outside the case to ignore the larger context of white supremacy. While Machado's conviction may seem like a triumph for the critical race perspective that places victims' accounts at the center of the analysis, on closer inspection it is, in fact, one of the few places that critical race theory and more absolutist interpretations of the First Amendment overlap. Even in the very limited number of instances in which white supremacy online does not constitute legally protected speech in the United States, the aggressive prosecution of such cases[24] seems to rely on racialized notions of who is suspect. There seems to be a disturbing difference between the class of citizen held suspect of such crime and the class of citizen whose speech is protected.

Conclusion

The Machado case represents an individual act of cyber racism and is significant for several reasons. First, it underscores that acts of cyber racism are not all committed by people involved in organized white supremacist groups. Indeed, just as the majority of hate crimes are committed by people who are not affiliated with any form of organized racism, it may be that subsequent empirical investigations into cyber racism reveal that the majority of these types of acts are committed by individuals who are not affiliated with any organization. The case-study method is limited by its inability to address such a conclusion based on these limited data.

This case study also illustrates a unique example of legal precedence. Machado remains the only person convicted of an Internet hate crime in the United States. The decision to prosecute Machado is consistent with current jurisprudence, which limits First Amendment protection of speech when it is joined with conduct that threatens, harasses, or incites illegality. However, the fact that the only person ever convicted of such a crime is a man of Mexican-American ancestry reflects the racism of the criminal justice system and the fact that it is overwhelmingly minority men who are regarded as suspects.

The Machado case study also highlights the interconnectedness of globalization, the Internet, and race. His crime was possible precisely because of two realities of the modern era: the global flows of people across borders and the Internet. Globalized migrations across national boundaries are partly responsible for landing Machado and his chosen victims at the same campus in Orange County and are part of what systematically set him at a disadvantage relative to his fellow students. Rather than fostering tolerance, this multicultural reality in the context of an intense pressure to conform and succeed in an Americanized and homogenous global culture negatively affected both Machado and the Asian and Asian-American students on campus. This individual act both retains many elements of the previous era of white supremacy (e.g., racist messages of hate) alongside some new features of the digital era (e.g., targets selected by user name, multiple messages sent from one to many over a short period of time).

The way that Machado was ultimately caught suggests how globalization and the Internet might combat online white supremacy. Upon receiving the racist hate e-mail, several students responded with e-mails of their own to the Office of Academic Computing (OAC). The staff at the OAC were able to identify Machado as the sender by tracing the e-mails he sent using SMTP (Simple Mail Transfer Protocol). Then, they identified the lab and located the individual computer from which the messages were being sent. When staffers went to the terminal, they found Machado still sitting there and asked him to leave. Surveillance cameras in the computer lab later confirmed that Machado was in fact the author of the threatening e-mail messages.[25] Part of what this technological hate-crime-busting story suggests is that there is the means to address similar individual acts of white supremacy where there is the will to do so.

This individual act of cyber racism also illustrates how certain minorities might choose to embrace the dominant white racial frame instead of choosing an oppositional, alternative epistemology. This has important implications for understanding both epistemology and how more extremist expressions of white supremacy are connected to the banal, everyday expressions of white identity. While Machado could have chosen to interpret his experiences and struggles in a way that aligned him with Asian and Asian-American students, he instead adopted the white racial frame and viewed them as racial Others. Adopting this white racial frame led to the production of a particular kind of knowledge—that is, seeing these students as Others. If he had adopted an alternative epistemology in which he critically evaluated his own social position and that of his fellow students within the context of globalization, Machado might have been less inclined to send those threatening e-mails. If Machado had adopted an epistemology that helped him clearly see the way that globalization relies on racism and racial inequality to operate smoothly, then that would have surely produced a different kind of knowledge about his fellow students.

While Machado acted individually and without any known affiliation to a white supremacist group offline or online, in order for us to understand white supremacy online more fully, we must move beyond the analysis of individual acts of white supremacy to examine organized white supremacist social movement organizations. Placing both the Machado case and white supremacist social movements within a global context, I turn next to the work of Manuel Castells, a leading figure in the sociology of globalization and the Internet.

Notes

Jameson 2002.

1. Raney 1998.
2. Feagin, Orum, and Sjoberg 1991. See also Yin (2003).
3. Hondageu-Sotelo 1994.
4. Douglass 2005. See also Olin (1991).
5. Kling, Olin, and Poster 1991.
6. Hess, Nero, and Barton 2001.
7. Gajjala 2003, Ignacio 2005.
8. U.S. Census Bureau 2007.
9. Almaguer 1994.
10. These enrollment figures are for UC, Berkeley; figures for UC, Irvine, were not available. Barlow 2003, 118.
11. Raney 1998.
12. Feagin, Vera, and Imani 1996.
13. McPherson forthcoming.
14. Nakamura 2002, 101–36.
15. A throwback to the print era, *cc* refers to *carbon copy*, and *bcc* refers to *blind carbon copy*, both notations added to documents produced using a typewriter and carbon paper.

16. Matsuda, Lawrence, Delgado, and Crenshaw 1993.

17. Even the extensive set of resources for the Machado Case History (for legal scholars interested in technology-related issues) at Computing Cases does not include any evidence from the Asian and Asian-American students about the impact on them of Machado's e-mail. I find this a telling omission.

18. Lubman 1998.

19. See Chou and Feagin's forthcoming book on Asian Americans.

20. Lubman 1998.

21. Levin 1999. See also Boeckmann and Turpin-Petrosino (2002).

22. Glaser and colleagues examine what motivates people who participate in racist online chat rooms to commit violence (their finding suggest that those in their study were most threatened by interracial marriage and, to a lesser extent, blacks moving into white neighborhoods), but they did not study the impact on the victims. Glaser, Dixit, and Green 2002.

23. Breckheimer 2002, 8.

24. For a similar analysis of the disproportionate enforcement of bias crimes, see Lawrence 2003.

25. Machado Case Materials 2007.

~

CHAPTER FOUR

White Supremacist Social Movements Online and in a Global Context

Social movements in the Information Age are essentially mobilized around cultural values. The struggle to change the codes of meaning in the institutions and practice of the society is the essential struggle in the process of social change in the new historical context, movements to seize the power of the minds, not state power.

—Manuel Castells

The Internet enables social movements to cross national boundaries in ways simply not possible in any previous era. In this new global era the existence of online white supremacist social movements has been scrutinized from three distinct angles. First, scholars such as Manuel Castells have examined how racial identity and globalization are connected in online social movements.[1] Second, others express concern about whether such social movements online threaten the broader political landscape, endangering the public sphere and democratic society.[2] And third, mainstream press accounts and certain scholars have voiced concern that white supremacists with an online presence are recruiting. Yet the reality of white supremacist movements online, I posit, is more complex than any of these perspectives suggest. A good place to begin my explanation is with a discussion of race, globalization, and identity.

Translocal Whiteness: Shaping Online White Identity through Global, Networked Social Movements

As Castells indicates in the epigraph opening this chapter, social movements in the digital era are centered on cultural values. For the most part, analyses of social movements and the Internet have concentrated heavily on progressive and left-leaning movements, while there has been far less attention given those of the far right. In the minority, Castells chose to write about the Internet and both progressive movements (e.g., feminism and environmentalism) and far-right social movements. Thus, Castells's voice is central to any discussion of white supremacist social movements on the Internet.

Sociologist Anthony Giddens has favorably compared Castells's three-volume *Information Age: Economy, Society, and Culture* to Max Weber's classic *Economy and Society*. Originally published in 1996, Castells's collective work presciently anticipated the enormous impact of the Internet and globalization on everyday life. Given that *The Power of Identity* (volume 2) addresses social movements in the Information Age and specifically refers to the patriot movement in the network society, Castells's work is particularly relevant to this discussion. He conceptualizes globalization and identity formation as conflicting trends,[3] a point similar to that made in Benjamin Barber's *Jihad vs. McWorld*. In two possible political futures—"both bleak, neither democratic"—Barber envisions McWorld as a commercialized, homogenized, depoliticized, and bureaucratized future, while Jihad is parochial, tribal, and factious.[4] For both Castells and Barber globalization is allied with tolerance, pluralism, and cosmopolitanism, whereas identity is implicated in racism, tribalism, and ethnic identities. In *The Power of Identity* Castells explicitly grapples with white supremacy, globalization, and the Internet in a segment he titles "Up in Arms against the New World Order: The American Militia and the Patriot Movement in the 1990s."[5] The section's primary source is the Southern Poverty Law Center's *Klanwatch/Militia Task Force* from 1996,[6] which today the SPLC publishes online and in print as *The Intelligence Report*.[7] Similarly informing Castells's work is Ken Stern's 1996 *A Force upon the Plain*, which discusses the American militia movement. These two sources buttress Castells's claims (1) that white supremacy is an extreme libertarian trend that identifies the federal government as a primary enemy, (2) that it perceives the new world order (i.e., globalization) to be a greater threat still, (3) that the movement features a backlash against feminism, gays, and racial or ethnic minorities, and (4) that it promotes an "intolerant affirmation of the superiority of Christian values."[8] Castells's larger point here is that along with the Japanese Aum Shinrikyo—the cult responsible for the 1995 sarin gas attacks in the Toyko subway—the patriot movement is *reactive*, reflexively resisting globalization. As such, he considers the movement to be a rebellion against the more cosmopolitan strains of globalization, quite similar to Barber's Jihad, which opposes McWorld.

Considering the global perspective, however, highlights a number of problems with Castells's analysis of online white supremacy. First, he misinterprets the patriot movement to be the umbrella organization under which all other white supremacist groups meet. He says

> The militia are the most militant, and organized, wing of a much broader, self-proclaimed "patriot movement," whose ideological galaxy encompasses established, extreme, conservative organizations, such as the John Birch Society; a whole array of traditional, white supremacist, neo-Nazi, and anti-Semitic groups, including the Ku Klux Klan and the Posse Comitatus; fanatic religious groups, such as Christian Identity, an anti-Semitic sect emanating from Victorian England's British Israelism; antifederal groups, such as the Counties' Rights Movements, Wise Use anti-environmental coalition, the National Taxpayers' Union, and the defenders of common-law courts. The patriots' galaxy also extends, in loose forms, to the powerful Christian Coalition, as well as to a number of militant right-to-life groups, and counts on the sympathy of many members of the National Rifle Association and progun advocates.[9]

While the patriot movement in the 1990s was certainly an important "force upon the American plain" for white supremacists, it did not then, and does not now, represent the epicenter of the "ideological galaxy" of white supremacist organizations listed above. Rather, the patriot movement is and always has been a single element, and increasingly insignificant one at that, of the broader white supremacist movement. Indeed, as the SPLC reports, the patriot movement is currently in free fall, suffering dramatically declining participation. According to the SPLC, at its peak in 1996 the patriot movement was comprised of 858 groups, yet by 2001 that number had declined by almost 82 percent to a mere 158 identified groups; even that number, characterized by the SPLC as "anemic," was perhaps inflated.[10] While the patriot and militia branches declined, other offshoots of white supremacy grew. As of the SPLC's spring report of 2008, there were an estimated 888 groups in the United States, up 48 percent since 2000.[11] Essentially, Castells mistook a dying limb of white supremacy to be the movement's heart. This first mistake in analysis begets another: for by making the patriot movement his index case study, on which his entire understanding of white supremacy is based, Castells erroneously locates the movement as an exclusively U.S.-based phenomenon, which it is not.

On the contrary, in the Information Age white supremacy is global and quite self-consciously so. Don Black, a white supremacist based in south Florida, established one of the earliest white supremacist websites, Stormfront.org, in 1995. Stormfront's tagline from the beginning has been "white pride worldwide," a motto that speaks to the global vision of the site's creators as well as to the current reach of the site. For some time, Stormfront has featured discussion rooms where supporters from across the globe connect, logging in from Australia, the Baltics, Belgium, Britain, Canada, France, Germany, Hungary, Italy, the Netherlands, South Africa, and Switzerland. As valuable a resource as the Southern Poverty Law Center is, its data about white supremacy in the global era are of limited value, since they restrict their scope to activity within the United States. Sources outside the United States, such as the French antiracist group J'Accuse, estimate there may be as many as sixty thousand racist websites worldwide, much higher than the SPLC's calculation of just under nine hundred sites based in the United States. The disparity can be explained in part by the French organization's global focus.[12] It is admittedly difficult for various methodological reasons to accurately estimate the number of white supremacist organizations or their individual supporters. Yet Castells forces an error by culling the primary data in this case exclusively from U.S.-based sources like SPLC and Stern's *Force upon the Plain*—a curious choice, in any case, given that his book is *about* globalization. White supremacy is a worldwide concern in the Information Age, not merely an American scourge.

Third, while Castells is quite right in his assessment that "identity is people's source for meaning and experience,"[13] because he situates his understanding of white supremacy by region rather than race, he overlooks the Internet's importance in forming a global white identity that transcends local and regional ties. For instance, following a lengthy discussion of militias,[14] Castells shifts to the role of the Internet:

> For conspiracy enthusiasts like militia members, unverified statements from cyberspace reaffirmed their set conclusions by providing an endless stream of additional "evidence." Also the frontier spirit characteristic of the Internet fits well with the freemen, expressing themselves and making their statement without mediation or government control. More importantly, the network structure of the Internet reproduces exactly the autonomous, spontaneous networking of militia groups, and of the patriots at large, without boundaries and without definite plan, but sharing a purpose, a feeling, and most of all an enemy. It is mainly on the Internet (backed up by fax and direct mailing) that the movement thrives and organizes itself.[15]

Castells is mostly correct here in terms of the linkages the Internet provides to social movement members, but he neglects an analysis of *race*, or more specifically, of whiteness and white identity and the way they are central to those linkages. To be fair, when *The Power of Identity* was written in the late 1990s, thinking in terms of linkages characterized popular understanding of the Internet. Since that time, however, a new field of scholarship has emerged that in great part draws on or is influenced by sociologist Sherry Turkle's *Life on the Screen: Identity in the Age of the Internet*.[16] This new interdisciplinary field examines the formation and reaffirmation of social identities online,[17] particularly tracing links forged by race and at racially dedicated social-networking sites.[18] This entire area of scholarship is unaccounted for by Castells or anyone who orients their understanding of white supremacy on region to the exclusion of race. Hence, Castells has no way to envision global white identity developing online.

Global white identity, which sociologist Les Back has referred to as *translocal whiteness*,[19] is crucial to understanding cyber racism in the Information Age. Writing about the racially motivated menacing of an Aboriginal community in Sydney, Australia, Suvendrini Perera illuminates the Internet's development of the phenomenon:

> The appearance of the "race-mixing" posters . . . was clearly designed to terrorize the long-standing and highly visible Aboriginal community in the area, as well as [to target] other racial minorities and people of color in the vicinity—notably, international students at the nearby universities and English-language colleges. The originating point for the poster was the website of the White Pride Coalition, from where it could be downloaded, along with a variety of other racist literature, images, and regalia. The availability of these materials on the website allows their owners to disclaim responsibility for their dissemination and public display on the street. It also enables individuals or small cells of people to act alone and in anonymity while drawing on the resources of a global white racist cyberculture.[20]

In Perera's account, a self-consciously white-defined group avails itself of racist materials courtesy of a white supremacist website—part of a global, white, racist cyberculture—to torment nonwhite community members. In the Information Age the Internet facilitates the formation of a transnational, explicitly racist white identity, as it has expedited the establishment of other transnational subcultural identities—queer identities, for instance.[21] (One of the key differences between these groups is that the formation of white racist identity portends terror for any outside that group, while the formation of queer identity often means terror for those *inside* that group.) The point here is that *translocal whiteness* is a racial identity shaped by global information flows, yet Castells's race and ethnicity are territorial identities (i.e., "religious, national, ethnic, territorial"[22]). By orienting racial and ethnic identity with a specific region, nation, or territory, Castells's analysis fails to account for the *digital diasporas*—that is, the way online communities shape racial and ethnic identities constructed at the intersection of technologies and globalization.[23] More to the point, Castells's analysis fails to account for the Internet's pivotal role in the formation of global white identities.

Castells further undermines his analysis by asserting that race, in addition to being tied to regional or territorial boundaries, is also configured as a demographic characteristic. For instance, he writes that "there is one clearly predominant characteristic in the patriot movement: in a large majority, they are white, heterosexual males."[24]

Castells dilutes the importance of racial identity, systemic racism, and the white racial frame when he categorizes race as merely one of many demographic characteristics rather than as a fundamental organizing principle of the movement. While he goes on to acknowledge that the angry-white-male theme "does connect with much older rejection of racial equality by white supremacist groups," his analysis concludes prematurely. Instead, he argues that:

> "*Rather, they are, fundamentally, a cultural and political movement, defender of the traditions of the country against cosmopolitan values. . . .* Right-wing populism is hardly a novelty in the United States; indeed, it is a phenomenon that has played an important role in American politics throughout the country's history. Furthermore, angry popular reactions to economic distress have occurred in both America and Europe in different forms, from classic fascism and Nazism to the xenophobic and ultranationalist movements of recent years. One of the conditions that can help explain the fast spread of the militia, besides the Internet, is growing economic hardship and social inequality in America. Men's average income has deteriorated substantially in the past two decades, particularly during the 1980s.[25] (emphasis added)

Once again, Castells limits his examination of white supremacy by focusing on geography—in this instance the United States—and then tying these movements to other forms of "right-wing populism" formed in response to "economic distress." Such class-based analysis is drawn from the classic Marxist view in which race is "epiphenomenal."[26] While Castells, a neo-Marxist, is careful in other sections of the chapter to not overinterpret the patriot movement with the language of class, he does not offer anything that might be considered a robust racial analysis. Indeed, as the passage immediately above illustrates, race is missing from his analysis. And the lack of something as critical as a thorough racial analysis substantially weakens Castells's overall argument, as becomes evident in the passage immediately following, when he asserts that economic inequality cultivated militias in the American West: "For instance, Montana, the seedbed of the new militia, is also one of the favorite destinations of the new billionaires, fond of acquiring thousands of acres of pristine land to build ranches from which to run their global networks. Ranchers in the area resented these moves."[27]

Perhaps Ted Turner and other billionaires grabbing up land in Montana have fomented resentment among some ranchers in the area, but this geographically specific example hardly seems adequate to the task of understanding white supremacy and globalization as a whole in the Information Age. Castells concludes with the following: "The social movements I have analyzed in this chapter are very different. And yet, under different forms, reflecting their diverse social and cultural roots, *they all challenge the current processes of globalization on behalf of their constructed identities*, in some instances claiming to represent the interests of their country, or of humankind, as well"[28] (emphasis added).

By drawing parallels between the Japanese Aum Shinrikyo cult and the white patriot movement, Castells asserts that reactive movements respond negatively to globalization, but he fails to explain the Internet's role in the identity formation of those individuals within these groups and demotes the Internet to a mechanism for providing "linkages."

Castells is to be commended for his farsighted sociological vision in recognizing the importance of the coinciding trends of globalization and the Internet for the transformation of social, economic, and cultural life. Yet, the analysis he puts forward in *Power of Identity, Vol. 2*, fails to adequately analyze white supremacy online in the global Information Age. First of all, he mistakenly takes the patriot movement as the ideal type for all other white supremacist organizations. He then uses the patriot movement as his index case study and thus erroneously locates white supremacy as a U.S.-only movement when, in fact, it is global. This focus on the patriot movement leads to a second error that emphasizes region rather than on race as the fundamental organizing category of the white supremacist movement. Thus, Castells misses the extent to which the Internet figures in the formation of a global white identity that transcends local and regional ties. And, finally, by adopting race as one among many demographic "characteristics" rather than a fundamental organizing frame, Castells misses the importance of racial identity, systemic racism, and the white racial frame for understanding white supremacy online.

White supremacy online in the global information era facilitates the formation of a translocal white identity, which is in turn shaped through global information technologies rather than in opposition to them. Here it is useful to return to Benjamin Barber's conceptualization of *Jihad vs. McWorld*. Rather than Castells's oppositional notion of globalization versus identity, Barber (despite the somewhat misleading title of his book) articulates a slightly more nuanced, dialectical view in which Jihad is enacted via McWorld; that is, in Barber's view racial, ethnic, and religious identities are constructed and affirmed through various mechanisms of globalization.[29] This is relevant to this discussion of white supremacy online as whiteness is constructed and affirmed through global information flows and in racially dedicated online communities committed to "white pride worldwide" (such as Stormfront.org). This leads to my next point of examination: namely, whether this kind of online activism endangers democratic society.

A Threat to Democracy? White Supremacist Social Movement Activism and the Internet in a Global Context

When it comes to political mobilization, the Internet undisputedly amplifies many messages, values, and ideas. People interested in the same ideas can easily connect using the Internet, and, as such, the Internet amplifies those connections and strengthens networks of like-minded people.[30] The neologism *cyberactivism* refers to the proliferation of social movement organizations that avail themselves of Internet technologies to further their goals, which often include promoting a more inclusive, democratic society.[31] Much of the scholarship about new social movements on the Internet is guided by a conviction in the liberatory potential of the Internet to transform society in more democratically[32] inclusive ways and therefore tends to focus on progressive movements.[33] For example, a good deal has been written about the Zapatistas uprising,[34] antiwar activism,[35] and feminist organizing.[36] New digital media (like blogs and wikis) and mobile computing technology (like SMS) have made formerly obscure activist subcultures accessible to more people and have created new inroads to political participation for those interested.[37] For activists in extremist white supremacist organizations, like others in obscure subcultures, the Internet provides a relatively inexpensive venue for widespread communication of their ideas unimpeded by monitors or wardens.[38] Whether or not this wider availability of white supremacy online politically mobilizes the movement remains to be seen. Jeffery Kaplan and his colleagues are among those who have taken up this question, and I believe their assessment comes closest to offering an answer:

> Internet or no Internet, barring some cataclysmic development, WAR, [and similar organizations] . . . currently seeking to take advantage of the new technology are unlikely to become serious political contestants. Nevertheless, the Internet does furnish them with a link, a way of circumventing the gatekeepers of the other channels of mass communication.[39]

A serious consequence of participatory media is its accessibility to specialist and nonspecialist users alike. And the very openness of the system invites anyone with a nefarious agenda to join in and author their own suspect content. It is key, here, that we parse the *actual* harm from the *potential*. I agree with Kaplan and his colleagues that the likelihood of a white supremacist organization emerging as a serious political contender is remote. However, the issue of communicating without gatekeepers is significant for the epistemology of white supremacy online and a topic to which I will return to in subsequent chapters. For the moment, let me continue to address why the larger political mobilization of white supremacists remains a distant, but nevertheless troubling, possibility.

In order to affect change, social movement organizations must mobilize resources, such as attracting financial backing, garnering media coverage, establishing organizational structures, and forming political alliances with those in power.[40] The Internet is an important new tool, because it increases the speed at which resources can be marshaled and then utilized to achieve the movement's goals.[41] Adopting a resource-mobilization framework, Noriko Hara and Zilia Estrada compared Stormfront.org's use of the Web with that of MoveOn.org, a website with a liberal-to-progressive political agenda.[42] They found that while there are some similarities between these two websites in terms of attempts at political mobilization, they are not equally effective: MoveOn.org is more popular and more effective than Stormfront.org for a variety of reasons. For example, Hara and Estrada point to the use of other media, such as print journalism and network news, to drive traffic to the websites and garner support for the respective movements. Both Stormfront.org and MoveOn.org have been featured in mainstream media reports, yet MoveOn.org has been much more aggressive in seeking out this media attention, and, Hara and Estrada argue, it is this strategy rather than content alone that has enabled MoveOn to sustain the broad-based political mobilization that has eluded Stormfront.[43] The broader appeal of MoveOn.org is borne out using additional data (figure 4.1).

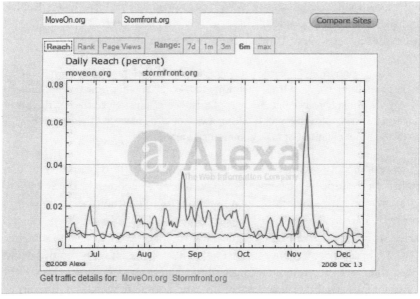

Figure 4.1. Comparative reach in millions for Stormfront and MoveOn.
Source: Alexa Web Service, www.alexa.com, 2008.

A comparison of the Web traffic to the two sites[44] confirms Hara and Estrada's analysis that MoveOn.org has broader appeal than Stormfront.org. As alarming as the Web traffic at Stormfront is, the fact that MoveOn remains consistently more popular than Stormfront should be heartening for those committed to democratic ideals. However, the fact that there are many people sufficiently interested in white supremacy to register at Stormfront should give those interested in social justice great pause to consider which civil rights goals have been achieved and which goals remain unfilled.

Online Recruitment: Distinguishing between a Registered User and a Member of a Social Movement

In a typical twenty-four-hour period there were 129,717 registered users online at Stormfront.[45] A number of writers have asserted that the Internet is a *potential* site for recruiting people to white supremacist groups; however, these claims are largely unsupported by empirical evidence. Instead, recruitment rhetoric plays on collective fears about the Internet and particularly fears about children's online activities. For example, in an article for the *Psychiatric News*, Lynne Lamberg writes that "hate websites aggressively pursue impressionable children and teenagers."[46] Compounding one apprehension with another, the author adds that "surveys show parents worry most about children's access to Internet sex sites and that many parents know little about hate websites."[47] Articles such as this suggest that recruitment into organized white supremacy functions like a virus, infecting vulnerable young people through brief, but deleterious, encounters. Given these concerns, what are we to make of the 129,000-plus people logged in at Stormfront? Are some members and others recruits? Or does some of this online involvement mean something else entirely for online social movements? My exploration of these questions and the issue of recruitment into white supremacist-movement organizations via the Internet builds on Abby Ferber's insights in her book *Home Grown Hate* that, taking into account the web, it may be time to rethink what constitutes a social movement.[48] In the following, I examine the empirical evidence of online white supremacist recruitment and draw distinction between varying types of participation in these groups, for which I suggest an analytic framework for different types of web participation.

Little data exist to support the claim that the Internet is an effective recruiting tool. The handful of research studies that do empirically question whether, and *precisely how*, white supremacists recruit young people online are inconclusive.[49] For instance, in their valuable study of the effects that hate sites' "persuasive storytelling" have on adolescents, Elissa Lee and Laura Leets found that adolescents who were infrequently exposed to explicit hate messages suffered only minimal effects.[50] By design their research neither followed adolescents repeatedly exposed to such messages nor examined how adolescents might be exposed in the first place. What the Lee and Leets study does show is that recruitment is a complex social process.

Traditional social movement organizations (formed before the Internet) consist of a formal organizational structure of *leaders* and *members* (think of labor unions, for example). New social movements are very differently organized, however, and are considered by sociologists to be less formal, consisting of loosely organized social networks of *supporters* rather than members, such as the Berkeley Free Speech Movement or the anti–Vietnam War movements. Membership in a social movement suggests formally recognized leaders, a somewhat rigid *member* status perhaps conferred through payment of membership dues, and a formal structure within the social movement organization. *Supporters*, on the other hand, may never be recognized as official members, may never pay dues, and may be only marginally involved in the activities of the movement but think of themselves as part of the movement. Thus, the *social movement member* has been defined by sociologists to have a narrowly constructed social identity.

This distinction between *supporters* and *members* is significant because it relates to the peripheral involvement of many online social movements. For example, in a well-grounded quantitative study of both online and offline environmental activists in the Netherlands, researchers found that online actions were more popular among those who did not take part in any traditional street actions; researchers thus suggest that online activism may be an easy entry point for more peripheral participants.[51] Whether or not peripheral online participants inevitably, or eventually, become supporters or more-fully involved activists, and what the mechanisms of that evolution might be, remain unclear. In terms of predicting offline collective action by those involved in white supremacy online, there is simply insufficient evidence to make such predictions at this time.

In order to better conceptualize the meaning of 129,000 registered users at Stormfront.org, I suggest the following schema for distinguishing types of Web participants (see table 4.1).[52] First, in the broadest terms there are *active* and *passive participants*; the primary distinction I draw here is between those who create content in some form or another and those who do not but instead only lurk.[53] Online communities in general rather famously suffer from participation inequality, in which an estimated 90 percent of those in any given community do not actively add to the dialogue but instead lurk (or read without posting),[54] and this trend holds true at Stormfront as well. Within the broad category of *passive* participants, there is a whole range of possible ideological stances, and here I have designated three: *passive supportive lurkers, passive curiosity-seeking lurkers,* and *passive oppositional lurkers*. What unites these types is that they are all nonposting, read-only participants. They are not registered users at the site and therefore are not counted as members in the website statistics; they instead appear as guests or visitors. I make no claim that there are only three types of passive lurkers, and there are, no doubt, many other types. Certain participants might, for example, move from one category to another over time. Others might find themselves curious, only to strongly oppose some of the views expressed but

Table 4.1. Distinguishing between Types of Web Participants

Passive *(guests or visitors)*	*Active* *(registered users)*
supportive lurkers	innovators, creators, and early adopters
	sustaining members
curiosity-seeking lurkers	supportive members
oppositional lurkers	oppositional members

also ardently support others. These are merely suggestive categories rather than an exhaustive taxonomy. My point here is that none of these categories of web participants at Stormfront meets the sociological definition of a *social movement member*, and only one category (the Passive Supportive Lurkers) might be considered a supporter in the traditional sense.

Active users comprise the second broad category: these are participants who create content, from building the technological architecture (e.g., creating the discussion board) to maintaining the community (e.g., discussion-board moderator), to creating new threads (e.g., topics of discussions) or fora (e.g., plural form of *forum*, usually an entire area for discussion threads around a related theme), to simply posting (e.g., an individual entry in response to another's thread). Within this broad category exists a range of possible ideological stances slightly less varied than among passive participants. It follows that the active participants are more ideologically similar than passive lurkers, as the people with the energy to devote to participating in the site are likely those most supportive of the site's ideological aims. I have designated four categories: *active innovators, creators, early adopters, active sustaining members*; *active supportive members*; and *active oppositional members*. As previously, I do not mean to pose these as an exhaustive taxonomy but rather a heuristic device for systematically considering Web participation. The first category, *active creators, innovators, early adopters*, includes people at Stormfront such as Don Black (the creator), David Duke (an early adopter), and Jamie Kelso (an innovator), the latter of whom is senior moderator and, according to at least one report,[55] is chiefly responsible for Stormfront's success as an online community. The second category, *active sustaining members*, refers to those who, in addition to posting, donate money to the site administrators. Some of these members also serve as moderators who guide the online discussion. The third category, *active supportive members*, includes those who are registered at the site, post regularly, and are generally supportive of Stormfront's ideological aims. And the fourth category, *active oppositional members*, includes the handful of members registered at Stormfront who do not identify as white and/or are not supportive of the site's goals. Of these four categories only the first two (shaded in table 4.1) meet the sociological criteria for social movement membership. In a typical twenty-four-hour period,[56] at Stormfront there were 129,717 registered users online, and of those 21,413 (approximately 16 percent) were designated active users by the site administrator (meaning they had posted at least once in the last three months) and there were 31,631 visitors (approximately 24 percent). Examining Stormfront's numbers indicates that there are actually more visitors (e.g., passive participants) than supportive, registered users (e.g., active participants). While I do not diminish the significance of over one hundred thousand people having registered at Stormfront, I do believe we need to think more carefully about what we mean when we talk about "recruitment."

The term *recruitment* is perhaps the wrong one here, because it reverses the online dynamic. The underlying issue, and the much more troubling one, is not that white supremacists online may be recruiting but that people are *seeking out* Stormfront and the message of "white pride worldwide." This speaks to the existence of cultural, embedded, and internal white supremacy rather than to an extremist one, external to the core culture. This embedded white supremacy is part of a white racial frame.[57] This is further reaching than an individual bigotry and reflects four centuries of systemic racism permeating all of our major societal institutions. The U.S. Constitution, recall, was substantially crafted by white male slaveholders, such as Thomas Jefferson, whose *Notes on the State of Virginia* discuss enslaved African Americans in fiercely racist language.[58] At Stormfront, one of the regular banner ads at the site (figure 4.2) features Thomas Jefferson and a quotation, which reads "Nothing is more certainly written in the book of fate than these [the Negro] people are to be free. Nor is it less certain that the two races, equally free, cannot live in the same government."[59]

The fact that some fifty years after the civil rights movement there are more than one hundred thousand registered users at Stormfront suggests that the message of white supremacy, far from being an anachronism, still resonates. Here again, the white racial frame is useful for understanding white supremacist social movements online. As individuals adopt the white racial frame, the racial foundations of the United States, such as these statements by Jefferson, get ignored because to pay attention to such passages would open up the possibility of an analysis of systemic racism. Opportunities for such analysis are forestalled by the white racial frame.

Additionally, there is widespread ignorance about the history of racist oppression extant in four hundred years of U.S. history. The legacy of this racial oppression includes a number of racial disparities in U.S. society, such as significant differences in poverty, educational attainment, and levels of incarceration between blacks and whites. When people who adopt the white racial frame begin to note these racial disparities and have only that frame to draw on to interpret these disparities, they misunderstand racial and social inequality as the result of individual inadequacy rather than the predictable result of systemic racism. Whether one identifies as racially white or not (e.g., Machado), trying to understand the inequality through the white racial frame leads down a cul-de-sac of misinterpretations. Thus the Thomas Jefferson quotation resonates deeply within this broader white racial frame. Jef-

Figure 4.2.   Banner featuring Thomas Jefferson.
Source: Stormfront.org.

ferson's expressly racist belief that two races cannot coexist under the same government confirms beliefs about persistent racial disparity for many who have adopted the white racial frame. And, having the Jefferson quote as a recurring banner on Stormfront confirms for visitors that they have found a source for true yet otherwise hidden information about race. The Jefferson banner also sends a message that allegiance to the white race above all others is consistent with the core values of the founders of the United States, and in that they are correct. In fact, the discussion forum at Stormfront.org includes a thread called "Thoughts of Thomas Jefferson regarding blacks" and features explicit statements from participants about what they see as the wisdom of the founders. For example, a participant at Stormfront using the screen name *kojac67* writes on April 11, 2006, that he is reading a book about John Adams that includes "real letters from the founding fathers as source material." Based on that reading, this participant concludes the following:

> The truth is that when our founding fathers spoke of all men being created equal . . . they had very certain ideas on what constituted "men." To them blacks were more animal in nature, and, therefore, not equal. How we have twisted the words of the constitution is criminal. The founding fathers created the foundation of a great society, with racial divisions. Who are we to say we know better? The more we pay attention to the men and the words of our nation's founders . . . the better off we will be. (*kojac67*)

Here *kojac67* uses moderate-sounding rhetoric and an appeal to the nation's founding ideals to make a point that runs counter to democratic ideals of equality for all. In this way *kojac67* shifts white supremacist rhetoric away from extremist expressions and places it within the more mundane, everyday expressions of white identity. In this passage, the two sit alongside each other. While some would argue we no longer live within an unequal system and that the values of the founders of the United States have been overthrown in favor of equality,[60] there is a large and growing body of evidence to suggest that the values of the slave-owning founders remain the core cultural values of this country.[61] In many ways, online participants in white supremacy are responding to core American values and extending them globally by logging onto "white pride worldwide."

The confluence of global linkages facilitated by Internet technologies means that through Stormfront true believers[62] in white pride can connect with their translocal and white identity. Those who view the world through a white racial frame may find that participating at Stormfront resonates in significant ways with the way they (mis)understand the world, but this is a different dynamic than being recruited into a social movement organization.

In contrast to the frightening, but mostly unrealized, *potential* of recruitment into white supremacy via the online world, *actual* recruitment into organized racism is a complex social process that happens primarily offline in face-to-face interaction. In his seven-year ethnography of white supremacist groups in the Pacific Northwest region of the United States, Blazak found that in face-to-face interactions the groups used "red flags of strain to guide recruiting activity."[63] Among these "red flags" are four main areas of strain: racial/ethnic (shifts to multicultural curricula), gender (feminist-activist groups), heterosexuality (gay-pride events), and economic (factory layoffs).[64] Youths, most often although not exclusively, young white males, experience cultural alienation or anomie,[65] because shifts in any of these areas of strain make them susceptible to recruitment and targeting by white supremacist groups. As Blazak describes it, this is a years-long process that happens almost entirely offline, in face-to-face social gatherings. The transformation from "white boys" to "terrorist men" also makes clear the ways gender and sexuality, and specifically heteronormative masculinity, are central to white supremacist discourse and recruitment.[66] This kind of young-white-male alienation predates the advent of digital media; to locate the harm in this we need look no further than to the 168 people killed at the Murrah Federal Building in Oklahoma City in 1995.

Conclusion

White supremacist social movements online are a complicated social phenomenon. First, rather than racial identity being constructed as oppositional to forces of globalization, white supremacy online in the global information era facilitates the formation of a translocal white identity. This translocal white identity, rather than being moored to extremist expressions, is often rooted in core American values and draws upon the rhetoric that self-consciously aligns itself with the "founding fathers," while simultaneously seeking to transcend national boundaries and exert a global reach. And this translocal white identity, as illustrated in the previous chapter about the Machado case, is one that is malleable and may expand to include individuals not considered white in other social or historical contexts.

Second, the likelihood that a white supremacist organization could pose a serious political challenge in a contemporary democracy is remote, though worrisome. The more serious threat to the democratic ideal of equality has to do with the epistemological challenge to the cultural value of racial equality, rather than with political mobilization of an army of extremist white supremacists. The emergence of white supremacy online allows for the possibility of knowledge communities where those who oppose racial equality can gather and affirm for each other their shared ideas about white superiority. And, within these online communities, they can engage in a self-perpetuating cycle of validating those knowledge claims. By asserting ideas in opposition to racial equality, then connecting those ideas to widely respected figures, such as Thomas Jefferson who also opposed racial equality, white supremacists lending further legitimacy to the effort to erode the knowledge base for the idea of racial equality.

Third, white supremacist social movements online cannot be adequately understood by drawing on facile and vague notions of recruitment via the Internet that play on people's fears. Instead, what it means to participate online is multidimensional and may or may not overlap with social movement membership. In this way, participation online in white supremacist forums overlaps with participation in other online forums. Some may participate actively and be true believers or passionate resisters; others may only lurk and may be supportive, nonsupportive, or fall somewhere else on a rubric of possible types of online participation. In general, the relationship between the multifaceted dimensions of online participation and active social movement involvement are not widely understood, and this is no less true for white supremacist social movement organizations. While the *potential* exists for a multinational white-pride social movement that organizes across national and geographic boundaries, this potential has thus far been unrealized.

I agree with Castells that social movements in the Information Age are mobilized around cultural values. White supremacist social movements are organized around the cultural value of whiteness, white identity, and the notion that the white race is distinct from and superior to all others. This is a value that the founders of the United States also shared, and now white supremacists, largely based in the United States, are using the Internet to reach across national boundaries to unite with others who value white identity as a marker of cultural superiority. Whether or not whiteness remains a core value in the American context or merely represents the values of an oppositional subculture depends on one's standpoint and epistemology for understanding racial equality—subjects I will address in greater detail in subsequent chapters. Next, I turn my analysis to the ways in which white supremacy is connected with gender and sexuality, because these are constitutive elements of cyber racism.

Notes

1. Castells 1997.
2. Tsesis 2002.
3. Castells says, "Our world, and our lives, are being shaped by the conflicting trends of globalization and identity" (1997, 1).
4. Barber 1996.
5. Castells 1997, 84–97; indexed references to white supremacists include pages 86 and 92.
6. According to Castells 1997, 84n18:

The main source of information on the American militia and the "Patriots" is the Southern Poverty Law Center, headquartered in Montgomery, Alabama. . . . As part of its program, it has established a Klanwatch/Militia Task Force, which provides accurate information and analysis to understand and counteract new and old, antigovernment and antipeople, extremist groups. For the most recent information, used in my analysis, see Klanwatch/Militia Task Force (1996, subsequently cited as KMTF). A well-documented account of the American militia in the 1990s is Stern (1996).

7. Kim 2005.
8. Castells 1997, 92–94.
9. Castells 1997, 85–86.
10. According to the SPLC,

In its annual count, the Southern Poverty Law Center's Intelligence Project identified just 158 antigovernment patriot groups that were active in 2001. That is down 19 percent from the year before, when there were 194 such groups, and the fifth consecutive decline since the movement peaked with 858 groups in 1996. And even the current numbers seem to overstate patriot activity, which for several years has been anemic at best. (Southern Poverty Law Center 2002)

11. Southern Poverty Law Center 2008.
12. Of course, these numbers reflect slightly different approaches—while SPLC focuses on groups organized on the ground, in face-to-face interaction, J'Accuse is measuring websites that may only reflect an individual's effort, rather than an entire group. This is an issue which I will return to at another point in the book.
13. Castells 1997, 6.

14. Castells 1997, 87–91.

15. Castells 1997, 91.

16. Turkle 1997.

17. Slater 2002, 533–46.

18. See, for example, Byrne 2007, 15–38. See also the edited collection containing Byrne's article by Everett (2008).

19. Back 2002, 365–77.

20. Perera 2006.

21. Alexander 2002.

22. Castells 1997, 2.

23. The study of digital diasporas is a large and growing field. One of the best volumes in this area is Gajjala's: *Cyber selves: Feminist ethnographies of South Asian women*. 2004. See also Bernal (2006).

24. Castells 1997, 94.

25. Castells 1997, 95–96.

26. For a recent discussion of this long-running sociological debate about whether race is an "essential social fact" or an "epiphenomal" artifact of class oppression, see Bonilla-Silva (1999). For those interested in additional discussions on this topic, see Cox 1948.

27. Castells 1997, 96–97.

28. Castells 1997, 108–109.

29. Barber 1996, chapters 10 and 11. Barber comes close to using the white supremacist movement as an example of an American-based Jihad (see, for example, pages 9 and 165), but this is not explicit in his text. In personal e-mail communication he shared with me, Barber agreed that the white supremacist movement could be considered an example of his conceptualization of Jihad.

30. Earl and Schussman 2003, 155–87.

31. McCaughey and Ayers 2003.

32. Jenkins and Thorburn 2003.

33. Bennett 2003.

34. Martinez-Torres 2001.

35. Kahn and Kellner 2004.

36. Sutton and Pollock 2000. See also Everett (2004).

37. Agre 2002c. See also Campbell 2006. And see Kahn and Douglas 2003, 299–314.

38. Brian Levin 2002. See also Thiesmeyer 1999.

39. Kaplan, Weinberg, and Oleson 2003, 155.

40. McCarthy and Zald 1977.

41. Kahn and Kellner 2004.

42. Hara and Estrada 2003.

43. Hara and Estrada 2003.

44. Using Alexa, a Web-trafficking service, found at alexa.com.

45. Numbers posted at Stormfront on April 11, 2008. These are included here as an illustrative example and are not intended to be a representative sample.

46. Lamberg 2001.
47. Lamberg 2001.
48. Ferber 2003b, 7.
49. Ray and Marsh 2001.
50. Lee and Leets 2002.
51. Brunsting and Postmes 2002. This is the kind of study that someone needs to undertake concerning the white supremacist movement but one I leave to future researchers, as it is beyond the scope of the current project. Statzel (2006), for example, argues that recruitment does happen online.
52. This is based on my ethnographic observations at Stormfront.org, where I would classify my own participation there as a *passive oppositional lurker*. While this is based on my observations at Stormfront in particulary, it also reflects my *active-support participation* at other websites. Such a schema raises methodological questions about how to study lurking behavior, to which I have no answer at the present time.
53. The term means to *read without posting or commenting*. In online jargon, there are various forms of this word: One who lurks is a *lurker*. One who decides to stop lurking and post may begin that initial post with "Delurking here to say. . . ." Lurking is part of the accepted atmosphere online.
54. See Jakob Nielsen's research on this (2006). Other research confirms this, such as Nonnecke and Preece (2000).
55. Southern Poverty Law Center 2008.
56. Numbers posted at Stormfront on April 11, 2008. These are included here as an illustrative example and are not intended to be a representative sample.
57. Feagin 2006b.
58. Thomas Jefferson 1787. Jefferson writes that enslaved black Americans smell bad, are natural slaves, are less intelligent, are uglier in skin color, are lazy, are oversexed, lack a sophisticated appreciation for serious music, are incapable of advanced learning, and can never be well-integrated into white America. It is for precisely this type of racist language that the white supremacists venerate him.
59. Thomas Jefferson 1821.
60. D'Souza 1995. See also Sowell 1984.
61. See, for example, the bibliography at racismreview.com/blog/bibliographies/.
62. Hoffer 1951.
63. Blazak 2001.
64. Blazak 2001.
65. *Anomie* is a term coined by sociologist Emile Durkheim and refers to a sense of normlessness in which one no longer knows what the rules, or *norms*, for acceptable behavior are. In extreme cases, Durkheim theorized, this condition can lead to anomic suicide.
66. Blazak 2001.

PART THREE

~

WHITE SUPREMACY ONLINE

CHAPTER FIVE

~

Gender, White Supremacy, and the Internet

Ask others not what a "woman's role [in] white nationalism" is; ask yourself what you can do for white nationalism.

—*MistWraith*

Bonnie Jouhari is a white mother of a biracial child who was harassed, forced from her home, stalked, and terrorized for years by a white supremacist. Jouhari is a former social worker who helped people file housing-discrimination complaints in the Reading, Pennsylvania, area; her work apparently enraged a white supremacist. In March of 1998 a white supremacist website published by Roy Frankhouser began posting pictures of Jouhari's workplace exploding amid computer-generated video flames. Jouhari and her daughter began receiving threatening telephone calls, and Jouhari found a flier on her car reading, "Race traitor, beware." The local police and the Justice Department declined to file criminal charges, citing Mr. Frankhouser's First Amendment rights to free speech. Jouhari moved first to another town in Pennsylvania, then to Seattle, and eventually to an undisclosed location in order to get away from this ongoing threat to her life and the life of her child.[1] It is important to understand the experiences of women like Jouhari and her daughter who have suffered the real harm of white supremacy online in their real lives. However, women are not only victims of white supremacy online; they are also creators of and participants in white supremacy online.

The 129,000-plus registered members at Stormfront have created an astounding 389,620 threads (e.g., discussion topics) with a staggering 4,833,278 posts (e.g., individual entries under each topic).[2] Within this vast arena is a small forum, linked off the main page, designated "For Stormfront.org Ladies Only." This ladies-only forum is popular with white women who frequent Stormfront and includes some 159 threads with 3,661 individual posts.[3] The women who post in this forum, such as *MistWraith*, quoted above, are committed to the cause of white pride worldwide; yet, it is white men who remain the chief architects of the white supremacy online.

The centrality of a white, heteronormative masculinity to white supremacy has extended from the print-only era to the digital era. Juxtaposing Bonnie Jouhari's experience as a target of white supremacy online (and the very real consequences in her real life) with the emergence of women-only spaces within larger white supremacist sites can illuminate different aspects of gender, white supremacy, and the Internet. However, by using these two examples I do not mean to suggest that we can understand gender by only looking at women.[4] Indeed, as I have argued elsewhere,[5] masculinity is constitutive of white supremacy; this characterized white supremacy in the print-only era as it does in the digital era. What I mean to suggest by using these two examples is that, first of all, Jouhari illustrates the impact in real life and the persistence of the miscegenation theme. Second, the designated ladies-only space within Stormfront.org illustrates both the growing engagement of women in white supremacy and in life online more broadly and the male dominance that is central to both. My investigation into these two gendered illustrations leads me to conclude that the print-only era of white supremacy featured a more top-down, tightly controlled ideological articulation, whereas white supremacy in the digital era, and particularly the involvement of women online, offers more openness and dissent within white supremacist discourse. However, this greater fluidity in white supremacist discourse does not lead to anything like a political critique that materially improves the lives of either women at Stormfront or women, who like Jouhari, are victims of white supremacy online.

In this chapter I examine white women, white men, gender, and sexuality as they are represented on a number of white supremacist websites, with a particular focus on Stormfront.org. I include illustrative examples from several case studies, such as the Jouhari case, and I focus primarily on Stormfront.org.[6] Stormfront is an important case of white supremacy online, perhaps *the case* (as discussed in the previous chapter) because it is the oldest and most successful[7] white supremacist site online and because it is an entirely participatory site in which a multitude of users, both men and women, almost all white and identifying as white nationalists,[8] create and post content. Thus, what I offer here is a preliminary gendered analysis of what white supremacy, enacted by both white women and white men, looks like in the digital era. My purpose in this chapter is twofold: (1) to suggest how white supremacy online might be gendered in ways that are similar to and different from both white supremacy in the print-only era and other sorts of online communication beyond those white supremacist sites and (2) to situate white supremacy online within a global context of inequality, particularly along lines of race, class, gender, and sexuality.

Choosing an Online Identity: Gender, Race, and Screen Names at Stormfront.org

White supremacy online is a male-dominated racial project as it is offline. In the print-only era, white men were the primary, but not exclusive, publishers of white supremacist newsletters. Although white women who qualified as "pure" (racially and sexually) figured prominently in the symbolic discursive universe of white supremacist rhetoric in print, *actual* white women played relatively small but still significant roles in the movement.[9] In order to understand the way white supremacy online is gendered, it is first necessary to examine some of the ways the movement is gendered offline.

Despite the male-dominance of white supremacy as a movement, some estimates suggest that white women may be the fastest-growing part of face-to-face organized racism, with some suggesting that women make up as much as 50 percent of new members.[10] To the extent that anyone has a stereotype of women in organized racist movements, the image conjured is probably one of a poor, uneducated woman with an abusive family history who has followed her racist boyfriend or husband into the movement. However, in her study of thirty-four women in the organized racist movement, Kathleen Blee found that there was no single racist type.[11] In fact, the women in her sample were educated and employed, and most were neither poor before joining the movement nor reared in abusive families.[12] While some of them did follow men into the white supremacist movement, not all of them did.[13] The majority of the women in Blee's research found their way into organized racism the same way others find their way into movement organizations: by meeting people who were already in those organizations. Once in the movement organizations, the women began to self-consciously identify as white, thus making explicit a racial identity that is taken for granted by most whites.[14]

Many of the gendered aspects of the movement offline carry over into on-line versions of white supremacy. While the men in white supremacist groups tend to emphasize a cult of heroes and martyrs,[15] Blee found that the women in the movement she interviewed express comparatively little interest in identifying with heroic figures; instead they report finding more satisfaction in feeling selflessly engaged in a struggle for what they see as right.[16] Evidence for a similar gendered phenomenon exists online in the sorts of screen names[17] (e.g., *nicknames, nicks, user IDs*, or *handles*) Stormfront.org participants choose for themselves. To illustrate this point, I conducted a content analysis[18] of screen names of users who posted on the Sustaining Members discussion board, where participants who made donations to Stormfront.org in 2005 were acknowledged by screen name. Participants who self-identify[19] as women choose names such as *MistWraith* (quoted in the epigraph that opens this chapter), *DrivenSno, WarMaiden, KinderKucheKirche, Classic Goddess, AryanAngel, cha0s_kkkitten*, and *Norwegian14Beauty*, which I coded as female. Participants at Stormfront.org who self-identify as men choose names such as *Charles A. Lindberg, Ironman1, Spartan*, and *Von Bismarck*, which I coded as male. Not all the nicknames are easily recognizable as gender-specific; a number of participants select user IDs that are gender-ambiguous, and users do not always self-identify by gender. Screen names such as *anglo saxon, Prepare*, or *Unconditioned Canuck* I coded as indeterminate vis-à-vis gender. I counted a total of 149 contributors. Of those, nineteen had clearly identifiable female screen names, eighty-two had male screen names, and forty-eight had screen names that could be either male or female. The pattern that emerges in the choice of screen names by Stormfront.org participants reflects the kind of distinction Blee points out in the face-to-face movement. That is, men tend to choose screen names that refer to and honor heroes and martyrs of the movement, while women mostly do not. The pattern in screen names at Stormfront.org is one that simultaneously reflects the broader gendered structure of society as it constructs gender identity and sexuality as well. This sort of pattern is consistent with other research that finds that these user-created nicks are important in shaping online interactions, because they offer an explicit indicator of gender identity and sexual availability.[20]

Screen names also signify racial identity in online interactions in general[21] and at Stormfront.org. Online at Stormfront.org racial identity is largely presumed, but there are ruptures in the assumed whiteness of participants. These ruptures are evident in thread called What Inspired Your Screen Name? In this thread members are invited by senior moderator Jamie Kelso, a.k.a. *Charles A. Lindberg*, to share the back story of their screen names:

> Screen names are fascinating. How did you dream up yours? Was your name inspired by a philosophy, a private meaning, an historical figure, a humorous idea, mythology, literature, history, a people, your work, your family, or some other idea? (*Charles A. Lindberg*, post dated 05-20-2003)

The hundreds of replies that follow in this thread (1,656 replies and 82,075 views as of March 1, 2008) reveal screen names chosen to signify national identity and racial *ideology* as well as racial and gender *identity*. For example, a participant that uses the screen name *diabloblanco14* (mentioned in chapter 3) describes the origin of the name this way:

> My name of course is Spanish for *Whitedevil*. I remember Muhammad Ali labeling us White Devils, and I thought to my self that that was exactly what we needed to be if we wanted to take our societies back and protect our women. So I turned it into a compliment and a badge of pride. The 14 of course is for the fourteen words "We must secure the existence of our race and a future for white children."
>
> My original diablo ID, which I still have on Yahoo, is Diabloblanco92, but it was lost in an earlier incarnation of Stormfront but remains on Yahoo. The 92 is for 92nd Street and Fort Hamilton Parkway in Bay Ridge, Brooklyn, the tough, white ethnic, VERY pan-Aryan neighborhood I grew up in (Italians, Irish, Germans, Norwegians, Greeks, Poles, white Hispanics, white Lebanese) where nearly EVERYONE was a racist.
>
> Although I'm Southern Italian rather than Spanish I used Spanish because I wanted to use a Med language to express white Med pride, and more people understand Spanish than Italian, and also as a tribute to some of the way hot and lovely WHITE Hispanic GFs I have had. (*diabloblanco14*, post dated 05-21-2003)

The lengthy description that *diabloblanco14* offers here of his screen name is laden with meaning that illuminates the malleability of the boundaries of whiteness. He identifies his ethnically diverse neighborhood in the Bay Ridge section of Brooklyn as a "VERY pan-Aryan neighborhood" in which he situates himself as not merely within the boundaries of whiteness but also Aryan-ness. This identification as white and Aryan is doubly ironic, given his Southern Italian heritage, which in a different context in the United States would have marked him and his neighbors in Bay Ridge as decidedly nonwhite. In fact, as late as the 1920s and 1930s most social commentators wondered publicly whether Southern Italians were even capable of ever fully assimilating into mainstream U.S. culture. By choosing a Spanish-language name to "express white Med pride," *diabloblanco14* effectively expands the bounds of whiteness here. Further, by including in his description a tribute to his sexual alliances with "WHITE Hispanic" girlfriends, *diabloblanco14* both challenges and affirms white supremacist rhetoric about the prohibitions on interracial sexual relationships. He challenges this by asserting his right to cross racial and ethnic boundaries to sleep with "Hispanic" women; yet, he affirms the white supremacist notions of the importance and value of same-race sexual relationships, along with the implicit message that only white women are attractive, by using all caps to emphasize the whiteness of the Latina women he dates. The underlying referent to "white devil" is intended to challenge a black-nationalist critique of white racism, while the number fourteen signals his identification with white pride. So, *diabloblanco14* is engaged in a complex identity construction through his choice of screen name. Each time he logs in and posts (a total of 7,762 posts from his join date of March 2002 through my last count in March 2008), his screen name appears alongside the post, affirming this complicated identity of race, nationality, region, gender, sexuality, and racial ideology.

British scholar Les Back has written about "translocal whiteness"—that is, the possibility that whites from a range of nations and disparate global regions choose to identify across those boundaries as, first and foremost, white. There is evidence of the construction of a translocal white identity from *Premisyl*, another participant in the What Inspired Your Screen Name? thread. *Premisyl*, who says that he is from Canada and "before then Czech Rep." writes, "My username should really be spelt *Premysl*, but I think that it somehow got messed up one day and I used this spelling. Anyway, Premysl was one of the first and greatest kings of Bohemia, although he is more legend than known fact now" (*Premisyl*, post dated 09-21-2003).

This prompts a much longer and referenced post from senior moderator Jamie Kelso (a.k.a. *Charles A. Lindberg*) who responds with the following:

> This is history that I did not know. Thanks Premisyl.
>
> Quote:
>
> The House of Premysl . . . also called Premyslid Dynasty . . . first Czech ruling house, founded, according to tradition, by the plowman Premysl, who was married to the princess Libuše. The members of the Premyslid dynasty ruled Bohemia and the lands associated with it from about 800 to 1306. The head of the Premyslid house was usually designated a prince, or duke (*kníže*), until 1198, when Premysl Otakar I raised Bohemia to the status of a hereditary kingdom within the Holy Roman Empire. Historical records of the early Premyslid

rulers are scanty. According to legend, Prince Borivoj is said to have been converted to Christianity by Saint Methodius (fl. mid-ninth century). Bohemia was consolidated politically in the tenth century, and the best known of its rulers at this time was Borivoj's grandson Vaclav, whose zeal for spreading Christianity in his dominions prompted his murder by his pagan brother Boleslav I (reigned 929–967). (*Charles A. Lindberg*, post dated 09-21-2003)

What happens here in this exchange between *Premisyl*, currently based in Canada and originally from Czech Republic, and Jamie Kelso, who is American based in South Florida, is that they enact translocal whiteness. That is, these two participants at Stormfront together reinforce their shared white identity across national boundaries (Canada and the United States) by drawing on a historical example from a third nation, the Czech Republic. While some may have configured each of these countries as ostensibly white in the print-only era of white supremacist newsletters, the digital era makes possible asynchronous exchanges such as this one between *Premisyl* and Jamie Kelso. What is happening in these exchanges is the formation of a new identity, a *translocal whiteness*, to use Les Back's term, which transcends national boundaries in favor of racial and ideological boundaries.

The women who participate in the What Inspired Your Screen Name? thread also cross national boundaries in favor of racial and ideological identification as white, yet the posts by women in this thread are markedly different from the posts by men. In the following post *White Rose* explains her screen name this way:

> I picked this name because I love roses, especially white ones, symbols of love, purity, and friendship. I'm proud of being white, and I love my English/Saxon heritage. The national flower of England is represented by the rose (depicted as either red or white). One of the most beautiful cities in England is Yorkshire, which is also called the City of the White Rose. The name also sounds very English to me. (*White Rose*, post dated 07-23-2003)

The women often describe their screen names in terms of beauty, in reference to their own appearance or to a beautiful flower and city, as *White Rose* does here. Like the men posting in this thread, *White Rose* is *doing* race by enacting a white identity that supersedes national and geographic boundaries. This post by *White Rose* is actually quite verbose compared to others by women in this thread. More commonly, women post using fewer words, tend to begin their posts with some form of self-deprecation, and are less likely to reference a larger historical or ideological point to describe why they chose their screen name. For example, this post from *Isabella* is typical: "I'm frightfully boring. I couldn't think of anything neat, so I signed up with my middle name" (*Isabella*, post dated 05-23-2003).

Note that she begins her post with a defensive claim that she is "frightfully boring" and then reveals that she used her own middle name. The post from *Isabella* draws no response from the moderator; yet when a man posts that his screen name is, in fact, his "real name" some months later, senior moderator Jamie Kelso steps in to praise the man for this "encouraging sign" and urges other participants to do the same (*Charles A. Lindberg*, post dated 10-08-2003). Another woman explains her screen name, *pixie*, in these succinct terms: "Mine is not real original—it's my nickname" (*pixie*, post dated 06-26-2003).

Like *Isabella*, *pixie* is defensive about not being "real original." Part of the defensiveness seems to involve not being overtly ideological in their choices of screen names, but this does not explain all of their reticence. When one woman with a strongly ideological screen name, *FEMALE14WORDS*, posts to the thread, her reply is exceptionally terse: "< —— Direct and to the point" (*FEMALE14WORDS*, post dated 07-02-2003). Here she economizes on words by using the keyboard to create an arrow that points in the direction of her screen name (which displays to the left). Even though she has a strongly ideological screen name, the gendered structure of online interaction serves as a constraint on a longer post.

Screen names are an important site of racial and gender-identity construction at Stormfront as well as an indicator of the male dominance of white supremacy online. Screen names suggest some of the ways that white supremacy has shifted from the print-only era to the digital era. White supremacist discourse is no longer contained by the one-way, top-down communication strategy of printed newsletters published by a few (mostly male) leaders. White supremacy in the digital era has expanded to include participation from many people in disparate geographic regions who are actively engaged in crafting a *translocal* white identity that privileges race and racial ideology over national identity. The gendered quality of screen names, as well as the gendered structure of online communication, illustrate some of the many ways race, nation, gender, and sexuality intersect for participants at Stormfront.

"For Stormfront Ladies Only": Liberal Feminism and White Supremacy Online

The fact that there is a ladies-only discussion board at Stormfront.org speaks to the gendered structure of online communication more broadly than just white supremacist discussion boards. Online communication in mixed-gender settings generally tends to disadvantage women,[22] and it is often the case that women and girls in mixed-gender online groups create a space of their own.[23] Women in mixed-sex online discussion groups post fewer messages and are less likely to persist in posting when their messages receive no response. Even when they do persist, women receive fewer responses from others (both females and males).[24] In addition, women do not generally control discussion threads except in groups where women make up a clear majority of participants.[25] In part, this lack of influence by women in mixed-sex groups explains why women-only online groups are common,[26] yet explicitly designated men-only groups are rare. This gendered pattern to online communication is evident in the item about screen names discussed above, and it explains the emergence of the ladies-only forum at Stormfront.

The white women involved in organized racism online, like the women in studies of white supremacy offline,[27] appropriate the discourse of white feminism to define their participation in the movement. The range of topics is familiar and incorporates a surprising amount of liberal feminist rhetoric. The threads started by women in the ladies-only forum is remarkably banal; many of the topics listed here could just as easily be found on a forum at iVillage.com or an afternoon talk show. The "ladies" at Stormfront.org are interested in health and beauty and dating and marriage and children and losing weight and feeling safe when home alone. There are also overtly racist ("hit on by negros!") and anti-Semitic ("Eliot Spitzer: Another Immoral Jew") threads, but these are much less common than the more pedestrian concerns of many women's lives. Of the 159 threads, 44 (27 percent) address some issue connected to women's roles as wives and mothers, 18 (11 percent) have to do with some version of health, and 8 concern issues related to beauty (5 percent).

In a thread within the ladies-only forum, a participant with the screen name *ConcernedKaia* (join date July 2007, fifty-four posts) started a new thread by posing this question: Should abortion continue to be legal? Her initial post mixes the overt racism of white supremacist rhetoric with a challenge to the pro-life rhetoric that "abortion is murder." She writes the following:

> I realize the commonly held view that abortion is murder and that white women should be having children instead of aborting them. However, black women are much more likely to have abortions than white women. It's as that joke goes, "What do you call an abortion clinic in Harlem?" "Crime Stoppers." LOL. Those fetuses that are aborted are oftentimes better off dead. Sorry, but

considering the environments that most of them would have been raised in, it's usually true. Plus, if I were ever raped by a black guy, I'd definitely want rid of what was growing inside of me. I don't think that abortion should be used as ordinary birth control, but under a lot of circumstances it seems justified. What's your thoughts on this issue? (*ConcernedKaia*, post dated 02-19-2008)

Here the rhetoric of an earlier white supremacy is transposed to the digital era unchanged from the print-only era in many ways. The view of reproductive rights through a racist lens that *ConcernedKaia* and others express here is little different than the kind of rhetoric I found in printed white supremacist newsletters. What shifts in white supremacy in the digital era is that now this sort of racist rhetoric is no longer simply ideology that is distributed in one direction, from movement leaders to movement followers, but instead is interactive and participatory. Following after this, thirty-five additional women read *ConcernedKaia's* initial post, and in reply, many of them ignore the racist rhetoric and respond in rather straightforward, liberal feminist terms, as in the following two: "Yes. End of story" (*Komrade Diktator*, post dated 02-19-2008); and this: "I'm firmly pro-choice, and, no, abortion is not nor should it ever be considered a method of birth control" (*Bubble2*, post dated 02-19-2008).

Of course, this is not the end of the discussion. Following several posts by women who identify as pro-choice, a participant with the screen name *AmberDawn88* writes, "Abortion cannot be kept legal. . . . So stop making excuses, and realize abortion for what it is, which is murder. By the by, pro-choice is not the opposite of pro-life. The opposite of pro-life is pro-death" (*AmberDawn88*, post dated 02-20-2008). Then another participant quotes the original post from *ConcernedKaia* and writes the following:

I fully agree with you. I do believe that abortion is and should be the woman's right. She should have the ability to abort the fetus if she is unable to care for it, or has HIV, or was raped, etc. . . . Nobody should have to live with the fact that they had a baby just because the law prevented the (early term) aborting of the fetus. . . . Bottom line: It's the woman's choice. She has to birth the baby, take care of it night and day, and if she is unable to do so either by mental or physical status or if she has HIV or some other kind of terminal illness, she should have the RIGHT to abort for her and her baby's own wellbeing." (*1bones3*, post dated 02-20-2008)

In this post *1bones3* articulates a stance that is indistinguishable from mainstream, liberal feminist rhetoric in support of women's right to control their own bodies when she writes "abortion is and should be the woman's right." Indeed, she recognizes the unequal distribution of childcare and housework in her assessment that the hypothetical woman in her example must "birth the baby [and] take care of it night and day." While *1bones3* concedes some ground to pro-life rhetoric when she alludes to late-term abortions (i.e., "the law prevented the [early-term] aborting the fetus"), even with this concession her overriding message is one that is consistent with the liberal feminism of organizations like N.O.W. and Planned Parenthood. The debate in this forum continues on with a volley of back-and-forth posts, such as this one, which immediately follows *1bones3*'s post: "Abortion is murder, plain and simple. It's blaming an unborn for mistakes that aren't theirs" (*chika4gw*, post dated 02-21-2008).

The conversation or, more accurately, the competing monologues is very similar to exchanges found outside white-supremacy groups. After the initial post in this thread by *ConcernedKaia*, few participants take up the racially charged implications of the original post until four days after the initial thread began, when another participant writes this:

Abortion should be legal in nonwhite countries who are populating the Earth so fast and at unsustainable numbers. They are crushing us in every which way. It is different with the white race, however. I am firmly PRO-LIFE. For those people justifying abortion in America because black women get them too, what you are saying is that abortions should stay legal because black females get them too but at the expense of unborn white children? No young white life is worth one hundred black abortions; am I wrong? Abortion has taken a toll on our worldwide numbers. One out of every two pregnancies in Russia ends in abortion. Do you know how many millions of babies that could have been? Think of all the Italian, English, Norwegian, and Swedish children growing in the womb who have been reduced to medical waste.

Naturally, the father of the baby gets no "choice"—his feelings don't matter one bit. Feminism at its best. She can go off and have your son/daughter vacuumed out or poisoned with saline with the snap of a finger. Have you ever seen the photos of a saline-induced abortion? Sorry, that's not what I want for my race.

Interracial rape, okay. It was a crime and can be taken care of in the hospital on an emergency basis. "For the mother's health"—and incest, how often does that REALLY happen? A hospital can take care of it; there is no need for abortion mills in every city or suburb across America and Europe.

Abortion should be severely curtailed for us. . . . And alternatives like adoption (white babies are in HUGE demand) should be considered. We have an obligation to protect the youngest of our race, because who else will? That is my opinion. (*whitebread*, post dated 02-24-2008)

Here *whitebread* directly challenges the implicit feminism in the others' support for abortion and more forcefully questions the feminist rhetoric of pro-choice when she asserts that "the father of the baby gets no 'choice,'" then charges that this is an example of "Feminism at its best." This post also addresses the racial questions raised at the beginning of the thread by *ConcernedKaia*. Despite her broad antiabortion stance, *whitebread* advocates for abortion in "nonwhite countries," which she perceives to be "crushing us" in "every which way." Such rhetoric clearly reaffirms white supremacy. Then she puts this white supremacy in stark numeric terms by asserting that "No young white life is worth one hundred black abortions," an assessment that white lives are a hundred times more valuable than black lives.

What *whitebread*, *ConcernedKaia*, and the other participants are negotiating in this ladies-only Should abortion be legal? discussion thread is what feminism viewed through a white supremacist lens means for the women who participate at Stormfront.org. In particular, they are creating space for both ardently pro-life and vehemently pro-choice articulations of white supremacy, thus effectively expanding the appeal of white supremacy beyond a narrowly conceived constituency. In contrast, white supremacist discourse in the print-only era was created almost exclusively by white men who published this in newsletters that left no room for negotiation or for women's voices. While it is certain that women read these newsletters in resistive ways, the discussion boards at Stormfront open up the production of white supremacist discourse to multiple voices and perspectives. In this gendered white supremacy online, enacted here by white women, the one-dimensional view of abortion in the rhetoric of white supremacy of the print-only era is broadened through a participatory engagement with the movement's discourse made possible by the Internet.[28]

This sort of negotiation around what feminism means when viewed through a white supremacist lens appears in a variety of different threads in the ladies-only forum. For instance, in a thread called 1943 Guide to Hiring Women, a participant links to a (not white supremacist) blog[29] that carries a scanned document that appears to be from the July 1943 issue of a magazine and features a laughably sexist list of ten instructions on how to hire and manage women.[30] The women at Stormfront.org are in on the joke intended by posting this dated article. Several women come through this thread and agree with the feminist message inherent in poking fun at such an article. It is clear from this thread and others that the women of Stormfront.org include many women who work outside the home and for whom such work is central. One woman uses the screen name *Future_Lawyer* to designate her occupational aspirations, although most of the women appear to hold jobs that they find less than fulfilling, as indicated by a thread called My Work Week Sucked, where women share stories from their work lives. The women participating in these discussions share a taken-for-granted acceptance of work outside the home and an expectation of being hired, paid, promoted, and treated equitably. This reflects the embrace of significant portions of liberal feminism, and yet, they resist other dimensions of liberal feminism, such as identifying as ladies and subtitling their forum Sugar and Spice and Everything Nice. Despite this embrace of some elements of liberal feminism, the women posting at the ladies-only forum continue to feel powerless in relation to the men in their lives in various ways.

Within the ladies-only forum, the most popular thread with 391 individual posts (and 12,957 views) is an item called Powder-Room Confessions. The title of the thread suggests a nostalgic period when restrooms were euphemistically referred to as powder rooms, and women engaged in a gendered practice of exchanging information away from the surveillance of men. Some of the confessions involve racist acts or encounters with people perceived to be nonwhite, but the vast majority of the posts in this item run to the mundane and cover routine confessions about watching television shows and movies that qualify as guilty pleasures and about acts such as eating entire boxes of cookies consumed in secret, childhood shoplifting, and revenge taken against deserving men. In this post one woman confesses to the way she left a job:

> Years ago, one of my bosses was trying to screw me over—wanted me to do the work of a supervisor without the PAY of a supervisor. I gave my two weeks' notice, and that made him so mad that he told me I should just leave right away. Later that evening I drove into the parking lot and took the personalized sign above his parking space. It still hangs on my wall. (*suepeace*, post dated 11-26-2007)

Here *suepeace* is clearly in a subordinate position at her job, and rather than negotiate a raise or a new position to address the inequity she encounters, she quits. And to take revenge rather than confront her boss, she steals his personalized parking sign late at night. Stealing a trivial but symbolically important memento from the workplace is an act of employee sabotage frequently committed by people who feel both aggrieved and powerless. The focus in *suepeace's* narrative in the context of Powder-Room Confessions is on "one of" her "bosses" who was "trying to screw" her over, suggesting both a series of similar sorts of petty, unfair (male) bosses and a lack of awareness of any sort of political consciousness about the structure of gendered inequality inherent in a segmented labor force. Thus, while the women posting at Stormfront.org embrace some elements of liberal feminist rhetoric and share similar expectations about work outside the home that it implies, like many women the material reality of their lives remains constrained by gender inequality.

The gender inequality that the women posting at Stormfront.org experience extends beyond the workplace to include intimate, heterosexual relationships. While many women express satisfaction with heterosexuality, as in the thread The Sweetness of Married Life (begun by *suepeace*, 12 replies, 577 views), many others articulate a different view. In an alternate view of heterosexual relationships expressed by the women at Stormfront.org, men figure in the women's lives as inattentive, unfaithful, sometimes abusive boyfriends and husbands. One woman describes a wave of revenge on an abusive boyfriend that is similar to *suepeace's* clandestine sign-stealing:

> I was in a crappy, abusive relationship up 'til last year, when I finally got away, so I got small acts of revenge. I put dirt in his food, sand in his side of the bed, cut up dog roll very thin and put it in his sandwiches, and lots of other things. It gave me great pleasure to watch him eat this stuff. Never mess with the person who cooks all the meals . . . hahahaha. (*littlemissevil*, post dated 11-21-2007)

This narrative of revenge mixed with the intimacy of food preparation is a familiar one and, like the sign stealing, suggests a surreptitious act of revenge carried out by someone who is relatively powerless who gains a sort of power in retelling the story. Another participant affirms *littlemissevil's* post by responding "Hahahaha," and the banter in the virtual Powder Room continues with others' confessions. A few hours later, another woman posts this confession about her unfaithful ex-husband: "When I found out that my ex-husband was cheating on me, I stopped cleaning the toilet. About a week later, before he came home from work to get his things and leave permanently, I used his toothbrush to scrub said toilet. I never told him" (*Untainted Truth*, post dated 11-21-2007).

Here the woman who goes by *Untainted Truth* gains a sort of victory in retelling this story in which she was both humiliated and relatively powerless but managed to humiliate her ex-husband from a safe distance. Like the other women, her revenge is exacted through a domestic chore that she continues to perform, and she takes pleasure, and, indeed, perhaps ensures her own safety, in *not* telling him. Like the sign-stealing revenge of *suepeace* and the food preparation revenge of *littlemissevil*, the woman posting as *Untainted Truth* exacts revenge in secret and gains power in the relative safety of a ladies-only confessional. The next day, the woman known as *littlemissevil* is back and responds to *Untainted Truth's* toothbrush confession with this post: "Hahaha, I sooo did that as well . . . but I thought people might think it's too mean. . . . LOL. Glad to see there is another vengeful women out there with clever ways of getting back at the bastards in their lives" (*littlemissevil*, post dated 11-22-2007). And *MadeinIreland* adds to the chorus when she responds, "Really? I thought all of us love when women get revenge! I know I do" (*MadeinIreland*, post dated 11-22-2007).

These confessions from the women posting at Stormfront.org suggest an acknowledgment of a gendered pattern of behavior on the part of the men in their lives as well as an acknowledged lack of power on the part of the women, yet the confessions fail to achieve a fully realized feminist critique because they lack any sort of connection to a larger political analysis of either the men's behavior or the women's position within society *as women* that makes them vulnerable to these men. In the Powder Room the confessions are merely personal, not political. Although the women draw strength from each other's confessions, they remain locked in a relatively powerless position within the gendered structures of both the online forum at Stormfront and the broader society. Still, this kind of discussion within the context of white supremacist discourse at Stormfront.org represents a significant rupture in the smooth, unvarnished representation of powerful, white masculinity. In the print-only era of white supremacist newsletters such a representation of white masculinity goes unchallenged, whereas in the era of participatory media, in which all users create their own discourse the fissures of white-masculine power are exposed.

Controlling Sexuality:
Heterosexual Miscegenation and Queer Sexuality

Controlling sexuality is a key feature of white supremacy,[31] and to better understand how this dynamic works online I need to first provide some background on how heterosexual miscegenation and queer sexuality were represented in the print-only era of newsletters. A core feature of white supremacist discourse of the print-only era was the sexual dominance of white men over others—of white women, to be sure, as well as controlling images and discourse of the sexuality of black men and black women and of Jewish men and Jewish women. A trope in extremist discourse and in mainstream American culture particularly in the nineteenth and twentieth centuries was the danger and allure of sexual contact between a black man and a white woman. The twist to this meme when viewed through a white supremacist lens is that such alliances (e.g., *miscegenation*) are viewed as part of a larger Jewish-led conspiracy to both degrade the white race and simultaneously distract whites and blacks from Jewish attempts at control.[32]

Along with the fear of heterosexual interracial contact, the pages of the print-only-era newsletters also contained an asymmetrically gendered view of racialized homosexuality. The rhetoric that expressed concern about queer sexuality took up a relatively small, but ideologically significant, space within white supremacist discourse in print. Specifically, rhetoric about male sexuality focused rather narrowly on bodily penetration, and white gay men were regarded as emasculated race traitors for their supposed willingness to be penetrated. In two line drawings on opposing pages of a white supremacist newsletter, a white man stands triumphantly over a black man as he anally penetrates him with a confederate flagpole; in another image, a white gay man (described as an "A.I.D.S.-Ravaged Fag") walks with a cane, his emaciated body visibly penetrated. In both these images and the surrounding text sexual dominance and white masculinity are inextricably linked.[33]

In the print-only era, homosexuality was also frequently linked to Jewish identity. Lesbians in the pages of the newsletters were universally configured as Jewish and as feminists. In keeping with the conspiracy theories of Jewish power, lesbian-Jewish feminists were represented as threats to the purity of white womanhood as temptresses who might lure otherwise heterosexual white women into a same-sex relationship or perhaps indoctrinate her with feminist ideas of gender equality, a threat no less sinister. Either way, the formerly pure and racially loyal white woman would be "spoiled for the white supremacist cause."[34]

This brief sketch of gender and sexual ideology in white supremacist discourse is one that was created by a handful of white men who published newsletters that sought to promote this ideology. In the digital era, and specifically at Stormfront, these views have been challenged, extended, and rearticulated in new ways made possible by the participatory quality of discussion boards. Unlike printed newsletters where a select few decide on one particular version of the ideology and print that, in the participatory medium of discussion boards, each individual participant writing at the boards is reading, evaluating, and reinterpreting white supremacist discourse for him- or herself. At the same time that the shift in print and new media has occurred, there have also been a series of social and political developments that have altered the discourse. First, the rise of a global, network society[35] and with it the global transfer of people, goods, and information across national borders has meant there are simply more and greater opportunities for international contact. Second, there is greater acceptance of interracial relationships and families in U.S. culture and society as a whole (including interracial adoptions, which are part of the global transfer of people, goods, and information) and, along with that, a significant increase in the visibility and political power of lesbian, gay, bisexual, transgender, and queer (LGBTQ) people, not just in the United States but globally. These two issues—interracial marriage and lesbian/gay rights—have dovetailed, sometimes quite uncomfortably, in the rhetoric of same-sex marriage. Some advocates for marriage equality have drawn an analogy between laws prohibiting same-sex marriage and those that prohibited interracial marriage. Thus, the combination of a changing social and political world along with the rise of new media have altered white supremacist discourse about interracial relationships and queer sexuality in the digital era.

There are new, unexpected, and complicated expressions of white supremacist concerns around interracial contact and homosexuality at Stormfront. In the white supremacist imagination interracial relationships remain a central concern and are now joined by an almost equal concern about homosexuality. Evidence for this is clear in the proportion of threads and posts dedicated to each subject. Using the search function built into Stormfront, I searched for terms related to interracial relationships and homosexuality. I then counted the number of threads returned on each of the search terms and calculated a mean number of hits (threads containing the search term) for each category; the mean for interracial terms was 576.5 items, and the mean for homosexual terms was 411.4.

Interracial relationships remain a concern, but what precisely constitutes *interracial* is up for negotiation. As in the example of *diabloblanco14* (discussed above in the section on Screen Names), he counts himself as not merely white but Aryan, despite his Southern Italian heritage. And he dates Latina women whom he describes as "WHITE Hispanic." Thus, a relationship that might be termed interracial by some is recast by *diabloblanco14* as one that stays within the boundaries of whiteness and upholds the standard that prohibits race mixing. While the question of who is and is not white comes up for discussion at Stormfront, there seems to be little doubt about who is black, as this is regarded as both immutable and plainly evident visually. It is interracial relationships involving blacks, and especially black men and white women, that remain a central concern. This centuries-old preoccupation of white supremacists has expanded to new, digital terrain, as in a thread called MySpace Advertises Interracial Sex. In this thread, started by forum member *White Garden*, he expresses grave concern about a banner ad at the social-networking site, MySpace.com. He refers to the site advertised (interracialromance.com), quotes from their advertising copy about their service for people who "enjoy interracial relations," and then writes:

> Truly disgusting. The filth should be removed from the Internet. Again, anyone age fourteen and over who registers on the site CAN SEE THESE ADS!
>   Special note: All the pictures I've seen on the site so far are of white women (with amazing face and body) with black males. (*White Garden*, post dated 02-29-2008)

Other forum members join in the discussion, each adding their own take on how "disgusting" they find black-male sexuality and reaffirming white supremacist prohibitions on interracial dating. While there is nothing new in this anti-race-mixing ideology, the digital era does suggest new forms for expressing both white supremacy and resistance to it. Here, the copy/paste function allows *White Garden* to copy advertising text paid for by InterracialRomance.com displayed on MySpace.com and paste it into Stormfront.org. In so doing, he effectively expands the reach of white supremacist commentary to include these other online spaces. In contrast to his reactionary judgment, the mere presence of the dating site Interracial Romance.com (and even MySpace.com) suggests a significant move away from societal norms that prohibit relationships across color lines. And global, networked connections make such relationships and interracial families even more likely. Thus, both the dating site InterracialRomance.com and Stormfront.org are engaged in a contested struggle, staking racial claims on the Internet, albeit on very different sides.

Along with shifts in discourse about interracial relationships, there have been profound changes in the discussion about queer sexuality within white supremacist discourse. To be sure, homophobia and virulent antiqueer discourse remain features of white supremacist ideology at places like Stormfront. People who identify as LGBTQ are routinely referred to as "disgusting" and "freaks," and all manner of bad behavior is attributed to gay identity. Alongside this hate-filled rhetoric, a new, more expansive version of white supremacy is being articulated by forum members who, while not openly gay or openly supportive of LGBTQ equality, are nevertheless quite reserved in their judgments of homosexuality. This rupture in white supremacist discourse appears in a number of threads that pose a question, such as one thread simply titled Homosexuality. The person who initiated the thread wonders, "What is it that makes homosexuals bad for the WN [white nationalist] cause?" Another thread poses a similar question: "Why exactly is homosexuality wrong?" A forum member responds with this:

> Homosexuality is not ideal because it doesn't produce white children, and its male version tends to spread disease. But homosexuality is a part of the white condition. There have been loyal prowhite homosexuals who have found ways to contribute, like donating lots of money to prowhite causes. Far, far too many whites aren't having children, yet singles, including homosexuals, are freed up to work for the cause in ways family men and women aren't. I think a healthy white society would not encourage it and would rightly seek to marginalize it but not criminalize it or do violence to those so inclined. (Hugh Lincoln, post dated 10-22-2007)

The response here from Hugh Lincoln sounds almost moderate compared to the universally hostile rhetoric about homosexuality in the era of printed newsletters. Hugh Lincoln's statement here about his willingness to consider the possibility of incorporating "prowhite homosexuals" into the cause is further evidence of the way that white supremacy in the digital era has changed. In addition, the strong connection between lesbian and Jewish identity seems to be missing, or at least much less prevalent than in print. Whether or not this represents a significant shift away from an intertwined homophobia and anti-Semitism in the digital era or simply the everyday invisibility of lesbians in discussions of homosexuality remains an open question. What seems clear is that rather than the one-way communication determined by a handful of movement leaders publishing newsletters for movement followers, the participatory forums at Stormfront allow for a multiplicity of white supremacist voices. And at least some of those voices express acceptance of a vision of white supremacy that includes openly gay members who are white and support the cause of white supremacy.

Consequences of Gendered White Supremacy IRL (In Real Life)

White supremacist rhetoric online can have very real consequences in real life. In the opening to this chapter I referred to the website that depicted Bonnie Jouhari's workplace exploding amid animated GIF flames and the very real harassment she suffered once her address and phone number were published on the site.[36] In this instance, the white supremacist rhetoric also had consequences for Roy Frankhouser, the self-described chaplain to the Ku Klux Klan in Pennsylvania, who terrorized Jouhari and her daughter. This sort of hate-filled targeting of an individual on the Web is part of what appears to be an emerging trend.[37]

In a 2007 incident with some striking similarities to the Jouhari case, a white supremacist from Roanoke, Virginia, with the redundantly appropriate name William White published the home addresses and phone numbers of the families of six Louisiana high school students known as the Jena 6. What became known as the Jena 6 incident started as a racially charged schoolyard brawl in which white youths hung a noose in a tree on school property as a way to warn black youths that the tree was designated as a whites-only hangout spot. A black youth challenged this, white youths retaliated, and several students were injured. The controversy heated up when the black youths were charged with felonies that carried long prison sentences for attacking a white youth while the white teens who had targeted their black schoolmates were released on very minor charges that involved no jail time. In addition to using a racial slur in the title of the posting, White also encourages readers to "get in touch, and let them know justice is coming."[38] In another posting, White is even more explicit about what he is advocating: "Lynch the Jena 6." As antiracism protests grew,[39] white supremacists grew increasingly enraged and violent. Retaliation for the antiracism protests were often expressed in violent, hypermasculine terms, as this quote from a white man posting to the Vanguard News Network illustrates:

> I think a group of white men with AK rifles loaded with high-capacity magazines should close in on the troop of howler monkeys from all sides and compress them into a tight group, and then white men in the buildings on both sides of the shit-skinned hominids shall throw Molotov cocktails from above to cleanse the nigs by fire.—NS Cat (post at Vanguard News Network)

This quote from an online forum reflects the militaristic swagger and tactics of bullying and intimidation that are characteristic of some branches of male-dominated white supremacy.[40] The website threatening Bonnie Jouhari and her daughter received over 97,000 visits in a three-year time period.[41] Thus, the Internet in both of these instances functions as a mechanism of harassment and as a force multiplier, expanding the reach of that harassment. In the Jouhari case, real-life harassment followed in the wake of the online harassment, yet local police and the Justice Department declined to file criminal charges against Frankhouser, citing his First Amendment rights. Eventually, the Department of Housing and Urban Development (HUD), under the direction of Andrew Cuomo, took action against Frankhouser in the form of a civil suit that ended in penalties and fines being levied against him.[42] In the Louisiana case, while there were reports that the FBI was investigating William White for the posting that threatened the Jena 6, as of this writing White has not been arrested or charged with any crime. If William White's threat had occurred in a number of European nations—say, Germany or Norway—the targeted families would have had legal recourse under antiracism laws (more about this in chapter 7). Consistent with gendered white supremacy, it is relevant to note that in each of these cases the online harassers were white males.

Mainstream news reports suggest there is growing apprehension that this kind of targeted harassment is becoming an all-too common practice.[43] In what some have termed *cyberbullying*,[44] schoolyard bullies use various digital technologies, such as MySpace pages and text messages sent from mobile phones, to target other young people for online harassment. This type of harassment is often based on physical characteristics (like size, disability, or age) or social identities (such as gender, sexuality, race, or ethnicity). Initial research in this area suggests that the targets of harassment are most often women and girls[45] and that the perpetrators of cyberbullying—whether children or adults—tend to be *white males*.

Even without this type of direct, overt harassment, there is additional evidence of a hegemonically white, heterosexual, masculine culture online. Lori Kendall argues in her richly nuanced ethnography of the gendered dynamics in the multiuser domain (MUD) BlueSky that digital technologies reproduce white, heterosexual, masculine cultures and hierarchies of power.[46] While this is by no means conclusive evidence, the preliminary research does indicate a pattern of white-male dominance of online spaces.

When viewed in a global context, it becomes clear that the ability of white women (such as *Concerned Kaia*, *whitebread*, and *Lycia*) to create white supremacist Web content—whether starting threads, reading and replying to others' posts, or serving as a discussion-board moderator—is at least partly the result of a privileged economic and geopolitical position in which those who live in industrialized nations are more likely to own computers and have Internet access than those living in developing societies.[47] This disparity in owning a computer and having Internet access reflects a parallel inequality in usage; together these have been referred to as "the digital divide." Although women still account for less than half of all Internet usage in a number of developing countries, globally women are rapidly catching up with increasing rates of participation online, often at faster rates than men.[48] One U.S.-based advocate for equal access to technology refers to the digital divide as "the civil-rights issue of the new millennium."[49] Others take issue with the *divide* terminology for a variety of reasons.[50] Empirical research indicates that most of the apparent digital divide in the United States concerning computer ownership and Internet access originally attributed to gender or racial difference is the effect of class (or socioeconomic status) more than gender and race.[51] As of 2006 in the United States Internet access has converged between men and women who are white.[52] Thus, white supremacists such as *Concerned Kaia*, *whitebread*, and *Lycia* are increasingly likely to be the online representatives of white supremacy but just as unlikely to be leaders.

Masculinity, the Internet, and White Supremacy

White men, such as Don Black, have led the way in the shifting white supremacist-movement rhetoric from print to the Web. This fact reflects the confluence of several others: the predominance of white men in leadership positions in organized racism, their dominance as early innovators in the fields of computer programming and Internet technology, as well as the continued dominance of elite white men in positions of power in U.S. political institutions and in global capitalism. Given the pervasiveness of white male dominance, in capitalism and in particular in the development of the Internet, it is perhaps not surprising that white men within organized racism were among the early adopters of this technology to advance the movement's goals.

The Internet has a history, geography, and demography grounded firmly in the material realities of gender, class, and race, and these shape the technology and influence our experience of the technology.[53] The collection of digital technologies that we now refer to as *the Internet* began as an initiative of the United States Department of Defense, called ARPAnet (Advanced Research Projects Agency Network).[54] The architects and early adopters of Internet technologies have predominantly been white men.[55] While the accomplishments of African Americans[56] and women across racial and ethnic categories have often been neglected, these exceptional individuals are frequently tokens in an otherwise white-male domain of computer technology. This white-male dominance of computer technology continues. Today the leaders of both the software and Internet-related industries and the cultural commentators who write most often for mass media outlets about digital cultures are predominantly men and exclusively white. The digerati, a play on the term *literati*, is a group of industry and cultural leaders appointed by the media (some might say "anointed") as spokespeople. To illustrate this point, one list of the digerati includes forty names, thirty-five of which are men, all of whom are white, and most of whom are from the United States.[57] The development of the Internet by white men as a communication technology for the military, along with the continued predominance of white men in the elite technoclass of both the digital economy and culture, has led some to argue that the Internet is inherently masculinist,[58] while many progressive activists, including many feminists, have carved out a space for resistance within this terrain.[59] This debate over gender and technology remains unresolved and reverberates through the racially charged use of the Internet.[60]

White masculinity informs the online practices of participants at Stormfront and the actions of individuals like Roy Frankhouser. While offline organized racist groups project a sense of hypermasculinity in their militaristic swagger and tactics of bullying and intimidation,[61] online participatory sites such as Stormfront allow for a variety of expressions of gender and sexuality. Although these new online expressions of white supremacy remain quite narrowly constrained, they simultaneously allow for reinvigoration of this ideology by including participation by white women who espouse liberal feminist rhetoric about equality, by including new interpretations of "interracial dating" and by offering limited support of "prowhite homosexuals." These digital, online expressions of white supremacy are embedded in the material structures of gender, race, and globalization. One of the ironies of masculinity and the Internet is that, even as the technologies reproduce masculine cultures and hierarchies of power, online space also enables women to engage in new forms of contestation.[62] And one of the ironies of white supremacy online is that, even as the broadcast television commercial aired touting the Internet as a "place where there is no race," Don Black and others were working to create Stormfront, a site that ardently advocates for a racist vision. Stormfront is not successful because there is a vast reservoir of pathological individuals ready to be recruited into a white supremacist army or because innocents are lured in by the dangers of the Internet. Rather, the forum owes much of its success to the effective deployment of the white racial frame that goes unacknowledged in the United States and the site's ability to use that frame to coalesce a translocal whiteness that ignores national boundaries. The white men who have led the white supremacist movement into the digital era, such as Don Black, David Duke, and James Kelso, are not the elite white men who are captains of global capitalism. Yet they are relatively privileged within a global context of economic, gender, and racial inequality. Similarly, white men who have led the innovations of cyber racism are not on a technological or entrepreneurial par with those creative individuals who first conceptualized the Internet, but they have translated the white supremacist movement into the digital era in ways that belie the conventional notions that white supremacists are backward and that technological innovations always bring progress. And, given that the white supremacist movement remains male-dominated, despite the greater inclusion of women's voices, it is not surprising that white men are the ones who translated white supremacy into the digital era.

The fact that white men have been the primary innovators in translating white supremacy into the digital era has had important implications for the material lives of women, girls, and those who are viewed as racial Others. In this way, the extremist expressions of white supremacy map onto the everyday expressions of white identity. The kind of cyber-racist attacks launched against Bonnie Jouhari, her daughter, and the young African American men of the Jena 6 case are the result of white men's use of Internet technologies to attack the perceived Other. This shares many features of the cyberbullying phenomenon, in which young children labeled Other along some axis of identity are targeted for attack online; the emerging research here suggests it is young boys who are most often the aggressors. Taken together, this indicates that white supremacy is inherently linked with white identity and that the Internet has been a particularly effective mechanism for furthering the goals of white supremacy. These goals corrode the ideals of equality in a democratic society.

Conclusion

The people who participate in and create white supremacy online actively shape their identity online in ways that are explicitly racialized, gendered, and, to some extent, sexualized. The participatory quality of Web 2.0, where everyone creates online content, opens up white supremacist rhetoric in ways that were simply not possible in the print-only era. While it is certainly likely that people reading white supremacist newsletters read those in ways that resisted the intended purpose of the author, that resistance never became part of the publication. The Internet, and specifically the participatory form of the Internet referred to as Web 2.0, changes that so the resistive read of the prevailing white supremacist ideology gets built into the medium. When the women of the ladies-only forum post responses that resist the views that male leaders of the movement espouse, they are both challenging and reaffirming white supremacist ideology through the medium of the online forum. In this way the resistive response gets incorporated into the medium and the movement ideology, and in this way it is different than movement discourse in print.

The women at Stormfront incorporate key elements of white liberal feminism into their rhetoric, thereby expanding white supremacist ideology and making the movement potentially more inclusive to those who hold a range of other political views along with a shared valued in white identity. Thus the women at Stormfront illustrate that white feminism is not in-compatible with key features of white supremacy. By resisting a more male-dominated version of white supremacy and articulating a form of white supremacy that is more inclusive and egalitarian along lines of gender, and even allowing for the possibility of a version of equal rights within white su-premacy for gays and lesbians, the women of Stormfront illustrate another way in which white supremacy is inherent in white identity. This suggests something troubling about liberal feminism. To the extent that liberal femi-nism articulates a limited vision of gender equality without challenging racial inequality, white feminism is not inconsistent with white supremacy. With-out an explicit challenge to racism, white feminism is easily grafted onto white supremacy and useful for arguing for equality for white women and pos-sibly for white gays and lesbians within a white supremacist context.

While there is a slight opening for the acceptance of queer sexuality within white supremacy, the vigilant protection against the perceived threat of miscegenation, or transracial heterosexual contact still predominates. Within the context of white supremacy online, miscegenation remains a pri-mary concern, even as the idea of the possibility of gays and lesbians within the movement gains more acceptance. Within this framework race and no-tions of racial purity trump sexuality and notions of sexual impurity. This shift toward greater acceptance (although this seems too strong a word) of gays and lesbians also suggests that the participants at Stormfront do not rep-resent a monolithically conservative ideology, in which racism, misogyny, and homophobia all line up neatly with a shared belief that the Holocaust was a hoax. Instead, the rather more disturbing news is that white suprema-cists at Stormfront are not as different from many white Americans in their views about gender equality and the acceptance of queer sexuality as we might prefer to believe.

Masculinity and whiteness are embedded in various ways in the Internet and in online communication. Race is, as one scholar puts it, "like an ever-present ghost in the machine" of American technology.[63] The emergence of the online community at Stormfront.org expresses what may be an authen-tic human desire for community, yet it is an expression of community that is articulated in ways that rely on the construction of a unified white, male, heterosexual subject and an explicit discourse of white supremacy.[64] The emergence of a ladies-only space provides for some participation by white women at Stormfront, but the very existence of the women-only forum speaks to the overriding male dominance of the site and online communica-tion as whole. The use of the Internet as a tool for harassment and intimida-tion by white supremacists like Roy Frankhouser, and more broadly in the culture by cyberbullies who are predominantly white and male, suggests that hate speech online has real consequences on- and offline.

Both the harassment of Bonnie Jouhari and the emergence of a ladies-only forum at Stormfront illustrate the way that the digital and the material are embedded in each other; in many ways, the online and offline distinctions are false. The digital world is embedded in the material world, and the material in the digital. White masculinity is a feature of Internet technology, and white masculinity is embedded in our culture, in our institutions, and, indeed, in globalization. At the same time that white masculinity operates as a "ghost in the machine," the participatory media of sites like Stormfront, where users create the content, mean that articulations of gendered white supremacy have opened in new ways that expand the scope of who might be included in such a world.

In the following chapter, I examine the presence of overt white supremacy online and explore the ways that movement rhetoric published in newsletters prior to the digital era has been translated to the Web. Then I explore the emergence of *cloaked* white supremacy online and the ways some white supremacist groups have taken advantage of the unique features of the Web to shift knowledge claims about race, racism, and civil rights. And following that, I offer a brief glimpse at the ways some young people in the United States make sense of these cloaked sites before shifting focus once again to white supremacy in a global context.

Notes

Signature file of a sustaining member of Stormfront.org

1. For more on this case, see Smith 2002. See also Marcus 2000 and Holmes 2000.

2. The discussion-board software that Don Black uses for Stormfront is vBulletin, and the software automatically generates these statistics (I discuss the features of this software in more detail in the following chapter). These numbers were observed March 12, 2008. While it is technically possible to inflate these numbers, they appear to be consistent with the number of threads and posts when counted manually. I did not verify these numbers for the discussion board as a whole, but I did verify them for the Ladies Only forum, and the user statistics displayed by the software is consistent with the manual count of threads and posts.

3. These numbers were observed on March 12, 2008.

4. As Abby Ferber notes, a gendered analysis cannot be reduced to the role of women in the organized racist movement: 2003, 10.

5. Daniels 1997.

6. The home of Don Black's White Pride World Wide, the largest white supremacist forum on the web.

7. By "most successful" here I mean that it has the most enrolled users; Stormfront.org had well over 129,000 registered users as of 2008. (See chapter 4 for a comparison to MoveOn.org).

8. The posters at Stormfront typically use *white nationalist* to refer to their worldview; I use *white supremacist,* because it is consistent with my previous analysis and because it suggests the translocal white identity that is an inherent part of white supremacy online.

9. Blee 2003.

10. Blee 2003, 4.

11. Blee 2003, 7.

12. Blee 2003, 9.

13. Blee 2003, 9.

14. Blee 2003, 71.

15. Aho 1990 and 1994. And see Ezekiel 1995.

16. Blee 2003, 69.

17. A handful of participants use their real names as their user IDs. These tend to be more prominent people in the movement, such as Don Black, founder of Stormfront.org, and David Duke, a leader in the contemporary white supremacist movement.

18. Selecting screen names from the Sustaining Members discussion board functions as a sampling strategy for selecting a subsample of the larger universe of all Stormfront.org members. The gendered pattern that emerged in this subsample appears to be consistent with the larger population of Stormfront.org users. I leave a more exhaustive analysis of all Stormfront.org users to the work of future researchers. For a longer discussion of the methodology I use in this chapter and throughout this book, see the methods appendix.

19. There is no way to verify gender in a primarily text-based online environment, so here I simply rely on each participant's self-disclosure in the context of posting about their preferred gender identity. While it is certainly possible that someone could deceive others about their gender, I do not know of a way to avoid the possibility of such deception. Furthermore, it is a moot point with regard to my argument here.

20. Greenfield and Subrahmanyam 2003.

21. Byrne 2007.

22. Kendall 2000.

23. Godwin 1998.

24. Herring. 1994, 278–94. See also Herring 1996, 115–45.

25. Herring 1993; Herring, Johnson, and DiBenedetto 1992, 1995; Hert 1997.

26. Balka 1993. Women's access to on-line discussions about feminism. *Electronic Journal of Communication* 3 (1). http://www.cios.org/www/ejc/v3n193.htm

27. While Blee makes reference to the increasing significance of the Internet for women in organized racism (Blee 2003, 15, 78, 138, 144), this is not the focus of her study.

28. And specifically by a particular version of the Internet often referred to as Web 2.0 where users create the content. Brochure sites, discussed in chapter 6, do not allow for this sort of participation but are closer to the one-way transfer of information in the print-only-era newsletters.

29. At http://iheartchaos.com/2008/02/23/how-to-hire-a-woman-how-to/.

30. For example: "#4. Retain a physician to give each woman you hire a special physical examination—one covering female conditions. This step not only protects the property against the possibilities of lawsuit but reveals whether the employee-to-be has any female weaknesses which would make her mentally or physically unfit for the job."

31. Ferber 2003.

32. All of the discussion here about sexuality in the print-only era of white supremacist discourse is drawn from Daniels 1997. See especially chapters 3, 4, and 5.

33. Daniels 1997, 49–51.

34. Daniels 1997, chapter 5.

35. Castells 1996, vols. 1, 2, and 3. See also chapter 2 in this book.

36. Smith 2002. Marcus 2000.

37. In a related form of online and hate-filled harassment, Fred Phelps's site (god-hatesfags.com) features animated GIF flames surrounding a picture of murdered hate-crime victim Matthew Shepard, with a daily counter marking Matthew's "number of days in hell." While the website in this case appeared after Matthew Shepard's murder and so did not contribute directly to his death, Phelps's rhetoric serves to justify similar hate crimes and is certainly a source of on-going harassment for Dennis and Judy Shepard, Matthew's surviving parents.

38. Thomas-Lester 2007.

39. The antiracism protests that emerged in response to the Jena 6 were largely possible because of online organizing by blacks and through a network of black bloggers. Unfortunately, exploring this much more progressive use of the Internet is beyond the scope of the current project.

40. Blee 2002, 4. Anahita 2006.

41. Smith 2006, cited in Daniels 2008a.

42. In 2000 a Pennsylvania judge ordered that Frankhouser pay 5 percent of his salary to Ms. Jouhari and 5 percent to her daughter in any year that he earns at least $25,000 for the next ten years; other penalties included promoting antidiscrimination efforts through recorded public-service announcements informing the public about laws against bias in housing to be aired on his television show "White Forum." In addition, Frankhouser was ordered to refrain from mentioning Ms. Jouhari or her daughter—except to apologize—in any public forum for the rest of his life, and he was ordered to stay at least one hundred feet away from Ms. Jouhari and her daughter for the rest of his life.

43. Harmon 2004.

44. Li 2005. See also Patchin and Hinduja 2006.

45. Li 2005. Patchin and Hinduja 2006.

46. Kendall 2000, 2002.

47. Norris 2001.

48. Sassen 2002, 376.

49. Carvin 2000. Mind the Gap: The Digital Divide as the Civil Rights Issue of the New Millennium. *MultiMedia Schools* 7 (1): 56–58.

50. A number of scholars have argued that the discourse of the digital divide configuring women, blacks, and Hispanics or the poor living in the global South as information have-nots is a disabling rhetoric (Everett 2004, 1280; see also Wright 2005). Others have argued that the term implies a technological determinism in which, if the divide is bridged, then all other social ills will be alleviated (Gunke 2003). Other scholars have critiqued the term because it suggests only one divide, when in fact there are many (Hargittai 2002).

51. Norris 2001.

52. While there remain some small differences in access and kinds of usage between Hispanic women and men and between African American women and men, these differences are negligible (Leggon 2006, 100).

53. Higgins et al. 1999, 111.

54. In the early 1960s J. C. R. Licklider, Ivan Sutherland, and Bob Taylor were working with researchers in Santa Monica, Berkeley, and Boston. In order to communicate with each of these sites, they had to use three separate computers with different log-ins. As Taylor recalls, after moving from one computer to another to discuss a project with a colleague at a different location, he said, "Oh, man, it's obvious what to do: If you have these three terminals, there ought to be one terminal that goes anywhere you want to go. That idea is the ARPAnet." (Janet Abbate 1999. *Inventing the Internet.* Cambridge, Mass.: MIT Press.) Taylor brought in Larry Roberts of MIT to work on the project, and in 1969 the two of them established the first ARPAnet connection between researchers at Stanford University and the University of California, Los Angeles (Abbate 1999). Over the next decade, the use of ARPAnet spread beyond the Department of Defense and became more widely used around the world, primarily at universities in developed countries. In 1973, researchers made the first ARPAnet connection outside the United States to Norway. In 1989, Tim Berners-Lee and Robert Cailliau separately presented ideas for a hypertext system for their employer, the CERN nuclear physics research facility in Switzerland. The first document that actually uses the term *World Wide Web* is dated November 12, 1990, and contains Berners-Lee and Cailliau's coauthored proposal for a system that would make it easier for nuclear physics researchers to share information (Berners-Lee 2000). See also Gillies and Cailliau (2000).

55. Adam 1998. See also Berners-Lee 2000 and Gillies and Cailliau 2000.

56. Taborn 2007.

57. See, for example, Who are "The digerati"? at http://edge.org/digerati/.

58. Adam 1998. Quinby 1999.

59. Many women working in global feminist organizations based outside the United States view Internet technology as crucial to the movement toward global gender equality (Harcourt 1999a, 1999b). Harcourt 2000. Purweal 2004. Merithew 2004. Jacobs 2004. In addition to global feminist organizations, many individual women, in the United States and transnationally, experience the Internet as a safe space for resisting gender oppression that they encounter in their day-to-day lives offline. Exploring this debate about whether Internet technology is inherently masculinist and oppressive or if it can be a mechanism for resisting such oppression, although compelling, is beyond the scope of the current project.

60. See Daniels, 2009a.

61. Blee 2002, 4.

62. Sassen 2002, 368.

63. Tara McPherson forthcoming.

64. McPherson (2000, 117–31) makes a similar argument about white men in neo-Confederate groups online, although for these white guys there is a reluctance to deploy a explicitly racist discourse of black inferiority and white superiority.

~

CHAPTER SIX

White Supremacist Discourse: In Print and Online

We want [our website] to give an accurate portrayal of The Knights. Most people base their opinions on what we call *comic-book research*. They go to the library and pick up a book written by someone who has his own agenda. They may watch a ridiculous Hollywood movie or watch the Jerry Springer show and then think they are experts on the Klan. Hogwash! Any good researcher goes straight to the source. On this website we offer our ideas, explanations, goals, agenda, beliefs, etc. for your examination—straight from the national headquarters of America's largest and oldest Klan organization—the authority on the subject.

—Thom Robb

In the fall of 1998, I was teaching at a predominantly white, suburban Long Island university. Those of us on the faculty who used computers as part of our teaching repertoire were involved in something called the Pioneer Program,[1] which encouraged technological innovation in the classroom. With that encouragement, I scheduled the Race and Ethnicity course I was teaching for a session in the computer lab. I had, I realize now with the clear vision of hindsight, a rather vague idea that students in that class would use the Internet to conduct research about their topics of interest, and I would help them develop websites rather than the traditional term papers for their final class projects (a pedagogical strategy I would probably not use today). On the first day in the lab, the class of thirty or so students, all white, mostly white ethnic from relatively prosperous Italian, Irish, Russian, or Jewish families, and most of whom were first-generation college students, filed into the state-of-the art computer lab and settled into the high-end office chairs, each one in front of a recently installed PC monitor. I watched in dismay as two of my students began surfing the Internet before I could even begin to give my instructions for the class assignment. One of those students was searching for information on Dr. Martin Luther King Jr. and encountered a cloaked site.[2] I looked on as another student typed the letters KKK.com into the first browser window he opened. This led him to the website for Knights of the Ku Klux Klan, hosted by Thom Robb, quoted in the opening of this chapter. Once at the website, my student laughed and pointed at the screen to share the image with his classmates.

The story of my experience with my students in that computer lab illustrates a number of themes that I want to address in this and the following chapters about white supremacy online. In this chapter I focus on the overtly racist white supremacist websites created by those that previously published white supremacist newsletters. My goal here is to offer a preliminary framework for studying social movement discourse in print and online and specifically to offer a preliminary analysis of how white supremacist movement discourse has been translated from print into the digital era. For instance, Thom Robb's printed newsletter, *The Torch*, was one of those I included in my previous study that examined movement publications of five different white supremacist groups,[3] and it was Robb's website that my student visited in the lab. To date there has been scant scholarly investigation that compares social movement discourse prior to and after the widespread adoption of the Internet[4]; and there is no research to my knowledge that offers a comparison of white supremacist movement rhetoric in print and online. According to scholar Les Back, such studies would contribute to "the qualitative understanding of how virtual fascism might relate to its previous media incarnations."[5] In this chapter I do this by examining how "virtual fascism," or what I refer to as *white supremacy online*, relates to its previous media incarnation in printed material. This analysis is by no means an exhaustive study of white supremacy online, as there is a growing body of literature already that examines this online discourse in interesting and innovative ways.[6] What I want to contribute to this ongoing scholarly discussion is an investigation into what I referred to in the opening chapter as a "naturally occurring experiment,"

based on the coincidence of my earlier research on white supremacist discourse in print (the sample for which ended in 1993) and the timing of the emergence of white supremacy online (circa 1994). As a result of this accident of timing, a unique opportunity for inquiry presents itself.

My focus here is on the broadest possible view of the five groups I examined in print and their transition to digital media. These five groups are: The Church of the Creator (COTC), the Ku Klux Klan (KKK), the National Association for the Advancement of White People (NAAWP), the National States Rights Party (NSRP), Christian Identity, and White Aryan Resistance (WAR). I selected these as the sample for my earlier study because they represented a broad ideological spectrum within the white supremacist movement and, while certainly not comprehensive, these groups continue to represent a wide range of perspectives within the white supremacist movement. I am primarily interested in investigating *whether or not the five groups I studied in 1993 made the transition from print-based newsletters to publishing on the Internet by 2007*. If they did not make this shift, I wanted to know why not. And if they did make the transition, I wanted to know what kind of Web presence[7] they have now. That is, if they are online, in what ways are they using digital media? Thus, I organize the discussion that follows according to the ways white supremacists have made use of the Internet, from the least to the most successful measured in terms of Web traffic.

404: Defunct White Supremacist Websites and Organizations

In the digital era an organization without a Web presence is barely recognizable as part of a viable global social movement. As a practical matter, a social-movement organization without a Web presence faces greater difficulty mobilizing social-movement resources than a group with a Web presence.[8] Three of the white supremacist organizations that once published newsletters have not made the transition from old to new media because the organizations themselves no longer exist. The COTC, the Invisible Empire of the KKK, and the NAAWP do not have websites, because their organizations are defunct. The violent white supremacist group Church of the Creator failed in their attempt to exploit the Internet to spread their ideology and build their organization. However, two of the individuals in those organizations, Thom Robb and David Duke, are active online elsewhere.

If you were to type the URL for the group Church of the Creator into a browser window (www.cotc.com), you would get a 404 message, meaning "file not found"— that website does not exist.[9] Ben Klassen founded COTC in 1973 and over the next twenty years shaped his own version of white supremacy based on his text, *The White Man's Bible*. In that text he formulated Creativity, a religion with the worship of the white race as the central tenet. According to Klassen's cosmology, the white race is "nature's highest creation," and "white people are the creators of all worthwhile culture and civilization."[10] From 1984 through 1992, Klassen published approximately[11] forty-six issues of *Racial Loyalty*, a printed newsletter dedicated to spreading his message of RAHOWA (which stands for "RAcial HOly WAr"), the publication's tagline, the group's motto, and later a URL. In the late 1990s COTC was among the most violent and quickly growing groups within the white supremacist movement.[12]

In the mid-1990s Klassen died, and Matt Hale took over the organization. Hale had global aspirations for COTC and added *World* to the name of the group. This was a choice that would later have serious consequences for Hale and his movement, but in the late 1990s it must have seemed easy and almost inevitable for someone with Hale's ambition to add "world" to the group's name and Web presence—a re-branding that Hale believed would connect him with others around the world who shared his views. In 1998 and 1999 Hale began establishing an early Web presence for his group by registering several domain names (rahowa.com, creator.com, and wcotc.com) and creating a variety of websites to spread the religion of Creativity and the message of white supremacy (see figure 6.1). However, Hale's communication strategy for his organization was not limited to websites and domain names.

For a number of years Hale crafted a public image as a clean-cut, suit-and-tie-wearing boy wonder of American neo-Nazism who played the violin and attended law school. In this guise Hale had a gift for attracting national media attention, both in print and from broadcast television, including the

Figure 6.1. Archived screen shot of Matt Hale's World Church of the Creator, 1999.
Source: Retrieved from the Internet archive www.archive.org/web/web/php, 2007.

major networks. After he graduated from law school, the Illinois bar blocked Hale's admission based solely on his ideology, and this case gained him a great deal of sympathetic media attention from mainstream news sources like GQ magazine and NBC's *Today* show. At the same time that Hale was cultivating his clean-cut public image through the mainstream media, he worked on recruiting followers through face-to-face meetings throughout the United States. When he spoke to small-town library audiences he savvily modulated his views for maximum appeal. During this time Hale was also cultivating a violent group of supporters by attending neo-Nazis rallies, urging participants to join the cause of white supremacy.

From 1999 to 2004 several violent, racist attacks were linked to COTC, including the 1999 shooting spree by Benjamin Smith that left two people dead and seven wounded; at first Hale was able to distance himself from these violent acts. During this time Hale also become entangled in a lawsuit over the use of the name World Church of the Creator, including his use of the corresponding domain name (wcotc.com). When Hale added *World* to *Church of the Creator* he was infringing upon the name of another group, a religious organization already in existence with no ties to white supremacy. Eventually, Joan Lefkow, a federal judge, ruled against Hale and in favor of the other group of the same name. This apparently enraged Hale and those in his group. Not long after the ruling, Judge Lefkow's husband and mother were killed in brutal attacks in their home (Judge Lefkow was not at home at the time). Hale was arrested, stood trial, and was convicted for soliciting the murder of Judge Lefkow.[13] On April 6, 2005, Hale was sentenced to forty years in prison for his involvement in the assassinations. As Hale went to trial, it became apparent that few of his former supporters would stand by him, and fewer still were interested in continuing the racist mission on his behalf. Once Hale was incarcerated and his organization was defunct, there was no one left to maintain the site, so COTC's public Web presence disappeared. As of 2007 the organization that Klassen founded when he was publishing *Racial Loyalty*, has all but ceased to exist and has no discernible Web presence, although a few sites do repurpose some of the COTC rhetoric.[14]

J. W. Farrands once boasted that his newspaper *The Klansman* was the "only publication for the white race that has never failed to publish." This publication did not make the transition from print to digital media. Farrands was the leader of the Invisible Empire of the KKK and publisher of *The Klansman* from 1976 to 1992. During those years he published an estimated 106 issues of the newsletter.[15] In 1993 he lost a civil lawsuit filed against his Invisible Empire by the Southern Poverty Law Center (SPLC) for the empire's violent attacks in 1987 on civil rights marchers in Forsyth County, Georgia. Farrands was ordered by the court to pay $37,500 in damages to the plaintiffs in the class-action suit. The settlement with the SPLC prohibited use of the Invisible Empire's name or the publication of their newspaper, *The Klansman*.[16] Conflicting reports suggest that Farrands has either reorganized his Klan forces under a new name, taken his operation further underground, or abandoned organized racism altogether.[17] While Farrands's Invisible Empire had a long-running print publication, as well as a reputation of being the most violent Klan faction in the United States, neither he nor the group he led has a visible, public Web presence today. Indeed, there is no evidence that Farrands or his organization ever created a website or had any discernible Web presence. Other white supremacists that previously published newsletters have made the transition to digital media, even though their organizations have not.

David Duke is a leader in promoting the cause of white supremacy online, yet his organization, the National Association for the Advancement of White People (NAAWP), no longer has a Web presence. Duke published forty-one newsletters for the NAAWP from 1980 through 1991. The ideology espoused by the NAAWP was couched in the moderate tones of a suit-and-tie brand of white supremacy (rather than the stridently extremist terms of the robes and hoods). Duke, a former member of the KKK, has transformed white supremacist rhetoric through the NAAWP by advocating for the rights of European Americans in ways that mimicked the language of civil rights.[18] Duke's organization dissolved beginning around 1998 due to internal struggles regarding the organization's ideology and rhetorical styles used to present that ideology to the broadcast media.[19] Duke never resolved those issues with his fellow members, and as of 2007 the former NAAWP website is 404 and now advertises the sale of the domain name.

Although his organization and its website are now defunct, David Duke maintains an extensive, interactive personal website (davidduke.com) and actively participates in white supremacy online elsewhere. Duke was among the first white supremacists to embrace the Internet as a key to the future of the white supremacist movement He set out this vision of how the Internet could be used by the movement in his essay "The Coming White Revolution: Born on the Internet," originally published online in 1998[20] about the same time that the NAAWP collapsed and still in the very early days of the Internet.

The examples of 404 websites and organizations—Matt Hale's COTC, Farrands's Invisible Empire, and David Duke's NAAWP—together illustrate that a prerequisite for any organization hoping to make the transition from print to digital media is the survival of the organization itself. White supremacist organizations disappear because of efforts by activists, such as the legal team at the Southern Poverty Law Center (as in the case of Farrands) or law enforcement officials who imprison the leaders with cause (as in the case of Hale), thus driving the organizations out of existence (as happened to COTC). And they cease to exist because of internal strife and dissention, as with the NAAWP. Whatever the reason for its demise, once the organization is defunct the website disappears shortly thereafter as well.

Copy/Paste: White Supremacist Brochure Websites

White supremacists Ed Fields and Thom Robb created websites that reproduced their printed publications virtually unaltered. The transfer of text from print to the Web is fairly simple using copy/paste commands, the set of keyboard commands that allow a user to copy text and images from one document or program and transfer or *paste* them into another.[21] *Brochure* websites are one-way static displays of information controlled by one content creator.[22] The use of brochure sites by extremists such as Thom Robb and Ed Fields to showcase racist propaganda has been a common application of the Web.

Ed Fields is a white supremacist and publisher of a newsletter called *The Truth at Last*. From 1978 to 1992 Fields published 102 issues of his periodical.[23] Fields is the founder of the National States Rights Party (NSRP), a segregationist-era organization. J. B. Stoner served as national chairman of the NSRP and was a popular figure among members. In 1983 Stoner was convicted of the 1958 bombing of Rev. Fred Shuttlesworth's church in Birmingham. Stoner's conviction and allegations of financial wrong-doing led to the disintegration of the organization in the early 1990s. Yet despite the dissolution of the group, Fields managed to maintain control of publishing the newsletter and remained throughout the 1990s "one of the busiest networkers on the far right," frequently attending rallies, conferences, and other face-to-face events organized by white supremacists.[24] In 2003 Fields joined the National Alliance, led by William Pierce.

Fields's Web presence is a rather literal translation of his newspaper, *The Truth at Last*, to a clunky brochure site of the same name (see figure 6.2). Once established in the late 1990s,[25] it appears that the site has never been updated. This is evident from a couple of places on the site, including the home page that has not changed since the site went up and reads "Now in Our 39th Year." Primarily, Fields uses the site to appeal for funds by selling back issues of and current subscriptions to the print version of *The Truth at Last*. In fact, a full half of the main page is taken up by text advertising the subscription rates (one-year subscriptions costing $18, six-month subscriptions $10, four-month subscriptions $6) with an assurance that "This

Figure 6.2.   Ed Fields's Truth at Last, 2007.
Source: www.stormfront.org/truth_at_last/, 2007.

newspaper is mailed in a plain, sealed envelope." Visitors to this site can also access Fields's particular version of white supremacist ideology, which includes denial of the Holocaust; references to the threat of supposedly unrecognized Jewish control of media, banking, and government; expounding on the perceived threat of civil rights advances like integrated housing and non-discrimination laws; and the corruption of mainstream white politicians who are complicit in allowing this state of affairs to continue unchecked. On the Web this ideological content is unchanged and nearly indistinguishable from the discourse contained in Fields's print publication.

It is also clear from the site that Fields does not maintain it or even go on-line, as the text on the contact page says that "Dr. Fields is not on line [sic]. To communicate with Dr. Fields, or for enquiries [sic] about book orders etcetera please use the U.S. mails." It then lists his P.O. box. If Fields had been digitally inclined, he might have used his famed networking skills to great advantage for the white supremacist cause. As sociologist Barry Wellman observed, "computer networks are social networks,"[26] and the internetworking capabilities of the Web could have solidified and expanded Fields's face-to-face contacts in white supremacist organizations.

There are several indicators that Fields's Web presence has been constructed for him by someone else. The URL for Fields's Web presence is stormfront.org/truth_at_last/, which indicates that Fields does not own his own domain name and that his website is in fact a subdomain of (or a page within) another white supremacist website. In addition, the reference to "Dr. Fields" in the third-person along with the indication that he is "not on line" together suggest someone else is writing the content and that Fields is not the creator of the site. Yet because it so closely follows the script of his printed newspaper, the site clearly represents his perspective. In this case, it is very likely that the actual copy-and-paste commands were executed by someone else on Ed Fields's behalf. Having a Web presence created by someone else is not the same as creating content of one's own, but the fact that someone else assisted with the transfer of *The Truth at Last* from print to digital media does not alter the fact that Fields is the author of the site, and it reflects his vision of the "truth." This highlights the difficulty in assessing authorship on the Web. And it points to the fact that Web authorship, even of a brochure site, is often a collaborative endeavor.

Thom Robb is a minister in the Christian Identity branch of the white supremacist movement and a member of the Knights of the Ku Klux Klan (although a different branch than the one Farrars led). Robb published approximately thirty-three volumes of his newsletter called *The Torch* from 1977 to 1991.[27] Robb owns the domain names for two related sites: kkk.com (1998–2000; no site active for 2001–2007) and kkk.biz (2004–2007) (see figures 6.3 and 6.4). The first site is one where he maintains a fairly active online presence with periodic updates; the second site, .biz, is a site that Robb

Figure 6.3.   Archived screen shot of Thom Robb's KKK.com, 2005.
Source: Internet archive, www.archive.org/web/web/php, 2005.

Figure 6.4.   Archived screen shot of Thom Robb's KKK.com, 2007.
Source: Internet archive, www.archive.org/web/web/php, 2007.

uses to sell kkk-themed merchandise (e.g., mugs, caps, t-shirts, and key chains). Robb was another white supremacist who was an early adopter of the Internet; his first website went up in 1998. While the site design and layout of his sites have changed somewhat since then, his sites still retain many of the characteristics of the text and imagery of *The Torch*. Robb's version of white supremacy favors rather aggressive Americana and Confederate iconography, such as the top banner that includes images of the Capitol dome, the American flag, Mount Rushmore, and the Confederate flag. The advance in digital media that Robb has over other brochure sites, such as Fields's, is that he has added some multimedia content, including digital video and audio. Despite this content, the site remains a brochure that re-produces *The Torch*, entirely copied and pasted onto the Web.

The copy/paste brochure sites of Thom Robb and Ed Fields illustrate a rather literal transition of white supremacist rhetoric from print to digital media, and neither are particularly artful or sophisticated adaptations of the available technologies. If the 404 sites were the least successful in terms of the transition from print to digital media, these copy/paste sites are at least more successful than those when measured in terms of Web presence and Web traffic. While it is not possible to measure traffic separately for Fields's site because it is a subdomain, the Web traffic for Robb's site is markedly lower than that of Tom Metzger's Resist.com.

C3: The Quasi-private Web

For committed extremists, the Internet has been useful for showcasing racist propaganda and for what Michael Whine refers to as "communication, command, and control" (C3).[28] The distinction here between the capacity for public showcasing and the ability to communicate in quasi-private ways through chat rooms, e-mail lists, and encrypted and/or password-protected Web spaces highlights what many commentators have noted are the limitations of using monolithic terms like *the Internet* or *the Web* or even, *cyberspace*.[29] In fact, there is not just one Web, but rather multiple forms of communication media contained under that umbrella term, some of them public and some of them quasi-private or altogether anonymous.[30]

Tom Metzger, a former Ku Klux Klan leader, a television repairman by trade, and a one-time candidate for Congress,[31] both showcases and exercises private use of the Internet at his website The Insurgent. He is one of the few that has renamed his newsletter in the transition from print to the Web. Metzger's former print-media incarnation was called "W.A.R.," an acronym for White Aryan Resistance. Metzger broke with the Klan when he formed W.A.R. in 1983 and developed a more radical analysis of political economy than the KKK and dropped any reference to Christianity.[32] To spread the message of W.A.R., Metzger created both print and broadcast vehicles: the W.A.R. newsletter, a cable-access television show called "Race and Reason," and a radio broadcast.[33] All these media are now showcased and available via The Insurgent (resist.com). The website includes position statements on a variety of topics, including immigration, international conflicts (most often involving Israel), homosexuality, and women. Prominently featured on the website is a link to purchase Aryan-branded merchandise (t-shirts, caps, key chains). The merchandise page includes the use of some forms that require a user login, but to actually place an order the end-user has to print out and mail in an order form with a check or money order. Aside from these forms, most of the website's features are primarily static, functioning only as one-way transfers of information.

Much of the content on Metzger's website is unique to the digital-media environment and was never available in printed form, although there is some overlap between his print and Web incarnations. A noteworthy and unique-to-the-Web feature of his site is an array of hate-filled computer games (see figure 6.5). These games—with names like "Drive By 2" where players can experience "what it is like in the ghetto," "African Detroit Cop," and "Watch Out Behind You Hunter"—situate gamers as shooters (in the convention of video games). In Metzger's racist and homophobic version of these

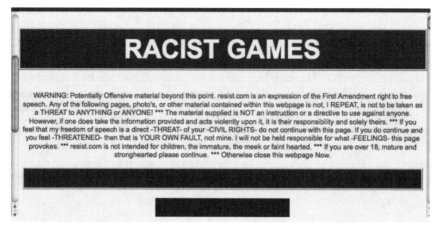

Figure 6.5. Metzger's computer games warning message.
Source: Internet archive www.archive.org/web/web/php, 2007.

games, players are instructed to "shoot the fags before they rape you"; in the game called "Border Patrol," with the tagline "Don't let those spics cross our border," gamers are encouraged to "shoot the spics." The games allow individual users to download and play the games on their own computers. In addition to being violently racist and homophobic, the computer games are also deeply gendered in ways that are consistent with more mainstream games; that is, the games socialize boys into misogyny and exclude girls from all but the most stereotypical roles.[34] Research clearly demonstrates that adolescents are more likely to play computer games than adults; among adolescents, boys are more likely than girls to be gamers.[35] Adolescents are also significantly more likely than adults to say that violence is their favorite part of gaming.[36] Metzger has included these computer games on his website to appeal to his core audience: young, white males. However, Metzger's computer games are crude bits of gaming code that barely adhere to standards in gaming[37] and seem unlikely to meet the minimum demands of sophisticated gamers who have grown up playing *Everquest, Mortal Kombat,* or *Grand Theft Auto.*

Without an evaluation of his internal website statistics, which are not publicly available,[38] it is impossible to know how popular Metzger's racist games are; there are some indications these games have been unsuccessful in reaching a wider audience since he recently removed them from the site.

Visitors to the site are also invited to sign up for a listserv and to get an e-mail address with an *@resist.com* suffix, hosted by Metzger himself. This type of feature points to the quasi-private Web technology of e-mail listservs, password-protected Web spaces, and encrypted communications. These are only quasi-private because the privacy used in these sorts of communication tools is easily breached, and I use this term to distinguish these modes of Internet-facilitated communication from the World Wide Web. It is to this use of encrypted Internet technology that Michael Whine refers when he speaks of the "communication, command, and control" used by extremists and terrorists.[39] The capacity of the Internet to facilitate relatively inexpensive means of communication between and among people in dispersed geographic regions of the world is certainly one of the primary benefits white supremacists see in the medium. Further, the fact that this communication can be encrypted and anonymous is appealing for many white supremacists,[40] although certainly not all, such as Metzger, who clearly relishes the spotlight.[41] At the same time that anonymity is appealing for some, networked communication also reinforces *translocal whiteness*[42]—that is, a form of white identity not tied to a specific location but reimaged as an identity that transcends geography and is linked via a global network.

The idea of "command and control" is based on a military style of leadership in which a designated authority figure commands and controls troops or followers. While encrypted communications may provide the capacity for using the communication technology for command and control purposes for groups with a cohesive ideological vision and a clearly stated goal, this does not accurately describe white supremacy online as a whole. The reality is that the potential destructive force of command and control is mitigated against by significant fissures in the movement along ideological, often religious, lines.[43] Metzger's split with the KKK over religion was no small matter within the movement, and religion is still a hotly contested issue that countervails the power of the communication technology to unify social movements (as discussed in chapter 4).[44] The command and control model is further weakened by the strategy of leaderless resistance advocated by other white supremacists. Metzger describes the philosophy behind The Insurgent this way:

> THE INSURGENT is a NETWORK of highly motivated White Racists. Each person is an individual leader in his or her own right. THE INSURGENT promotes the Lone-Wolf tactical concept. Made up of individuals and small cells. Each INSURGENT associate serves the idea that what's good for the White European Race race is the highest virtue. Whatever is bad for the White European Race is the ultimate Evil. Each Associate works at whatever his or her talents allow. ([original emphasis]) (resist.com/audio.htm)

The notion of a "leaderless resistance," in which small, covert cells acting independently work toward one shared political goal, has been popularized by another white supremacist, Louis Beam (louisbeam.com), and widely adopted within the movement. The strategy of leaderless resistance has been wildly popular among extremists beyond white supremacists, including extremist environmentalists and Islamic jihadists. The actions of Timothy McVeigh, the white supremacist who bombed the Murrah Federal Building in Oklahoma City, are perhaps the best-known example of leaderless resistance in the white supremacist movement. The presence of quasi-private hate speech online, and the sort of overt hate speech that Metzger showcases, is disturbing because of the potential it has for translating into violent attacks.[45] Measured in terms of Web traffic, Metzger has been the most successful in making the transition from print to digital media of the five groups I examined in print; yet Metzger's Web presence is a distant second to the giant in the field of white supremacy online, Stormfront.org (see figure 6.6).

Virtual Community: "White Pride World Wide"

The white supremacist Internet portal[46] and virtual community[47] at Stormfront.org (discussed in the previous chapter) represent a qualitative shift in the Internet and the greatest success for white supremacy online. Don Black

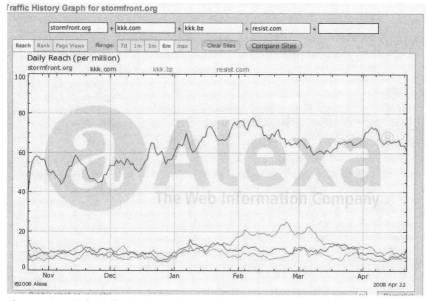

Figure 6.6.   Web traffic for Stormfront, resist.com, KKK.com, and KKK.bz, November 2007 to April 2008.

Source: Alexa Web Trafficking, www.alexa.com, 2008.

founded Stormfront in November 1996 and established it as a simple brochure site that explained his views on white supremacy. Since approximately 2002, David Duke has also participated actively at Stormfront; he and Don Black host a weekly online "radio show" or audio broadcast that is available through the website both live (available to anyone at the site, including guests) and in archived, downloadable format (available only to registered users). In addition, a number of other white supremacists prominent in the print-era, such as Ed Fields and Thom Robb, also maintain a Web presence at Stormfront—Fields through his brochure website, which is hosted there, and Robb through a weekly audio address. As with other forms of promotional marketing online, having a recognizable brand will attract participants. For people who are fans of David Duke, knowing that he posts and reads regularly at Stormfront may encourage them to spend time there if they think that they might have the opportunity to interact with someone that they respect and admire.

The central feature that makes Stormfront.org qualitatively different from other efforts at white supremacy online is that it has adopted the technological features that characterize Web 2.0 in that it allows the kind of interactive member participation and content creation highlighted in the analysis of the "ladies-only" forum discussed in the previous chapter. By opening up his Web space for participation, Don Black, along with the "senior moderator" Jamie Kelso, has built something exceedingly rare on the Internet: a successful virtual community.

Virtual community, a term popularized by Howard Rheingold,[48] describes the complex set of relationships between people who hang out online and sometimes meet face-to-face as well. This is a fairly complicated social phenomenon, and while it is widely regarded as a new one, there are historical antecedents in other media. For example, Benedict Anderson describes how national newspapers of the print-only era contributed to the development of national and regional consciousness among early nation-states.[49] Barry Wellman was the first sociologist to study the Internet version of virtual communities with his "community liberated" study in 1979. More recently, sociologist Peter Kollock,[50] among several other scholars and writers, has set out various rules, guidelines, and principles for how virtual communities work and what makes some successful and others not. Mike Godwin, for example, suggests nine principles for how to make online communities work, admonishing us to "use software that promotes good discussion," to not "impose a length limitation on postings," to "front-load your system with talkative, diverse people," and to "provide a space for kids."[51] Kollock's understanding of why people participate in online communities includes a sense of efficacy, reciprocity, and recognition that their participation yields.[52] Marc Smith adds another motivation, which is significant for the analysis here: a sense of community. The quest to understand virtual community is motivated, at least in part, by a desire for commercial profit by U.S.-based entrepreneurs.[53] What research by sociologists and attempts by marketers clearly demonstrate is that a successful online community is exceedingly difficult to achieve. This makes the success of the virtual community at Stormfront an all the more compelling example of white supremacy online. Online communities are often formed around a common interest or purpose. In this instance, people that seek out Stormfront are looking for others who share a belief in the value of whiteness as a distinct and inherently superior racial identity.

Unlike the white supremacist brochure sites described earlier, the registered users at Stormfront can post opinions, read responses from others, then post more feedback for all to read. The potential for dialogue is built into the software, and, indeed, without this user-created content, there would be nothing at the site to read. Stormfront uses a software program called vBulletin (www.vbulletin.com), a standard, off-the-shelf software that facilitates online discussion. This software is not free ("freeware") but is relatively inexpensive ($85 to $160) compared to newer, more feature-rich software used by online communities.[54] The vBulletin software is a widely used commercial software package for online communities, and a number of corporate enterprises use it, including *Sunset Magazine* and *MacWorld*. The fact that commercial ventures use this software to facilitate their online communities contributes to the normalization of Stormfront as an online community. If a user is accustomed to visiting one of these commercial sites and then seeks out or stumbles upon the vBulletin interface at Stormfront, the site appears as legitimate as any other forum the user has encountered online.

Jamie Kelso joined Stormfront in approximately 2003 and transformed the virtual community. He pushed for leading white supremacist movement leaders to start posting. Furthermore, Kelso is an expert online community manager who seems to be well versed in the principles that contribute to a successful online community. Kelso regularly moderates the boards at Stormfront and often initiates innocuous threads to encourage people to join the conversation; softball questions include "Where is your home?" or "What inspired your screen name?" (discussed in chapter 5). This is a reliable strategy for getting "lurkers" to move from passive to active engagement. By asking a question that nearly everyone has an answer to and nobody minds sharing, people may feel more at ease "de-lurking" and posting a response instead of just reading. Kelso also brought emoticons (smiley faces) to Stormfront, added a feature to recognize members' birthdays on the main entry page, and created essay contests with $2,000 scholarships for white kids. Emoticons allow for a greater range of personal expression, birthday celebrations enable people to build relationships with each other, and contests draw registrations and participation. Kelso's initiatives in the area of online community have paid off rather spectacularly for Stormfront in terms of number of registered users. In January 2002, Stormfront had five thousand registered members. A year later, membership reached eleven thousand. A year after that, in early 2004, it had twenty-three thousand members. By January 2005 membership hit the forty-two thousand mark and climbed to fifty-two thousand in June 2005.[55] Since then it has more than doubled, to over 129,000 registered users. To put these numbers into perspective, I again employ the comparison to MoveOn.org (their tag line is "Democracy in action"), which claims to have 3.2 million members at their site; yet, there is no virtual community dedicated to civil rights and racial equality that has a reach anywhere near Stormfront's.

Understanding White Supremacist Groups' Transition to Digital Media

There is a great deal of variation in white supremacist groups' transition from print to the digital era, and this has to do with a variety of factors relating to social movement organizational resources, white supremacist ideology, and the Internet (see table 6.1). Websites do not exist apart from the people and organizations that support them, so the first requirement for the transition from print to digital media is access to organizational resources, such as stable leadership, a small amount of capital to invest in the necessary hardware, software and Web-hosting services, and members or volunteers (or hired hands) with the technical knowledge to coordinate all these. So part of understanding the range of success has to do with the variation in mobilizing social movement resources, such as people, money, and, in the digital era, technology.

The second reason for the variation has to do with different types of white supremacist ideology within the movement. The white supremacist movement is notoriously sectarian, and there are frequent battles over the minutiae of ideological debates. Religion is a frequent point of disagreement, as when Ben Klassen wanted to retire from his Church of the Creator operation and approached Tom Metzger about taking it over, only to have Metzger refuse because he is "opposed to religion" (even when the white race is the object of worship). In light of these sorts of turf wars, it is telling that the NAAWP failed to make the transition from print to digital media because of

Table 6.1. White Supremacists' Transition from Print to Digital Media, 1997–2008

Organization Name	Content Author	Published Newspaper prior to 1997	Web Presence as of 2008 (with multiple domain names registered to one person)*	Site Type
WCOTC	Matt Hale	x		404
KKK	J. W Farrands	x		404
NAAWP	David Duke	x		404
Truth at Last	Ed Fields	x	x	BR
Christian Identity (KKK)	Thom Robb	x	x	BR
WAR	Tom Metzger	x	x	C3,G
White Pride World Wide (Stormfront)	Don Black, David Duke, and James Kelso (with Thom Robb, Ed Fields)		x x x x x	P, CLK, DV, DR

* David Duke has been an early adopter of the Internet for the white-supremacist cause and has his own individual Web presence—as well as being a leader at Stormfront— but his group NAAWP does not.
404 maintains no Web presence
BR is a brochure site, containing one-way transfers of information
C3 contains elements of the private Web
G includes games
P is a participatory site
CLK indicates cloaked subdomains
DV includes digital video
DR includes digital audio

an internecine feud that was never resolved. The transitions from print to digital media in the middle range, the copy/paste and the C3 sites, have managed to maintain a Web presence through their ability to mobilize the necessary resources but have not grown at anything like the pace of Stormfront because they have remained ideologically isolated from others in the movement. Stormfront owes much of its ability to attract and retain a large number of registered users to the fact that it pitches a very broad ideological tent and tries to include as many variations of white supremacy under that tent as possible.[56] In addition to looking at the *within-group* differences among all those who previously published in print, it is important to examine the sharp distinction between them and Stormfront, which did not have a print incarnation.

All five organizations that I examined in print shared a conceptualization of the Internet as primarily a mechanism for one-way transfers of information. This is evident in the failed attempts of the 404 sites and in the literal translations of the copy/paste sites. Even Tom Metzger's C3 site has many elements of his newsletter (such as the racist line drawings and jokes) that are reproduced wholesale from his printed newsletters. This assumption about the Internet is rooted in the way previous forms of media, such as broadcast or print, work based on a one-to-many model. But this assumption seems to have constricted their view of the possibilities of the Internet for new and innovative approaches to social movement discourse. The question remains, though, as to why Stormfront has been so successful in terms of generating traffic when other attempts at white supremacy online, bound to print media in significant ways, have failed to or have received much less traffic (see figure 6.6 above).

Stormfront succeeds because the people who participate in this form of white supremacy online seek it out. They return because it offers them something meaningful. People seek out Stormfront because it resonates with a white racial frame, and they return because they enjoy a sense of community built on a collective white identity. For a virtual community such as Stormfront to thrive, people have to not only seek it out, they also have to invest time and energy in order to sustain it. Also, Stormfront's remarkable success at creating and sustaining a virtual community suggests a very different online dynamic than the brochure sites or even Metzger's moderately interactive site that mainly showcases racist propaganda. The presence of a long-running and robust virtual community for "white pride worldwide" suggests that this online space offers something that a large and growing number of people desire and find worth returning to repeatedly. People that participate at Stormfront can be sure they will find other people who share their value of whiteness as a separate and superior racial identity and can freely express that idea and have it affirmed by others.

Old and New Media Forms of White Supremacy Converge

This investigation into the transition of white supremacist ideology from print to digital media is by no means exhaustive, but one that is meant to offer a broader framework for similar analyses of other social movements' transition into digital media. Using a different social movement's discourse, locating a physical archive of that movement's documents prior to 1993 or so could supply a sample for the print-only analysis. Then that analysis could be analyzed alongside contemporary digital media versions of the movement's discourse. Such an analysis would expand our understanding of both digital media and social movement discourse. While I see this as a worthwhile and much-needed area of research, I do not want to overstate the disparateness of old print media and new digital media, for these forms are increasingly converging.

The Internet represents an important transformation in a number of ways, not the least of which is how people create, publish, and distribute social movement discourse. Yet it would be a mistake to draw a broad line of distinction between print and digital media as if these were discrete categories. They are not. Ed Fields, for example, uses his website (digital media) to sell his newspaper (print media), not unlike mainstream publications in the digital era (e.g., most magazines and newspapers now have an online presence where you can also sign up for a print-based subscription). Several of the sites—Robb's kkk.com, Metzger's Resist.org, and Black's Stormfront.org—include a variety of multimedia elements that incorporate old and new media forms of white supremacy. Stormfront has a number of discussion threads dedicated to mainstream popular culture, such as Hollywood films in which participants offer detailed analyses of these cultural products through a rather matter-of-factly racist interpretive lens. And, in 2001, someone from COTC cross-posted a link from a Creator website onto Stormfront. The link included Leni Riefenstahl's classic documentary *Triumph of the Will* "online in its entirety" and available for download. All of these are examples of what Henry Jenkins refers to as *"convergence culture,"* which represents as a paradigm shift within the Information Age in which media flow across platforms, there is an interdependence of communications systems, and multiple methods are used to access content.[57] Riefenstahl's film is old media (printed on celluloid) converging with new media (made available online). Thus, rather than think in terms of print as completely separate from digital media, the two are converging together in new ways.

Even white supremacists like Thom Robb, who created one of the clunky copy/paste websites that my student in the computer lab encountered in 1998, are aware of the multiple forms of media converging in the Information Age and the place of white supremacy online within it. Robb makes reference to these multiple media forms on the FAQ (frequently asked questions) page on his web-site. In the quotation that opens this chapter, Robb refers to a hypothetical in-dividual who "may watch a ridiculous Hollywood movie or watch the Jerry Springer show" and, based on that information, claim to have some knowledge of the Klan. Robb challenges this way of knowing, contrasting it with an old media, print-based forms of gaining knowledge. He grumbles, "They go to the library and pick up a book written by someone who has his own agenda." In Robb offers an alternative means of knowing by going to his website, a path that leads "straight to the source." And, presumably, this is what my student was do-ing in the lab that day when he typed KKK.com into the browser window. In the following chapter, I address the type of site my other student stumbled upon when looking for information on civil rights—cloaked sites.

Conclusion

White supremacy in the print-only era included the voices of a few white men who represented the leadership of the movement. Now, as the message has been converted into digital media, white supremacy online is increas-ingly multivocal and less one dimensional than when it relied primarily on printed newsletters for movement communication. In some ways the partic-ipation of women in white supremacy online is more pronounced and more noticeable than in the print-only era. Yet, white male supremacists remain the primary producers, publishers, and architects who have led the charge of translating white supremacy into the digital era.

It is important to note that not all white supremacist organizations or indi-viduals have been successful in translating their rhetoric onto the Internet. A number of those who published printed newsletters simply failed to understand either the mechanics of how to establish and maintain a Web presence or failed to see its value for their cause. The translation of printed texts to new media, despite hyperbolic references to materials being available at the "flick of a switch," can be a challenging, even daunting, task. Causing even greater con-sternation, as anyone who works in the Internet industry can attest, is figuring out how to drive traffic to a site. Internet marketers talk about this in terms of "eyeballs," as in "how many eyeballs can we get to the site." And, indeed, an en-tire cottage industry has sprung up of Internet marketers offering "search engine optimization," the industry's term for boosting a particular site's ranking in most search engines in order to maximize the number of "eyeballs" that see it. Given the complex (and often mysterious) algorithms that many search engines use, these consultants are well paid for their services. My point in raising this here is to suggest that directing Web traffic to an individual website is a complicated business. Thus, the rather simplistic notion that white supremacists can simply put up a plain text brochure site and successfully recruit scores of new members is a misunderstanding of how the Web works.

Still other white supremacist organizations and individuals have successfully translated their movement into the digital era, and it is worth noting some of the reasons for this success and what it can tell us about racism and the Internet. The quasi-private and overtly violent racism of Tom Metzger's Resist.com falls in the middle range of white supremacist organizations that have successfully converted their print endeavors into a Web resource. Metzger, like many of his brethren, has primarily established a copy/paste website that reproduces wholesale many of the features of his previous newsletter "White Aryan Resistance." The difference here is that Metzger has been able to use the Web to merge in one place several other media forms, including his radio broadcast and telephone hotline. The Internet also offers Metzger the opportunity for quasi-private communication and command and control with loyal followers intent on violence. Given that Metzger has once already been found liable in a civil case for inciting racial violence, the threat of violence from a site like Metzger's poses a real danger to those he counts as his enemies. While the overt racist rhetoric that Metzger airs on his site's public forum may be considered passé among many middle-class whites, the fact that they can access and possibly laugh at Metzger's racist "jokes" in private is consistent with the data indicating how whites who are not involved in organized racism behave in private, backstage settings.[58] In terms of attracting Web traffic, Metzger's site is not nearly as successful as the virtual community at Stormfront.

A successful virtual community of any kind with over a hundred thousand visitors is difficult to achieve. The fact that Stormfront has been able to accomplish this feat speaks in part to a general need among human beings for community; and, specifically, it speaks to the fact that Stormfront is meeting a real desire among its participants for a community that values whiteness and white identity above all else. By retreating into this white-dominated chimera, participants at Stormfront produce and validate knowledge claims that affirm the value of whiteness by drawing on an epistemological tradition that stakes a claim on "truth" with the intended goal of undermining the hard-won political value of racial equality.

Notes

1. I remain grateful to Celina Morejon for her technological wizardry in and out of the classroom and to my colleague Chris Toulouse (and cofounder of teachtools.com), who encouraged my early forays into technology and education.

2. I recognized the site as cloaked for a number of reasons, mostly because I asked the student to scroll all the way to the bottom and saw the small text that read "Hosted by Stormfront," which I knew to be a white supremacist site. My student, who was not familiar with Stormfront, did not initially discern the politics of the site's creators. In many ways I have been trying to make sense of this experience in the lab since 1998. I explore cloaked sites such as this one in great detail in the following two chapters.

3. Daniels 1997.

4. There is a growing field of scholarship that examines how social movements are making use of digital media. See, for example, Atton 2003. See also Olesen 2005, Salazar 2003. But none that I am aware of that specifically compares the discourse of one social movement organization in print to that in digital media. I find this gap in the literature somewhat curious, given the growth of the Internet and its increasing importance for social movements.

5. Back 2001, 96.

6. Adams and Roscigno 2005.

7. *Having a Web presence* refers to whether or not an individual or an organization has an established existence on the World Wide Web through a Website, e-mail, blog, or collection of Web files.

8. Part of why the Internet has been so popular with social movement organizations, as discussed in chapter 4, is that it makes the routine activities of organizing much easier. Certainly social-movement organizations can and do effectively engage in activism by relying solely on non-Internet-based forms of communication, such as landline telephones and printed materials sent via fax or postal mail. And this is how much of white supremacist organizing was done in the past and continues to be done today. Social movement organizations that use entirely analog (non-Internet) forms of communication may have greater difficulty reaching potential supporters and already committed members to coordinate their activities and to distribute information about the organization. Of course this assumes that the potential supporters and already committed members are online. On a more existential level, in the digital era an organization without a Web presence is often said to not exist. However, this is not how I use the term here. I am interested in whether or not the organizations exist in the material, face-to-face world *and* whether they "exist" on the Web. These are connected, as I will demonstrate.

9. In a practice known as *cybersquatting*, speculators buy up domains that have not been renewed by their owners and put up a placeholder site to sell the Website to someone else. Cybersquatters have taken over Matt Hale's former domains, and they are now for sale. The religious organization that filed suit against Hale is now the owner of the domain name www.wcotc.com and maintains a Website there.

10. Anti-Defamation League 2005b.

11. All the numbers referring to the total number of volumes of white supremacist newsletters published in this chapter are approximate. I based these estimates on the printed versions of these documents housed in the Klanwatch archive at Southern

Poverty Law Center in Montgomery, Alabama, where I did original research (Daniels 1997). All the estimated numbers in this chapter are drawn from Daniels 1997, 145–56, Appendix B: Publications Inventory (N = 369).

12. Daniels 1997, 30 and Appendix B: Publications Inventory.

13. I am skipping over a vast amount of detail about the intricacies of this branch of the movement in service of my theoretical question here, which is about how these groups did or did not make the transition to digital media. For readers interested in a more thorough account of this recent history, I suggest they turn to a number of excellent online resources. The Southern Poverty Law Center has an extensive collection of materials that document the demise of Hale and the COTC, available here: splcenter.org/intel/news/item.jsp?aid=11. The Anti-Defamation League's *Extremism in America*, Matt Hale, offers additional information, adl.org/learn/ext_us/Hale.asp?x picked=2&item=6. For a detailed genealogy of the broader movement, I recommend Berlet 2006.

14. There are a few Websites that mention *Creativity* or *Church of the Creator*, but there is no active movement anymore according to monitors at the ADL and SPLC. As of February 2009, the URL for Rahowa (www.rahowa.com) was live again but does not seem to represent an active organization apart from this limited, brochure Website. The registrant info is anonymized but a search at AboutUs.org (www.aboutus .org/Rahowa.com) reveals a West Palm Beach address for the Website's owner. It is possible that Don Black, a resident of West Palm Beach, or one of his associates is responsible for the renewed Web presence of Rahowa. My thanks to Charles Cameron for alerting me to this development.

15. Daniels 1997, 27 and Appendix B: Publications Inventory.

16. Ross 1995.

17. Ross, in her Public Eye report (previous note), suggests that Farrands has reorganized his Invisible Empire and continues to carry out racist activities, while an online journalist and blogger writes that Farrands may still be engaging in racist activities or he may have "found Jesus" and taken a new path (thetroublemaker .blogspot.com/2006/05/carolina-KKK.html). If Farrands has a public Web presence, I was not able to find it.

18. Daniels 1997, 27 and Appendix B: Publications Inventory.

19. There are interesting elements of this story concerning media and the extremist-versus-mainstream versions of white supremacy. According to the SPLC, the split and eventually demise of the NAAWP has its origins in a 1997 report by ABC's *Prime Time Live*, showing Klan members consorting with NAAWP followers at the Florida ranch of NAAWP official Dan Daniels. It also featured an interview with Paul Allen—the Duke crony who headed the NAAWP through the mid-1990s—in which Allen appeared awkward and defensive. In the aftermath of the report, Daniels, the former sheriff of Polk County, Florida, resigned "to spend more time with his family." Allen then sent all NAAWP local leaders a contract in which they were to promise "to never publicly express themselves in an extremist racist manner" or to

be connected to anyone who did. Allen also complained that NAAWP members were brainwashed into leaving the group by the ABC report. See Southern Poverty Law Center 1998.

20. Anti-Defamation League 2001.

21. Learning the one-handed keystrokes for these commands (control + C, control + V) is often included in basic computer-literacy courses. And at least one researcher has suggested that *copy/paste literacy* may be integral for digital literacy in the future (Dan Perkel, UC Berkeley, personal communication). The term (along with its corollary *cut and paste*) comes from the print-only era, in which people cut printed text apart by hand with scissors and glued pieces of text back together in a different order. Students and their teachers are familiar with the ease (and pitfalls) of Web-to-print copy/paste strategies. Less frequently discussed are the ways that print-to-Web copy/paste technology has facilitated the spread of so-cial-movement discourse. The use of the copy/paste commands allows white su-premacists to take documents that are already in digital format, such as a word-processed document, and simply copy that text into a Web-based format, such as HTML.

22. Brochure sites are characteristic of the early days of the Web and stand in stark contrast to the multiple user-created sites that characterize Web 2.0, such as Craigslist or Wikipedia, where anyone can add content to the site.

23. Daniels 1997, 29 and Appendix B: Publications Inventory.

24. Fields is connected in some way to nearly every other figure in the white su-premacist movement discussed in this chapter. For instance, in 1988 he taped an in-terview for Metzger's "Race and Reason" cable-access show. In 1991 Fields organized a Klan rally in Montgomery, Alabama, along with Thom Robb of the Knights of the KKK. In 1996 Fields spoke at the Second Annual White Rights Rally of David Duke's National Association for the Advancement of White People. In 1998 Fields began organizing speaking engagements for Holocaust denier David Irving. Fields also connected with those in the COTC, while it was in existence. See Anti-Defamation League 2005c.

25. This is an estimate on my part, based on my recollection that the first time I encountered Fields's Website was around 1998, and it has not changed since that time. It is not possible to confirm this through the Internet Archive, as I have done with other Websites here, because Fields's site is a subdomain and therefore does not appear as a separate site (with individual dates) in the archive.

26. Wellman 2001.

27. Daniels 1997, 29 and Appendix B: Publications Inventory.

28. Daniels 1997, 29 and Appendix B: Publications Inventory.

29. See, for example, Agre 2002b. See also Dean 2003 and Hull 2003.

30. Wellman 2004.

31. In 1979 Metzger won forty-three thousand votes in a losing bid for a Demo-cratic Congressional seat in a San Diego primary.

32. For an in-depth analysis of Metzger, there are a number of good resources, most notably Ezekiel 1995; Langor 2003. For a broad overview of many of the groups discussed here, including more about Metzger, see Marks 1996.

33. Dees and Fiffer 1993. See also Turner 1986.

34. Cassell and Jenkins 2000.

35. Cassell and Jenkins 2000.

36. Griffiths, Mark, and Chappell 2004.

37. Salen and Zimmerman 2004.

38. In my analysis I have chosen to use only publicly available data. I discuss the logic and ethics behind this decision in further detail in the methods appendix.

39. Whine 1999.

40. Whine 1999.

41. Bostdorff 2004. See also Thiesmeyer 1999.

42. As discussed in chapter 4 (and elsewhere in the text) and originally conceptualized by Les Back 2001, 94–132.

43. The literature on the divisions within the white supremacist movement is vast. Some notable work in this area includes the following: Barkun 1997, Dobratz 2001, and Dobratz and Shanks-Meile 1995.

44. Kaplan, Weinberg, and Oleson 2003.

45. However, there is scant empirical evidence that clearly demonstrates when and how white supremacy online might relate to such attacks. Unfortunately, this is the sort of evidence that is often accumulated in hindsight rather than predicted reliably in advance.

46. An Internet "portal" is a Website that offers a variety of services, pathways and links to other sites.

47. I am grateful to Kellie Parker, Online Community Manager at PCWorld and MacWorld, for her careful review of this section on "virtual community." She provided invaluable feedback and some key insights about the type of software Stormfront uses.

48. Rheingold 1993.

49. Andersen 1983.

50. Kollock and Smith 1999.

51. Godwin 1994.

52. Kollock 1999.

53. Hagel and Armstrong 1997.

54. It is not clear how much Don Black pays for using vBulletin, but it is in the range of $85 (one-year lease) to $160 (own).

55. Kim 2005.

56. Kim 2005.

57. Jenkins 2006.

58. Picca and Feagin 2007.

~

CHAPTER SEVEN

Cyber Lies: Cloaked Websites

Fascist [propaganda] has by now come to be a profession, as it were, a livelihood. It had plenty of time to test the effectiveness of various appeals and . . . only the most catchy [sic] ones have survived. Their effectiveness is itself a function of the psychology of consumers. . . . The surviving appeals have been standardized, similar to the advertising slogans which proved to be the most valuable in the promotion of business.

—Theodor W. Adorno

Propaganda analysis is an antidote to the excesses of the Information Age.

—Aaron Delwiche

Shortly after the biopolitical disaster that followed Hurricane Katrina in August 2005[1] a wide constellation of websites with domain names like KatrinaFamilies.com and ParishDonations.com appeared on the Internet featuring digital photos of distressed people in the flooded Gulf Coast region. Beyond the digital photographs, exclusively featuring white people, the sites contained no overtly white supremacist or racist rhetoric and appeared to be legitimate appeals to help people in the devastated coastal area. Web traffic to those sites was redirected to a single site, InternetDonations.org, which also appeared to be a rather generic site, except for the fact that the domain

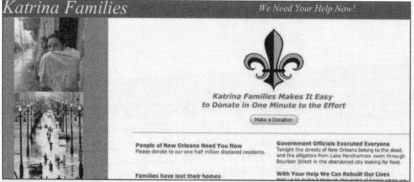

The Web site katrinafamilies.com is one of several with ties to a white supremacist group that has been ordered to stop fund-raising activities.

Figure 7.1. Screen shot of KatrinaFamilies.com, published in the *New York Times*, September 8, 2005.
Source: New York Times, September 8, 2005.

name was registered to Frank Weltner, a white supremacist based in St. Louis, Missouri. The state of Missouri sued Weltner, a member of the neo-Nazi National Alliance, in September 2005 for violating state fund-raising law and for "omitting the material fact that the ultimate company behind the defendants' websites supports white supremacy" (see figure 7.1).[2] Weltner's Katrina-related sites are no longer on the Internet because of the prohibition in Missouri's fund-raising law, but he continues to maintain a number of other websites, including the overtly anti-Semitic JewWatch.com and the cloaked site AmericanCivilRightsReview.com.

The emergence of websites such as Weltner's KatrinaFamilies.com and AmericanCivilRightsReview.com are illustrative of one aspect of white supremacy online: the emergence of hard-to-detect racist propaganda in the digital era. While many writers have expressed much concern that unsuspecting Internet users are in danger of being recruited into white supremacist groups online,[3] in my view, these sites present a different kind of danger. Rather than being lured into social-movement participation through overt white supremacist sites (such as those discussed in the previous chapter), it is much more likely that the casual Web user will inadvertently encounter white supremacy through *cloaked* websites.[4] I define *cloaked websites* to be those published by individuals or groups who conceal authorship or intention in order to deliberately disguise a hidden political agenda.[5] The danger in cloaked websites is less about recruitment into social movement organizations within organized racism and more about a threat to the cultural value of racial equality. Cloaked sites call into question the value of racial equality by challenging the epistemological basis of hard-won political truths about the civil rights era, about the Holocaust, and even about the end of slavery. By that I mean that the cultural values about race, racism, and racial equality that many consider to be settled by the victories of the civil rights movement, going back to the end of slavery, are, in fact, open for debate once again as white supremacy online offers an alternative way of presenting, publishing, and debating ideas that take issue with these cultural values. Taken together, this alternative way of presenting, publishing, and debating ideas constitutes an alternative way of knowing—that is, an alternative epistemology. It is this epistemological threat to the cultural value of racial equality, along with the absence of both critical thinking about race and a vibrant movement toward racial equality, that I see as the most insidious threat posed by white supremacy online—a threat that is especially pernicious for generations born after the civil rights era. Before I examine how young people make sense of cloaked white supremacy when they encounter it online (which I do in the next chapter), I analyze cloaked websites in some detail. In this chapter I explore a wide variety of examples of cloaked websites and situate them within the study of propaganda more generally, and then I turn to the specific issue of racist propaganda in a digital era.

Cloaked Websites: Propaganda in the Digital Era

Cloaked websites are similar to previous versions of print- and electronic-media propaganda in which the authorship, source, or intention of a publication or broadcast is obscured.[6] So-called "black" propaganda is false material in which the source is disguised, "grey" propaganda is that in which the source is not identified, and "white" propaganda is that in which the real source is identified.[7] For example, in a study of revolutionary and counterrevolutionary electronic communication using radio the authors[8] distinguish between these three types of propaganda: (1) white propaganda, in which stations openly identify themselves (e.g., Radio Free Europe); (2) grey propaganda, in which stations are purportedly operated by dissident groups within a country although actually they might be located in another nation (e.g., the supposedly anti-Castro La Voz del CID[9]); and (3) black propaganda stations, which transmit broadcasts by one side disguised as broadcasts by another (e.g., the Lord Haw-Haw broadcasts of the English voice of Nazi Germany[10]). While the crudely color-coded designations of white, grey, and black are problematic linguistic constructions,[11] the distinctions drawn by these conceptualizations are useful for understanding cloaked websites. Websites, like radio broadcasts or printed media, can be used to advance the goals of propagandists,[12] and, as with black and grey propaganda, cloaked websites are rendered more effective precisely because they conceal their intention.[13] There has been a good deal of attention, both in the mainstream press and in scholarly journals, to the use of the Internet to advance political agendas in support of marginalized subcultures. Generally, this is seen as a good thing because of the participatory aspect in the face of large, corporate monopolies controlling media.[14] Yet relatively little has been written about websites that intentionally conceal, disguise, or obfuscate their authorship in order to advance a political agenda.[15] A few examples of cloaked websites other than those published by white supremacists follow to illustrate my point.

Cloaked Websites: Some Examples

Cloaked websites arise from a variety of political agendas. Perhaps the most widely known example of a cloaked site is that of www.GWBush.com,[16] which was set up in the early days of the junior Bush's first presidential campaign. The activist group behind this project, known collectively as ®™*ark*, holds views that would be considered far left-wing on the American political landscape as they are primarily interested in drawing attention to the system of corporate power and challenging the legal convention in the United States of corporate personhood.[17] This cloaked site was very effective, in part because of the clever use of a domain name similar to the official campaign's URL, and in part because it used the exact same graphics from the official site. Initially a number of reporters were taken in by the site and phoned the Bush campaign to ask for clarification on policy issues. Bush and his campaign advisors objected strenuously to the site, going so far as to issue a cease-and-desist letter to the site's creators and file a complaint with the Federal Election Committee.[18] And it was in response to this cloaked site that George W. Bush twice remarked that "there ought to be limits to freedom."[19] One of the ironies here is that the GWBush.com site was arguably more engaged with actual issues, such as corporate responsibility and the war on drugs, than was the official Bush campaign site.[20]

On the other side of the political spectrum from the ®™*ark* activists, corporations utilize cloaked websites to counter criticisms of corporate practices and to give the appearance of grassroots support, a practice known as *astroturfing*.[21] In 2006, corporate giant Wal-Mart launched Working Families for Wal-Mart (forwalmart.com) and Paid Critics (paidcritics.com), two thinly cloaked sites written by a public relations firm, Edelman, employed by Wal-Mart.[22] Wal-Mart launched this aggressive online disinformation campaign after receiving scathing criticisms for its global-business practices from a number of sources.[23] While even a casual Internet user is sure to pick up on the shill-like tone of the corporate rhetoric on this site, the company nevertheless tries to disguise its involvement with this text on the About Us page: "Working Families for Wal-Mart is a group of leaders from a variety of backgrounds and communities all across America." The site describes their mission as "fostering open and honest dialogue with elected officials, opinion makers, and community leaders that conveys the positive contributions of Wal-Mart to working families."[24] It is deeply ironic, not to mention disingenuous, that a site that hides its intention and authorship states that its mission it to foster honest dialogue. Perhaps most brazen here is the second site, which attempts to discredit any critics of Wal-Mart by labeling them paid critics when in fact it is Wal-Mart who is paying people to write and publish both sites. This is a profoundly cynical move on the part of Wal-Mart and Edelman that betrays their assumption about the lack of sophistication of Wal-Mart customers, whom they presume will be duped by the cloaked sites. By establishing these cloaked sites, Wal-Mart and Edelman are attempting to manipulate customers into ignoring the criticisms, regarding the company more favorably, and, thus, continuing to spend money there. And they are betting there will be very little resistance.

Cloaked sites are not exclusive to the United States. In a site called Youth for Volpe,[25] Canadian politician Joe Volpe's alleged corruption is the target of this cloaked site, intended as satire. In 2006 Volpe was a liberal Member of Parliament, who was also campaigning for a leadership position. The cloaked site, which features images of children who are supposedly pledging donations to Volpe, appeared sans authorship after news reports about illegal campaign donations surfaced. Volpe later said he would return five contributions made to his campaign after it was revealed that eleven-year-old twins had each donated more than $10,000 and a fourteen year old had given another $5,400, but by this time the site was already up. Volpe, like Bush and global corporate giant Wal-Mart, was not amused; and, unlike the other two, Volpe could use Canadian laws and his political power to have the site shut down. An additional site has been launched that he has not been able to remove.[26] Whether or not cloaked sites can actually sway an election or influence consumers remains an open question. Still, these three examples suggest that powerful politicians and corporations clearly see both danger and opportunity in cloaked sites. Politicians worry that their lack of control over cloaked sites not of their own creation could mean a rupture in a highly crafted public persona and influence constituents to vote against them. Public-relations firms try to use cloaked sites to shape public perception of their client corporations in order to influence consumers. In both instances what is at stake with cloaked sites is managing a public identity.[27] At risk is the potential loss of votes, money, and power.

Cloaked websites can also conceal a hidden political agenda connected to reproductive politics, such as Teen Breaks (teenbreaks.com). This site is very sophisticated in its use of domain name, graphic user interface, professional-looking design, layout, and moderate-sounding rhetoric. To all but the most astute political observer and experienced Internet veteran, the site appears to be a legitimate source of reproductive-health information. In fact, it is a disguise for pro-life propaganda. Nowhere on the site does it reveal the political affiliation of the publisher nor even who the publisher is beyond a vague mention of the Rosetta Foundation, which is a front for a pro-life activist.[28] On a page called Complications for Girls, the site quotes literature from the conservative group Focus on the Family to support the notion that there are many (and exclusively) negative physical and emotional consequences from abortion,[29] part of a "post-abortion syndrome." This supposed syndrome is not a medically recognized condition but rather a rhetorical strategy of the pro-life movement to advance its agenda. This cloaked site is in many ways a digital version of the brick-and-mortar Women's Health Clinics advertised in the phone book alongside legitimate clinics, intentionally concealing the fact that all the counselors and information are designed to prevent women from accessing abortion services.[30] The danger in a cloaked site of this type, as with the brick-and-mortar locations, is that young girls or women looking for reliable reproductive-health information might be persuaded that post-abortion syndrome is a reality and, in the worst case scenario, that they would endure an unwanted pregnancy and childbirth rather than end a pregnancy for fear of the fictitious syndrome and lack of access to services. The tautological strategy here of using conservative sources to substantiate conservative "facts" is a commonplace tactic of the right-wing propaganda machine in the United States. Indeed, a cottage industry of conservative think tanks and pundits churning out scientific distortions has created what one writer calls a "war on the Enlightenment" ideal of rationality.[31] Whatever one's personal politics might be concerning the right to abortion, the fact that this site presents itself as neutral and conceals its authorship and political agenda qualifies it as a cloaked site.

Deception is not a new rhetorical strategy, but some features of the digital era can make it more difficult to discern which sites are legitimate and which sites disguise a hidden political agenda. Of course, designating a site as legitimate or cloaked is at some level a political distinction, similar to calling some organizations front groups and others legitimate social movement activism.[32] Shying away from such political distinctions in evaluating information online only serves to obfuscate the key issues. Rather, I contend that the kind of critical consciousness that enables one to make these kinds of judgments possible is urgently needed, particularly when it comes to the racist propaganda of cloaked white supremacist websites.

The cloaked white supremacist websites I explore in the rest of this chapter conceal political agendas intended to subvert civil rights and affirm white supremacy through an audacious deployment of the rhetoric of the civil rights movement. Indeed, a number of these sites deliberately seek to disguise the racist motives of the website's author by using carefully chosen domain names, deceptive graphic user interfaces (GUIs), and language that is not only less strident than what appears in overt hate speech online but also mimics the language of civil rights.

Cloaked White Supremacist Sites

Frank Weltner, mentioned in the opening of this chapter, is perhaps most widely known for his overtly anti-Semitic website JewWatch.com.[33] Weltner also maintains a cloaked site called American Civil Rights Review (ACRR) (see figure 7.2). The main page of this site features blue and red text on a bright yellow background, an audio file upon loading, and inexplicable animated GIFs throughout. Across the top of the main page is an image map—that is, a series of images that link to other pages within the website. The featured images, from left to right, include a black and white digital photo of Malcolm X (linked to an interior page called Civil Rights Positions), a digital reproduction of a Currier and Ives painting of a plantation (with a link to a page titled Cotton Plantation by the Mississippi River, High Self-Esteem for Many Slaves), a black and white digital photo of Ché Guevera (with a link to Diversity and Multiculturalism in International Areas), and a graphic of a sign with stenciled letters that reads "St. Louis—No Trespassing—No Loitering" (with a link to a page called St. Louis Home Page, with further links to pages about the devastation wrought by urban renewal at the hands of Housing and Urban Development). The blue highlighted text above the image map reads "American Civil Rights Review," and the smaller, red text beneath says, "Speaking Out for the New Civil Rights Movement." Below that is another heading in red: "Civil Rights/Human Rights SUPER-NEWS Search," which invites visitors to "Access Daily Happenings in Major NEWS Sources." These all link to an external site, the search engine Yahoo, by the category noted in the linked text. Only this is visible from most Web browsers without scrolling further down the page. If the Web user does scroll down (and usability research indicates that only about 10 percent of users scroll all the way to the bottom of a page), the page does continue below this

Figure 7.2. Archived screen shot of cloaked American Civil Rights Review, 2007.
Source: Internet archive, www.archive.org/web/web/php, 2007.

where there is more linked text in blue, this headlined with "Civil Rights/Human Rights Web Resources on ACRR," which links to internal pages. Further down are still more animated GIFs, a number of badges or emblems ("Made on a Mac"), and at the very bottom, red all-caps text that reads "COPYRIGHT NOTICE," with a link to an external page hosted at Cornell University Law School with language about the fair-use provision within U.S. copyright law. There is no identification anywhere on the page (even scrolling all the way down) of the author or publisher or the intended message of the site beyond speaking out for the "new civil rights movement." And, indeed, determining authorship of this site is impossible without going to an external source.[34]

It would be a mistake to dismiss the harmful potential of the cloaked ACRR based on its crude graphic design. While it is true that the unappealing text and background colors, use of animated GIFs, screaming all-caps headlines, and default font settings give this site away as a first-generation or "last century"[35] website, the racism and anti-Semitism on the cloaked site are fairly nuanced in some unexpected ways. On the interior page linked through the Currier & Ives painting, Weltner describes the "High high Self-Esteem" of "Many Slaves" and goes on to make an argument for slavery as an "idyllic" social system in which plantations were "sanitary, happy, and humane" places rather than sites of a cruel, dehumanizing system of brutal torture and forced labor that they were. Weltner further erodes the historical reality of the racialized system of slavery by arguing that "Europeans" were equally mistreated by bad working conditions as enslaved Africans and African Americans were by chattel slavery. Weltner's argument defending slavery as a "humane" system is not particularly new and harkens back to centuries-old versions of white supremacy, such as that found in Thomas Jefferson's *Notes on the State of Virginia*.[36] The nuance here exists in the combination of the use of digital media and the evidence Weltner selects to make this argument. Weltner draws on oral histories of former slaves recorded by WPA workers in the 1930s and provides links to audio files and transcribed texts.[37] The Library of Congress has championed the collection and archiving of oral histories, and oral histories have been used by educators to engage students about slavery, abolition, and the civil rights struggle, as on another Library of Congress project website, "Voices of Civil Rights,"[38] which features oral histories of the civil rights movement. However, in Weltner's hands the oral histories take on a different meaning. On his cloaked site, he selectively compiles excerpts on a page titled "Forgotten Black Voices," such as this quotation from "Adeline, 91": "I wants to be in Heaven with all my white folks, just to wait on them and love them, and serve them, sorta like I did in slavery time." Here, he uses the oral-history data to support his revisionist[39] claim that slavery was a "humane" institution in which enslaved people were not mistreated. This is a remarkable use of digital media to undermine the cultural value of racial equality. With this repurposing, Weltner takes an oral-history project created by the Library of Congress intended to valorize the African American experience of surviving the horrors of slavery, a legitimate and laudable project by most standards, and twists that same source material to call into question that very experience and the struggle to overcome it. Weltner uses the oral-history data from the Library of Congress and reinterprets them though a white racial frame to suggest that chattel slavery was, after all, a humane system and thereby diminishes both the harm done to African Americans in this system and white Americans' culpability for that system. By using language such as "forgotten black voices," Weltner draws on the language of multiculturalism. This rhetorical choice further complicates Weltner's attempt at revising the history of slavery because it offers the patina of credibility by suggesting black authorship (and, thus, authenticity). This language also serves to further disguise Weltner's political intentions and avoid waving any red flags that overt white supremacist rhetoric might raise. However, Weltner's attempt at retelling the history of slavery falls short of being thoroughly successful.

There are a number of features characteristic of digital media that make Weltner's strategy both potentially very effective and a failed attempt. Weltner's appropriation of civil rights discourse on the Internet is potentially much more effective than if it were published in a printed newsletter of the pre-Internet era. While there were (and still are) vanity presses that publish books and newsletters without review, the cost and distribution function as built-in constraints. In addition, recognizing some forms of racist propaganda in printed media is easier in part because they are distributed outside conventional channels.[40] The fact that Weltner deploys language that mimics civil rights using digital media, and does so on a cloaked website that conceals his authorship and political agenda, means that without the gatekeeping of editors, publishers, and broadcasters Weltner's rhetoric takes on a veneer of legitimacy. Furthermore, Weltner's appropriation of oral-history source material from another online source, the Library of Congress, further blurs the line between legitimate and revisionist history. The link to the Library of Congress connects Weltner to a credible source; then his interpretation of the data from that source reinterprets and subverts long-established historical facts. Finally, the Internet has a kind of leveling effect that renders one source as valid as another because they are both accessible via the same media—the same connection and browser window that delivers the Library of Congress or *The New York Times* also offers up Weltner's cloaked site.[41] This leveling effect makes other evidence, such as visual cues like graphic design and page layout, even more important for assessing the credibility of websites.[42] This is where Weltner's site fails dramatically; his crude page design and layout render all the text-based content at the site suspect. But this particular kind of failure is an easy one to fix by either a person with good graphics-design skills or by downloading a generic website templates[43] and customizing it to include white supremacist political content. This also means that Weltner is one good graphic designer away from a much more pernicious Web presence.

Don Black, the white supremacist who maintains Stormfront.org (discussed in previous chapters), also publishes a number of cloaked sites, including one called Bamboo Delight (bamboo-delight.com) (see figure 7.3). The Bamboo Delight Company website purports to offer visitors "Acupuncture Lessons, Kung-Fu, Alternative Medicine, Weight-Loss Secrets," and guidance in "Chinese Wealth Secrets." The headline on the top of the page tells visitors that by "Combining Aryan Knowledge with Chinese Medicinal

Figure 7.3. Archived screen shot of Bamboo-Delight, 2007.
Source: Internet archive, www.archive.org/web/web/php, 2007.

Exercises" an unidentified "we" have been able to develop "healing and Exercise methods superior to all others." The word *Aryan* is the only clue on this portion of the page that this is a white supremacist site; the author or publisher of the site is not disclosed.[44]

As with the previous cloaked site, the graphics and page layout are all amateurish. The anti-Semitism of the site's author is evident as one scrolls down the page. At the bottom of the page the text situated between animated flashing multicolored horizontal bars suggests that "diseases are never cured but only treated" because Jewish physicians are religiously prohibited from treating non-Jews. This cloaked site supposedly offers information about alternative medicine and conceals its anti-Semitism by disguising the authorship, placing the overtly anti-Semitic text at the bottom of a long page, and distracting the user with the unexpected reference to "Chinese medicine" not typically associated with white supremacy.

Don Black also hosts a site called Martin Luther King: A True Historical Examination, which is, in many ways, the archetypal cloaked site (see figure 7.4). Black registered the URL martinlutherking.org in 1998 and has maintained this cloaked site continuously since then.

Figure 7.4.   Archived screen shot of MartinLutherKing.org, 2007.
Source: Internet archive www.archive.org/web/web.php, 2007.

At first glance, the website appears to be a tribute site to Dr. Martin Luther King Jr., albeit one intended for a younger audience as indicated by the link at the top ("Attention, Students: Try our MLK Pop Quiz,") and the one further down the page indicating that there are "Rap Lyrics." There are a number of clues that something is amiss. The first is the description of the website as a "A True Historical Examination." The use of the word *true* here suggests an uncovering of some formerly untold truth about Dr. King. And the inclusion of this version of the truth is an additional clue about the intention of site's author. The main page features an unflattering quote of clandestine FBI audio tapes recorded while King was engaged in sexual activity with a woman other than his wife. The fact that this quotation is taken from actual recordings and was originally published in *Newsweek* (and this source is noted on the website) works in a similar fashion to Weltner's use of oral-history material from the Library of Congress. It is possible to read the transcript of King's conversations taped by the FBI within the larger context of systemic white supremacy in which nascent civil rights movements are routinely stamped out by the government,[45] within the context of this cloaked site the quotation is intended to undermine King's legitimacy as a civil rights leader and with that the racial equality that he stood for.

Once on the website, there are a number of additional indications as to the source of the information, including a link in the right margin that reads "Jews and Civil Rights," thus hinting at its anti-Semitic agenda.[46] Clicking on that link leads to a page that more than suggests anti-Semitism, as it includes a chapter called "Jews, Communism, and Civil Rights" from white supremacist David Duke's book *My Awakening*. For the astute Web user this is a giveaway about the ideological orientation of the website's author. Still, for many younger, less-experienced Web users or those unfamiliar with recent U.S. racial political history, the name "David Duke" may have no resonance. Going back to the first page, there is one more clue if a casual Web user wanted to know the origin of this "True historical examination." Scrolling down to the very bottom of the first page, there is a link that reads "Hosted by Stormfront," and clicking on that link takes the user to Don Black's "White Pride World Wide" at Stormfront.org. Although these clues might seem fairly obvious to some relatively savvy Web users, other users can easily miss them. What makes this cloaked site archetypal is only partially about what is on the site itself; just as significant is the domain name and the place the site appears in search-engine results.

Using a standard search engine[47] and the search terms *Martin Luther King*, this website regularly appears third or fourth in the results returned by Google. Before even viewing the content of this site, the URL makes it appear to be legitimate, in part because the main Web reference is made up of only the domain name martinlutherking, and the URL ends with the suffix .org. The decision to register the domain name martinlutherking.org relatively early in the evolution of the Web was a shrewd move for advocates of white supremacy and similarly a lost opportunity for advocates of civil rights. Recognizing that domain-name registration is now a political battleground, a number of civil rights organizations have begun to reserve domain names to prevent them from being used by opponents of racial justice. For example, the NAACP registered six domain names that include the word *nigger*, and the ADL registered a similar number of domain names with the word *kike*.[48] However, registering offensive epithets is only a small part of the struggle. The move by opponents to register the esteemed symbols of civil rights as domain names, such as Martin Luther King, and use them to undermine racial justice is one that was clearly unanticipated by civil rights organizations. To be effective, cloaked sites with domain names such as www.martinlutherking.org or www.AmericanCivilRightsReview.org rely on the naïveté of their target audience, a predominantly white audience that each year moves further away from the experience of the civil rights era.

The presence of cloaked sites raises important questions about white supremacy in the digital era. One of these questions has to do with whether someone could stumble upon virulent anti-Semitism or racism online. It is not only possible but likely that casual or novice Web users could inadvertently come across white supremacist rhetoric while looking for legitimate civil rights information (see chapter 8). The cloaked Martin Luther King site is a case in point. Using the Web monitoring service Alexa, I charted the traffic to this cloaked site and to the legitimate civil rights website The King Center, published by the King family's organization in Atlanta, and then I also charted them comparatively (see figure 7.5). The estimated traffic for both sites is in the tens of millions in terms of number of hits, and the traffic patterns for the two sites are strikingly similar. Not surprisingly, traffic to both sites peaks annually, around the time of Martin Luther King Day (toward the end of January) and during Black History Month (February). There is also one noticeable difference in traffic between the two sites, evident when looking at the graphs side-by-side.

Here, there is evidence of a spike in traffic to the King Center site (the legitimate site) on January 31, 2005, the day Mrs. King died. Other than this one rather dramatic difference the traffic patterns for the two sites are remarkably comparable. The patterns are so similar, in fact, that it suggests that Web users who are looking for legitimate civil rights information may very well be ending up at the cloaked white supremacist site.

The online home of the Institute for Historical Review (www.ihr.org) is a cloaked[49] site that may be more nefarious for its skillful graphic user interface

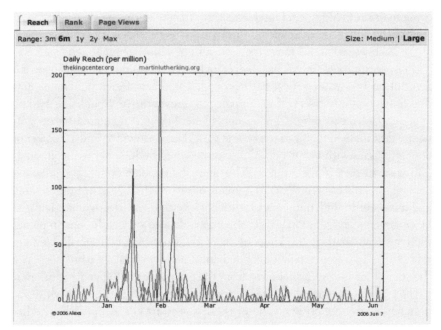

Figure 7.5. Comparative reach in millions for TheKingCenter.org and MartinLuther King.org.
Source: Alexa Web Service, www.alexa.com, 2006.

(see figure 7.6). Here the GUI is much more polished than on any of the previous sites discussed. There are no audio files or animated GIFs as there were with Weltner's site, and none of the amateurish background colors or fonts as with Black's sites. There are books and tapes available for sale on the left and right sides of the page, and down the center is a list of brief, paragraph-long descriptions of various news stories, each accompanied by a hyperlink and a photo. Across the top of the main page is a row of links to other pages on the site. The rhetoric on the site appears quite moderate, at first glance, and the mission is described as "dedicated" to "truth and free speech." The structure, graphic design, and language on this page look completely benign; of course, they are not.

As critically aware readers will know, the Institute for Historical Review (IHR) is an organization that seeks to deny the existence of the Holocaust published by Mark Weber based in Orange County, California. IHR touts itself as a source of scholarly information to which "countless scholars, researchers, and journalists have turned" for "solid and reliable information."[50] The Web users who know who Mark Weber is or who are already aware of the mission and deceptive nature of the IHR will not be misled by the cloaked website, but, for the uninitiated, it is very likely that the combina-

Figure 7.6. Archived screen shot of The Institute for Historical Review, 2007.
Source: Internet archive, www.archive.org/web/web/php, 2007.

tion of professional-looking graphic design and nonextremist-sounding rhetoric can be disarming and effectively deceptive. The historical revisionists of IHR adhere to a philosophy that their pursuit of "solid and reliable information" is stigmatized knowledge, similar to the revisionist history of slavery according to Weltner and the "untold truth" about Dr. King according to Don Black.[51] When this commitment to "uncovering" stigmatized knowledge coincides with anti-Semitism as it so often does, precyber frauds such as the *Protocols of the Elders of Zion* find a renewed life in the digital era.[52] Thus, while historical revisionists, conspiracy theories, and white supremacy certainly existed in the print era, the Internet offers a new terrain for those who seek and produce stigmatized knowledge, blurring the lines between history and propaganda.

Racist Propaganda in the Digital Era

The emergence of cloaked white supremacist websites illustrates a central feature of racist propaganda in the digital era: the use of the Internet to spread difficult-to-detect lies that are intended to undermine racial equality. Cloaked white supremacist websites take issue with historical facts in sometimes oblique ways. By concealing authorship and intention, such sites combine old forms of black and grey propaganda with digital media. This combination of racist propaganda and digital media constitutes a new way of presenting, publishing, and debating ideas about race, racism, and racial equality. To better understand racist propaganda in the digital era, we can learn from critical theorists who wrote about propaganda in another era shaped by an earlier medium.

In a 1951 essay about American fascist propaganda, Theodor Adorno, writing about the persuasive tactics of a broadcast media, points to the similarities between mass culture and fascist ideology. In the epigraph that opens this chapter Adorno critiques the manipulation inherent in both advertising and fascism when he writes that fascist propaganda has "by now come to be a profession" that relies on consumer psychology in which propagandists "test the effectiveness of its various appeals" and only the catchiest ones survive.[53] In a similar fashion, cloaked white supremacist sites repackage overt racism in the language of multiculturalism, thus deploying public-relations-savvy rhetoric intended to appeal to a large audience in order to manipulate and subvert previously agreed-upon facts. This is a strategy that extends beyond extremist white supremacist cloaked sites to the larger, mainstream culture. Evidence of this in the digital era is clear in sites such as Conservapedia (conservapedia.com), created by Andrew Schlafly (Phyllis Schlafly's son) and intended to be an antidote to the supposedly liberal bias of the popular Wikipedia (wikipedia.org), the "free encyclopedia anyone can edit."[54] Such attempts by the more mainstream branches of the American right to use digital media to challenge the "liberal bias" of encyclopedia definitions is similar to the strategy of cloaked white supremacist websites use of digital media to challenge racial equality. Both strategies use digital media to call into question cultural values in favor of changing the audience's mind and persuading them of the site's political views. In this new political landscape, conservatives and white supremacists use the guise of cultural tolerance and a variety of digital media to engage in an assault on "fact-based reality."[55] This strategy draws on a fairly radical postmodern deconstructionism in which truth is no longer possible. When claims to knowledge and truth are entirely relative, then there can be no basis for equality or social justice in a democratic society.

Adorno and other critical theorists associated with the Frankfurt School responded to similar challenges to a democratic society by reasserting the capacity of reason as a crucial strategy in the liberation of human beings from oppressive regimes of domination.[56] Adorno's articulation of the connection between reason and liberation represents a precursor to epistemologies of Black/Chicana feminist thought,[57] and both are particularly relevant for understanding and resisting racist propaganda in the digital era. To the extent that racist propaganda on cloaked websites succeeds, it does so in part by relying on the assumption that what they are presenting is unbiased and objective. In fact, every website, just like every book, film, work of art, or other cultural product, has an author and a particular point of view. Rather than seeing point of view as bias and therefore discrediting it, critical race feminists argue instead that it is *only* by taking standpoint into account that we can arrive at the truth. The experiential knowledge of those at the bottom of multiple hierarchies of oppression provides an understanding of the "systemic forces at work in their oppression" that is less available to those at the top of those hierarchies.[58] Along with lived experience as a criterion of meaning, this alternative epistemology places an ethic of caring central to the process of arriving at the truth. The goal of such a process of arriving at truth is self-conscious struggle that empowers women and men to actualize a humanist vision of community.[59] An epistemology that envisions lived experience, an ethic of caring, and a humanist vision of community as integral to the process of arriving at the truth is what is required to uncover the racist propaganda concealed by cloaked white supremacist websites.

Conclusion

Cloaked websites represent a unique new form of white supremacy online because they disguise white supremacy in the rhetoric of multiculturalism and civil rights. While David Duke and others attempted to mimic the discourse of civil rights in print (e.g., the National Association for the Advancement of White People), the deception inherent in cloaked sites is a new twist, made all the more effective because of the medium of the Internet. This new form of cyber racism shares a number of features with traditional propaganda. The epistemological challenge to the value of racial equality in a democratic society is that the landscape of the online universe is a relatively flat one, in which all content appears virtually equivalent without the critical ability to distinguish between sites. Thus, without at least some critical awareness of racial inequality, detecting and evaluating cloaked sites is difficult.

One of the many promises of digital media is that it opens up the possibility for multiple perspectives. Understanding multiple perspectives is an important corrective to the racism, sexism, and homophobia generated by corporate-owned media outlets, and this is a vital contribution of participatory media.[60] However, the idea of valuing multiple perspectives does not mean all perspectives should be valued equally. If valuing multiple perspectives is the only standard, then we have no basis on which to critically distinguish between a cloaked website and a legitimate civil rights website, no way to evaluate the content at The King Center site or the material on Don

Black's cloaked Martin Luther King site. The cloaked white supremacist sites examined here are grounded in an epistemology of white supremacy that seeks to undermine hard-won political battles for racial and ethnic equality by rearticulating an essentialist notion of white racial purity and, along with it, a sense of entitled privilege based on that whiteness. The usual approach of "understanding multiple perspectives" is simply inadequate to the task of critically evaluating cloaked sites. Valuing multiple perspectives without regard to content means that there is no way to distinguish between white supremacy and racial equality, no basis for a vision of social justice.

The shifting terrain of white supremacy online raises important questions about epistemology, how we know what we say we know, and knowledge claims in the digital era. In the following chapter I investigate how young people, many of whom have come of age in the digital era immersed in Internet technologies, find and evaluate information about civil rights online and how they make sense of the cloaked white supremacist websites that they encounter.

Notes

The first epigraph is from Theodor W. Adorno. 1951/2002, 118–37. Freudian theory and the pattern of fascist propaganda. In *The essential Frankfurt school reader*, ed. Andrew Arato and Eike Gebhardt. Oxford: Blackwell Publishing.

The second epigraph is from *Agenda-setting, opinion leadership, and the world of Web logs. First Monday* 10 (12) (December).

1. Lavelle and Feagin 2006. See also Giroux 2006a.
2. Zeller 2005. And see Anti-Defamation League 2005a.
3. See the lengthy discussion about this in chapter 6.
4. Daniels 2008a, 1–31; Daniels 2006. The term *cloak* first referenced a website, as far as I know, in Ray and Marsh 2001. In this article the authors refer to martinlutherking.org as "cloaked." I am adopting the term *cloaked website* and am expanding the term to include other types of sites. While I recognize that others have used the terms *counterfeit, hoax,* and *urban legend* to refer to some of these sites (e.g., Piper 2000), in my view these lack a conceptual clarity that I hope to offer with the term *cloaked.* I am grateful to Andre Oboler for pointing out that the term *IP cloaking* refers to a questionable search-engine-optimization (SEO) technique designed to show a search engine one page and the people who visit the page another. This is not the practice I'm referring to; I reference websites designed to disguise political intent.
5. Daniels in press.
6. Cull, Culbert, and Welch 2003. See also Jowett and O'Donnell 2006.
7. I am grateful to Glen Blankenship for making me aware of these different types of propaganda. Soley and Nichols 1986.

8. Soley and Nichols 1986.

9. Frederick 1986.

10. Doherty 1994.

11. Unfortunately, such language shapes and reinforces patterns of thought suggesting that black is bad and white is good.

12. "Propaganda is the deliberate, systematic attempt to shape perceptions, manipulate cognitions, and direct behavior to achieve a response that furthers the desired intent of the propagandist," Jowett and O'Donnell 2006, 10.

13. Stauber and Rampton 1995.

14. See, for example, Kahn and Kellner 2003. See also Kahn and Kellner 2004, Langma 2005, and Jenkins 2006a.

15. Daniels 2006; Daniels, 2009. Cloaked Websites: Propaganda, cyber racism and epistemology in the digital era. *New Media & Society* 11 (5).

16. The site is no longer active, but the creators have a Web page that chronicles the saga and offers screenshots of some earlier versions of the site, along with audio of Bush's "freedom ought to have limits" reaction. (At http://rtmark.com/bush.html.) Two culture-jammers who call themselves The Yes Men also collaboratorated on this project, and their involvement is chronicled in the documentary film *The Yes Men* (2003).

17. Meikle 2002, 114–15.

18. Meikle 2002, 116–18.

19. Meikle 2002, 118.

20. Meikle 2002, 118.

21. *Astroturf*, used to describe fake grassroots campaigns, is a term that predates the Internet and was coined by Sen. Lloyd Bentsen. Today it is most often used to refer to online efforts to propagate word-of-mouth interest in a political candidate or a consumer product. See Mayer 2007.

22. CNNMoney.com 2006.

23. Bianco 2006. See also Norman 2004, Quinn 2000, and Spotts 2005.

24. http://forwalmart.com/about/.

25. Now youthforvolpe.blogspot.com, formerly youthforvolpe.ca, until Volpe took action to have the original site removed.

26. Weber 2007.

27. The Yes Men have an interesting take on public identity; they use cloaked sites to enact culture-jamming "identity correction," in which "Honest people impersonate big-time criminals in order to publicly humiliate them. Targets are leaders and big corporations who put profits ahead of everything else." At http://theyesmen.org. I am grateful to Ryan Button for pointing out the use of cloaked sites by The Yes Men.

28. According to several online sources, Sandra Choate Faucher is president of The Rosetta Foundation; however, so little information is available about her or the foundation online that it's possible she is a sock puppet—that is, a fictional character created by someone else.

29. http://teenbreaks.com/abortion/complicationsgirls.cfm.

30. Ginsburg 1998.

31. Goldberg 2006, 80–105.

32. Mayer 2007, 106.

33. Marc Levin interviews Weltner in the documentary *Protocols of Zion* (2005). The ADL describes Weltner's site like this:

> Jew Watch organizes its anti-Semitic materials much in the same way a popular Web directory might group more benign information. Weltner presents accusations that Jews were behind the terrors caused by Russia's Communist regime in "Jews, Communism, and the Job of Killing Off the USSR's Christians." "Jewish Genocides Today and Yesterday" describes an alleged Jewish plan to deport non-Jews from the United States in 1946. "90 percent of All United States Newspapers Are Owned and Run by Jews" repeats the oft-heard charge that Jews run the media, and "The Rothschild Internationalist-Zionist-Banking-One World Order Family" claims that Jews control the world of finance. Adolf Hitler's writings, transcripts of Father Charles Coughlin's anti-Semitic radio broadcasts, and the text of Henry Ford Sr.'s bigoted *International Jew* are all available at Jew Watch as well.

Anti-Defamation League 2001b.

34. External sources to check domain registration include the Who Is look-up registry, but it is possible for registrants to disguise their ownership. One can also use Web-tracking services, such as Alexa, to vet sites and check authorship. Or one can use a link analyzer to see what other sites link in to the site. All of these have limitations, thus making discerning authorship when the author intends to conceal it that much more difficult.

35. Flanders 1998. See also Flanders 2002.

36. Feagin 2006b.

37. *Born in slavery: Slave narratives from the federal writers' project, 1936–1938* contains more than 2,300 first-person accounts of slavery and 500 black-and-white photographs of former slaves. These narratives were collected in the 1930s as part of the Federal Writers' Project of the Work Projects Administration (WPA) and assembled and microfilmed in 1941 as the seventeen-volume *Slave narratives: A folk history of slavery in the United States from interviews with former slaves*. It is available as an online collection, sponsored jointly by the Manuscripts Division and the Prints and Photographs Divisions of the Library of Congress, with funding provided by the Citigroup Foundation. At http://memory.loc.gov/ammem/snhtml/snhome.html.

38. This is one of the sites that I discuss in chapter 8. Because they both use oral history data, I pair this legitimate site with Weltner's cloaked site and ask young people to evaluate them. The legitimate site is available online at voicesofcivilrights.org.

39. The term *revisionist*, as I use it here in the narrowest sense, refers to the white supremacist project that seeks to revise history in a way that denies the facts of the Nazi genocide of Jews, homosexuals, and Roma peoples under the Third Reich. While I realize that some historians have used *revisionist history* as a term to refer to other kinds of projects, such as feminist revisions to male-dominated history, this is not how I use the term here.

40. Of course, pseudo-scientific publications like Herrnstein and Murray's *Bell Curve* create a compelling counterexample to this point. Herrnstein and Murray 1994.

41. Metzger and Flanagin 2007.

42. Metzger, Flanagin, Eyal, Lemus, and McCann 2003.

43. There are dozens, if not hundreds, of services online that offer professionally designed website templates that anyone can download for a nominal fee (around $50) and customize with their own content. See, for example, monstertemplate.com.

44. As with ACRR, the author of Bamboo Delight is only discernible through an external source. For this example I am indebted to the work of the ADL and their report Poisoning the Web: Hatred Online (2001a), at http://adl.org/poisoning_web/black.asp.

45. Feagin 2006b.

46. Here, again, context is the key. The word *Jew* is not, by itself, anti-Semitic; but when that term is used, rather than *Jewish people* or *Jewish tradition*, it raises suspicions.

47. The most popular search engine today is Google, but other popular search-engine tools, such as DogPile, return similar results.

48. Festa 2002.

49. The IHR site represents a slight variation on cloaked sites since it does reveal the names of the sites authors while still cloaking their politics under a veneer of legitimacy. The rhetoric at the site emphasizes that it is a source for "solid and reliable" historical information, when in fact the goal of the site's creators is to undermine the agreed-upon historical reality of the Holocaust.

50. http://ihr.org/main/about.shtml.

51. Barkun 2003.

52. Weitzman and Jacobs 2003. See also Barkun 2003 and Bonner 2000. Due to limitations of space, I am not including a discussion of the cloaked sites that deal with the Protocols; see Weitzman, Mark, and S. L. Jacobs. 2003. *Dismantling the Big Lie: The Protocols of the Elders of Zion.* Los Angeles: KTAV Publishing House.

53. Weitzman and Jacobs 2003, 133.

54. Decker 2007. See also *Cleveland Leader* 2007.

55. Rich 2006. See also Goldberg 2006, 102. Under the Bush regime, *truth* has been replaced by *truthiness*, and late-night talk show host Steven Colbert's riffs on truthiness are meant to skewer this right-wing strategy.

56. Adorno, Theodor W. 1951/2002. Freudian theory and the pattern of fascist propaganda. In *The essential Frankfurt school reader*, eds. Andrew Arato and Eike Gebhardt. Oxford: Blackwell Publishing.

57. Anderson 1993, 39–52. Collins 1998. Guba and Lincoln 1994. Scheurich and Young 1997.

58. Pizarro 1988.

59. Collins 1998, 255–71.

60. Jenkins 2006a.

CHAPTER EIGHT

~

Searching for Civil Rights, Finding White Supremacy: Adolescents Making Sense of Cloaked Websites

> It is essential in a democratic society that young people and adults learn
> how to think, learn how to make up their minds. They must learn how
> to think independently, and they must learn how to think together. . . .
> So far as individuals are concerned, the art of democracy is the art of
> thinking and discussing independently together.
>
> —The Fine Art of Propaganda, 1939[1]

The art of democracy is intricately linked to critical thinking, and both
are facing new challenges as white supremacy moves into the digital era. An
anecdote from a colleague illustrates these challenges. In 2005 I attended
a small conference in New York hosted by the Anti-Defamation League
and the International Network Against Cyberhate. The conference was
attended by a range of academics and law-enforcement officials concerned
about the presence of white supremacy online. I ended up chatting with
scholar/activist Ken Stern,[2] who told me a story that illustrates just how
effective cloaked sites can be. While Ken's son, Daniel, was attending He-
brew school, Daniel's teacher, a rabbinic student, gave the sixth-grade students three Web resources for a research project on the Holocaust. The
Web resource the teacher highlighted as the best of the three was IHR.org,
the Institute for Historical Review. Fortunately for Daniel, his father is an

expert in recognizing white supremacy and anti-Semitism and was able to intervene in this assignment; that Daniel's teacher, a rabbinical student, could be fooled by a cloaked site indicates just how effectively deceptive such sites can be. Ken's story about his son's experience is anecdotal evidence to be sure, but this story resonated with my own experience with students in the computer lab who stumbled upon the cloaked MLK site (chapter 7). These sorts of experiences with cloaked sites stand in sharp contrast to the popular perception of young people as "digital natives," an unfortunate turn of phrase meant to suggest that those who grow up with digital media have a greater facility with it (as opposed to "immigrants," who become familiar with digital media later in life).[3] Perhaps young people who are fluent[4] in digital technologies could easily detect cloaked white supremacist sites and distinguish them from legitimate civil-rights sites, or perhaps not. I wanted a more systematic approach to investigate how young people make sense of cloaked white supremacist sites. What follows is a small, qualitative exploration intended as a beginning toward such a systematic analysis.

Examining the text of Web pages, discussion forums, and newsgroups is the method that has come to dominate the study of white supremacists online.[5] More difficult and less prevalent are investigations into the connections between online interaction and face-to-face social networks among extremists.[6] Most vexing still and least common are studies of the Web user. In other media, this type of research is called *audience reception* and explores how the listener, viewer, or reader interprets the text, whether that text is visual (as in films or television shows) or printed (as in novels or newspaper articles). A number of critics have suggested that while this is an important area of study, the terms *audience* and *reception* are rooted in old, broadcast media and do not work well for digital media for a variety of reasons.[7] When it comes to empirical explorations of how people find, read, and interpret extremist rhetoric on racist websites, there is scant research. An important exception to this is the work of Lee and Leets, who examine how adolescents respond to what they call "persuasive storytelling" online by hate groups.[8] Lee and Leets found only minimal effects on adolescents who were infrequently exposed to explicit hate messages. However, their research did not explore how adolescents might be exposed to these messages, and it only focused on explicitly racist sites and not on cloaked websites. This chapter is intended to address this gap in the emerging body of knowledge about race and the Internet and examines how teens find information online about race and asks how they interpret cloaked websites.

For young people who have come of age during the digital era, the notion of "doing research" does not mean going to a library: it means going online to use a search engine to find information.[9] This shift in how young people look for and find information has a number of far-reaching consequences about digital media and learning.[10] Race and racism are part of this new digital era in ways both predictable and unexpected. Many adolescents, like many adults, in the United States are naïve about matters of race and racism, and this naïveté makes discerning cloaked white supremacist websites even more difficult. I contend that both digital literacy and critical race consciousness are necessary for understanding race in the digital era. How young people look for information about race, racism, and civil rights and how they make sense of that information once they find it are the questions to which I now turn.

Searching for Dr. King and Finding David Duke

Using a combination of experiments and interviews, I analyzed how a small sample (N=10) of racially and ethnically diverse young people (ages fifteen to nineteen) made sense of cloaked white supremacy online.[11] I recruited participants via the Internet, asked them to use any search engine and any search terms they chose to find information about Dr. Martin Luther King Jr., and then asked them to do the same to find information about the goals of the civil-rights movement, "as if doing a report for school." Following that, I paired a series of legitimate and cloaked sites and asked the participants to tell me which of these sites they would use "if doing a report for school." During both, I asked the participants to "talk aloud," describing their decision-making process. Nine of the ten participants selected the search engine Google (the remaining participant used the search engine Yahoo.com). All of the participants used the same search engine throughout their interview and did not switch to another search engine. The participants also used similar search terms. The most commonly used search terms for the first scenario were *martin luther king* or *martin luther king + biography*. And, for the second scenario, the most commonly used search terms were *civil rights*, *civil rights movement*, and *civil rights goals*.

When asked about how they evaluate the search-engine results, most said that they relied on the order that search results appeared on the screen as a valid and reliable way to evaluate whether or not a site was trustworthy. This was a consistent theme across the interviews and is reflected in this quotation from a participant, reporting that she would "never" go beyond the first page of results in her research of a topic:

> I actually have never, I think, in my life gone to like the third page, or the second page, because I just stop at the first page. . . . Because, I mean, there must be a reason why everything's on the first page and the rest of the stuff is later. (study participant, age sixteen)

In a sense, this young woman is correct when she says that "there must be a reason" for the results on the first page to be listed there. There is a reason, and it is an algorithm created by software engineers at Google. Given the huge popularity of Google as the search engine of choice by so many, we might expect that there would be familiarity with how the search engine works. As it turns out, this is not the case. Actually, different search engines work differently, and the way Google works is through a fairly complex algorithm that includes a Web-crawling robot, the Google indexer, and a query processor. PageRank is Google's mechanism for ranking one Web page higher than another based on the results. Central to this mechanism are links from outside pages; each link from an outside page to a website is, in Google's evaluation schema, a vote for the importance of that site.[12] So, while there is a reason that those results appear on the first page, it is not because someone sitting in an office at Google headquarters has read and evaluated each site and rank ordered them based on an agreed upon set of criteria. In fact, because of the way Google's algorithm works, it is possible to intentionally manipulate the ranking of a site by linking to a page using consistent anchor text. This is commonly referred to as *Google bombing* and has been used a number of times as a form of political critique of the Bush administration; thus, because people on a number of websites across the Internet have repeatedly used the same linking anchor text, in 2006 anyone who typed the search terms *miserable failure* into Google would find that the first result was a link to the biography of George W. Bush.[13] When I asked the participants if they had ever heard of a Google bomb, not one said that they had and were perplexed and amused when I showed them the George W. Bush results for the *miserable failure* search. Trusting the results on the first page of Google might not be an issue for understanding race, except in two key circumstances: (1) when searching for information on race, racism, and civil rights, cloaked white supremacist sites appear alongside results for legitimate sites, and (2) people like the young woman quoted above implicitly trust the order of results as a valid and reliable mechanism for assessing trustworthiness.

The cloaked site www.martinlutherking.org consistently appears third or fourth on the first page of results in Google when using the search terms *martin luther king*, and this, along with the URL, has implications for how young people find information about race, racism, and civil rights. Typical of the way participants in this research evaluated the cloaked site when it appeared in search engine results was this young woman's response (responses from participants are indicated by A, questions and prompts from the interviewer by Q, and descriptions of what is displayed on the computer screen by italic script):

[COMPUTER SCREEN: *Opens Google, uses search terms* martin luther king *without quotations. Once the search results are returned, she scrolls the page quickly, using the mouse button.*]

A: Right now, I'm just reading the sites, to see what they're about, to see which ones are easier for me.

Q: Okay, and what kinds of information do you look at? What pops out at you?

A: I guess maybe something like this would pop out, an article from . . . about his life and impact.

Q: Okay. And is that a link that you might click on?

A: I would just look at it; I wouldn't click on it yet. . . . But this one . . .

[COMPUTER SCREEN: *Points her mouse to the martinlutherking.org link returned third in the list of results from Google.*]

A: . . . this one looks good.

Q: You think you would click on that one?

A: Yeah, because the site itself, it says, "Martin Luther King dot org," so I guess they're dedicated to that. (study participant, age eighteen)

Here, in the span of just a few seconds after typing in the search terms looking for information about Dr. King, this young woman has come across the cloaked white supremacist site and evaluates it positively, along with a legitimate site about Dr. King hosted by *The Seattle Times* newspaper. In part, this participant is responding to the anchor of the site's universal resource locator (URL); in other words, the fact that the Web address is comprised of the civil-rights leader's name makes it seem legitimate. She is also responding to the suffix or ending of the Web address, the .org. This kind of response to the URL martinlutherking.org was a consistent theme throughout the interviews. Participants understood the suffix *.org* to mean that a site was a legitimate source of information, as this young woman explains:

> [COMPUTER SCREEN: *Scrolls up and down the list of search results, including the martinlutherking.org link returned third in the list of results from Google.*]
>
> Q: Okay. Anything else about the URL that lets you know it's trustworthy?
>
> A: That's about it. Basically, like the source where it's coming from. I mean, if it's like a personal Web page or something, they just have information about him, I wouldn't go there.
>
> Q: And how do you know when it's a personal Web page? How can you tell?
>
> A: Well. . . . Okay, like if it's dot edu, then you know it has to do with education, like a university or something. And, you know, like this one. . . .
>
> [COMPUTER SCREEN: *Scrolls over the results for a legitimate site, hosted at Lucid Café, a Web portal created and run by Robin Chew, a Web developer and marketing executive in San Francisco.*]
>
> A: Lucid Café. That doesn't look too . . . I don't know . . . the title looks serious, but the URL. . . .
>
> Q: Alright, based on the URL you wouldn't go there even though the title and the description look okay.
>
> A: Yeah. And dot org, too. . . .
>
> Q: Yeah, and what does that mean for you?
>
> A: I don't know what it means, actually. . . . *[laughs]* . . . Organization?
>
> Q: No, it's fine. . . . I don't mean What does it actually mean, I meant, What does it indicate to you?
>
> A: Oh, okay. . . . Again, it's more of a trustworthy website. Because dot coms are everywhere, and dot org and dot edu are more specific. (study participant, age eighteen)

The fact that URLs ending in .com are more common ("everywhere") leads this participant to conclude that the less common .org websites are more trustworthy. For the most part, Internet literacy skills–based classes have instructed Web users to read the URL as a first step for evaluating the legitimacy of a website and to trust URLs ending in .org more than those ending in .com. Thus, this participant is doing precisely as she has been taught. While it is possible to read the URL of a site and sometimes ascertain where the site is hosted or who is sponsoring it, it is also possible for the site creator to disguise the nature of a site using a clever or nefarious domain-name registration. In the case of the martinlutherking.org site, the cloaking of white supremacist political and ideological goals began when Don Black registered the domain name and launched the site in 1998. This suggests that racial politics in the digital era have shifted to a new location: domain-name registration. It also suggests that typical approaches to teaching Internet literacy skills are inadequate on their own to meet the demands of this new form of struggle over meaning in racial politics. Also necessary is a basic understanding of racism and the struggles against it; without at least a basic understanding of this, the possibility of being duped by a cloaked white supremacist site is much greater.

The lack of understanding about racism and the civil-rights struggle can contribute to an inability to recognize a cloaked site and is illustrated in the following interview. This is an account of the first four and a half minutes from the time the participant begins the search scenario looking for information about Dr. King:

[COMPUTER SCREEN: *Google results for search terms* martin luther king]

A: And see what results come up? Am I looking for any particular website?

Q: No, just any website that comes up, maybe the first three.

A: Okay, and I'm finding information on his life history?

[COMPUTER SCREEN: *Stanford University's site about Dr. King*]

A: Okay, this is a website by Stanford University, so I think it would be pretty well-established and accurate. His biography is on here. Other sites that we found included . . .

[COMPUTER SCREEN: *back to Google results*]

A: . . . *The Seattle Times* on Martin Luther King on the civil-rights movement, and . . .

[COMPUTER SCREEN: *Clicks on the* Seattle Times *page . . . then, back to Google results.*]

Q: Could you try clicking on some of those links and see what they say also, like once you get inside of the website?

[COMPUTER SCREEN: *Clicks on the www.martinlutherking.org main page.*]

A: Sure. . . . There's a Martin Luther King pop quiz, there's some historical writings, essays, sermons, speeches, . . .

[COMPUTER SCREEN: *Clicks on what seems to be a broken link on www.martinlutherking.org, to* Historical Writings; *the link takes more than a couple of seconds to load, and she abandons it as a broken link. Then she skips to the* Truth about King *link without comment and clicks on* Death of the Dream *link, subtitle* The Day King Was Shot.*]

A: . . . There's information here about the day he was shot. It has some photographs of Dr. King the day before his death . . . and some information about
what happened the night before he died, which is not apparently public knowledge, or, yeah, it's not like common knowledge. . . .

[COMPUTER SCREEN: *Goes back to scrolling over the links on the right. Clicks on*
suggested books, and on that page several titles appear, including a picture of David
Duke on the cover of his book My Awakening.]

A: . . . Then there's some information on some books that were written by Dr.
King and biographies that were written by– about him by other people. . . .

[COMPUTER SCREEN: *Clicks on* Truth about King *page.*]

Q: Do you know who that person was? [*referring to David Duke*]

A: No, I have no idea.

[COMPUTER SCREEN: *Clicks back to the* Suggested Books *page.*]

Q: David Duke, have you ever heard of him?

A: No.

Q: You've never heard of him?

A: Uh-uh [*no*]. Who is David Duke?

Q: He's a Klan leader.

A: Oh, is he? I had no idea. I actually don't know much about the civil-rights
movement at all.

[COMPUTER SCREEN: *Reading Duke book description more closely now.*]

A: Hmmm. . . . Interesting. It's interesting how that would be on Martin
Luther King's website. (study participant, age eighteen)

In less than three minutes from when she began using a search engine to
look for information about Dr. King, this young woman has selected a
cloaked white supremacist site and is reading a page that contains the views
of David Duke, an avowed white supremacist, yet she does not recognize that
this site is cloaked. Consistent with conventional Internet-literacy skills
training, she is reading the URL as legitimate. What is lacking here is not her
Internet-literacy skill; it is her understanding of the historical context of
racism in the United States and David Duke's place in it. As she says, "I actually don't know much about the civil-rights movement at all." Although it
may be possible to have an understanding of racism and the civil-rights struggle against it in the United States and still not know who David Duke is, not
knowing seems to suggest a lack of critical awareness about contemporary
racial politics. This young woman is certainly not alone in her lack of criti-

cal awareness, and it is not surprising given the push toward a mediocre, testing-based educational system that lacks critical thinking in general[14] and is completely absent any analysis of racism, either historical or contemporary.[15]

Evaluating Civil Rights Online:
Photographic Evidence and Visual Cues

When asked to evaluate the differences between the legitimate site and the cloaked site participants used a variety of strategies, including examining digital photographs and visual cues. The Web is a visual, as well as (hyper)textual, medium.[16] As such, those who have grown up using the Web expect to find visual and photographic images in their search results. Indeed, they rely on these as important sources of information, as this young man explains while exploring the (legitimate) Voices of Civil Rights website:

> This site looks good. I mean, it has a lot of pictures and photos, so you can see for yourself what happened. (study participant, age eighteen)

Seeing photos as a window into what happened was a consistent theme across the interviews. Here another participant describes her initial impression of the cloaked Martin Luther King site:

> First thing I notice is the colors. . . . And although the colors are more, are duller, they're in black and white. And, his picture, the picture of Martin Luther King, that makes a major difference. Because, you know, it's this picture that attracts all your attention to it. (study participant, age seventeen)

And a third participant describes her impression of *The Seattle Times'* use of photographic images this way:

> A: Well, they have a photo gallery which I would probably click on, because photos are, photography interests me, so. . . .
>
> Q: Okay, and would that be useful to you in doing your report on King, and if so how?
>
> [COMPUTER SCREEN: *Clicks on a black-and-white photograph of Mrs. King kissing a smiling Dr. King; there is a caption to the right.*]
>
> A: Well, like this photo: Without even reading the caption . . . I already know what he looks like, so I know that's him, that's his wife, and it looks like a good occasion. (study participant, age sixteen)

Visual images are not simply decoration for a site but carry messages, convey meaning, and suggest connotations for these participants. This expectation of and reliance on visual images was consistent across all the interviews. Without visual images, a particular website was not only deemed less reliable, it was simply less interesting and often discarded as a possible resource, as this participant describes in her assessment of a site that was text-only:

> This site seems awfully wordy. . . . I don't know that I would use this one. (study participant, age fifteen)

In particular, images that appear to be *historical* were a significant part of what the young people in this study were looking for and expected to find when they went online to search for information about Dr. King or the civil-rights movement. And photographic images seemed to carry the weight of authenticity for them, because they reportedly allow one to "see what happened." This reliance on the supposed veracity of photographic images is ironic at a time that some have referred to as the postphotographic era.[17] In the digital era, the widespread use of software that can alter photographs in ways that are virtually imperceptible to the untrained eye makes photography less a window to the truth and more of an act of interpretation. That this has significance for racial politics became evident in 1994 when O. J. Simpson was arrested and a photograph of him appeared on the cover of *TIME* magazine in which the color of his skin had been tinted several shades darker than his actual skin tone.[18]

Aside from photography, the teens reported that they relied heavily on other visual cues when evaluating civil-rights information online. Background and text color, font, layout, and the entire graphic user interface (GUI) of websites were primary criteria used to evaluate whether or not a site was trustworthy, as this participant describes in her assessment of one of the cloaked sites:

> This site looks like someone, you know, just an individual created it. It doesn't look very professional. (study participant, age seventeen)

Here, a site that does not look "professional" is deemed an untrustworthy source of information. Conversely, a site that has a GUI that gets positively evaluated is deemed to have trustworthy content. The distinction between a site that is "professionally" designed and one that "an individual" created is the important distinction here, as this participant illustrates in her evaluation of the paired websites:

[COMPUTER SCREEN: *Clicks on the cloaked MLK site.*]

A: This one certainly looks less professional.

Q: And what tells you that it looks less professional?

A: Uhm, it doesn't have a clean layout, like this one. . . .

[COMPUTER SCREEN: *Clicks back to the King Center.*]

Q: Okay, and so . . . what does that mean? What do you believe about the site or the people who created it?

A: Well, this one was designed– like, they hired someone to design it. . . . (study participant, age sixteen)

In these examples both the participants take visual cues from graphic design about the trustworthiness of the information contained there. While visual cues are important elements in evaluating Web content, they can also be easily manipulated. If the cloaked websites under investigation here made use of "more professional" Web-design graphics and layout, it would make them much more difficult for these young people to distinguish their illegitimacy.

Critical Race Consciousness and Assessing Bias Online

Thinking critically about race is crucial to being able to distinguish cloaked websites from legitimate civil-rights websites, because this is, ultimately, a political distinction. Unless we are able to think critically, all websites are reduced to the level of personal opinion without reference to the power relations that imbue racial politics. And without a critical race consciousness, one website is just as "legitimate" or "biased" as another. A number of the young people in the study evaluated websites in a way that reflected a lack of critical race consciousness, and it made evaluating the sites more difficult:

[COMPUTER SCREEN: *Clicks from cloaked site to the King Center site.*]

Well, you know, in looking at this site, it appears to be created by his widow, or his family, so, it could be biased. (study participant, age seventeen)

In this instance, the legitimate civil-rights website sponsored by the King Center is evaluated as a less than reliable source of information because it is affiliated with Mrs. King and therefore likely "biased." This young woman is doing what she has been taught in skills-based approaches to Internet literacy, to "look for bias." Yet in this instance it leads to the erroneous conclusion that the King Center site might not be a good source of information about civil rights or Dr. King. While the King Center site certainly presents information from a point of view, it is precisely this point of view—situated in the struggle for civil rights and against racism—that gives it credibility. Another teen assesses bias in a cloaked site:

> Q: Do you know who published this site, who's behind it?
>
> [COMPUTER SCREEN: *Looking at graphic on the top of* High Self-Esteem for Many American Slaves *page on American Civil Rights Review.*]
>
> A: Uhm, Currier and Ives?
>
> Q: No.
>
> [COMPUTER SCREEN: *Spends some time clicking through the site . . . then comes to a page that has all those badges on it and a copyright link to copyright legalese on a page hosted by Cornell University.*]
>
> A: Is it by Cornell?
>
> Q: No.
>
> [COMPUTER SCREEN: *Reading from the text on the page about slavery, American Civil Rights Review.*]
>
> A: I mean, I don't think I would disagree with it. I'm sure there are some slaves that were treated well. So, I can understand their point of view. There's always two sides to everything. (study participant, age seventeen)

In this case the young woman determines that this site represents just another "point of view," another "side" of a two-sided argument. She is also unable to ascertain who it is that's publishing the site, which is hosted by anti-Semite and racist Frank Weltner whose rewrite of history would have us believe that plantations were "sanitary, humane, and relaxed" workplaces rather than institutions predicated on human misery. As in the previous example, this illustrates how a lack of critical thinking about racial politics offline can lead to misreading online.

For young people who possess critical race consciousness, recognizing cloaked websites is within their reach. The following is how another teen approached the same cloaked website created by Frank Weltner:

> A: So, I'm looking at the URL, and it says, American Civil Rights Review slash slavery, so I'm looking at the main thing; it says American Civil Rights, so it's probably something that I would depend on. And now I'm looking at the picture of a cotton plantation on the Mississippi River, and, you know, plantations and slaves are related a lot, so that relates to slaves. I'm going to just scroll down. . . . There does seem to be useful information.
>
> [COMPUTER SCREEN: *Reading from the American Civil Rights Review.*]

A: "Idyllic View of American Slavery" . . . they just have pictures; I would rather have– Oh, they're actually talking about how the artist basically portrayed the slaves.

[COMPUTER SCREEN: *Reading from the American Civil Rights Review.*]

A: "Now notice how the artist has painted the slaves in relaxed positions."

[COMPUTER SCREEN: *Pause; reads silently.*]

A: It kinda sounds like– like, I'm reading this, "Were the slaves mistreated?" It says "Sometimes." . . .

[COMPUTER SCREEN: *Points to screen.*]

A: . . . and that just throws me off, because I think, Yes, slaves were mistreated all the time. And then it says "Sometimes."

Q: And so what does that mean? What do you think now that you've read that?

A: Now I don't think it's accurate anymore! Because it says . . .

[COMPUTER SCREEN: *Reading from the American Civil Rights Review.*]

A: . . . "Sometimes, but most probably no more than were other workers including whites." I highly would disagree with that; it sounds so false to me, because most of the slaves, they were all black. And white people would not have been treated the same way. And then it goes into *[reading]* "Europeans were sometimes given the hardest jobs." When you're talking about slaves and then they're going to Europeans which were obviously not treated the same as slaves because the slaves weren't even treated like people. So, that just throws off everything.

Q: So now what do you do with this site? You said before that the URL looked good and it might have some useful information.

A: I wouldn't use it.

Q: You wouldn't use it?

A: No, because even if I find other information that seems accurate, this just makes the whole thing biased to me. Because, to me, the answer would be "Yes." There's no "Sometimes" or "No." It's "Yes." So, I wouldn't even use this. (study participant, age eighteen)

Here the participant decides to not use the cloaked site based not on an evaluation borrowed from her Internet-literacy skills, but rather on her ability to think critically about race. She reads the text about slaves being mistreated sometimes and says, "That just throws me off." Ultimately, she decides the site is not a credible source of information and she would not use it. And even with her negative evaluation of this site, she uses the same language as the previous two interviews when she says that the site is "biased," slipping back into the skills-based language of Internet-literacy curricula. New ways of thinking about racism in the digital era will have to move beyond two dimensional notions of bias, in which there are "two sides to everything."

Epistemology and White Supremacy in the Digital Era

The way that the young people who participated in this study do or do not make sense of cloaked white supremacist websites tells us something about epistemology and white supremacy in the digital era. For example, the effectiveness of cloaked domain names, such as www.martinlutherking.org or www.AmericanCivilRightsReview.org, rests in part on the racial naïveté of their target audience, particularly a white audience unaccustomed to taking racial matters into account. If the technical cues of rudimentary graphic design and layout are resolved, reliance on the usual hints about Web credibility will not be enough to distinguish cloaked sites from legitimate ones. Instead, it will become that much more difficult to parse the white supremacist rhetoric that exploits the vocabulary of multiculturalism and political victories that championed racial equality and social justice. In the digital era discerning white supremacy online requires an epistemology that recognizes the importance of the standpoint of those making claims to "truth," incorporates the lived experience of racial (and multiple) oppressions, and places an ethic of caring and human community at the center. Obviously, unsuspecting or racially naïve white people are not the only ones who read these cloaked sites.

People of color, particularly youth of color, also read cloaked sites. For young people of color reading cloaked sites means having their own culture and history distorted in the retelling, and this is characteristic of the epistemology of white supremacy. This, however, is not new or unique to digital media; people of color have had their culture and history distorted by whites, both those with and without good intentions, for many centuries. This is where youth of color who can draw on their lived experiences of racism may have an advantage in critically evaluating these sites. If they draw on lived experience of everyday racism and do the critical work of evaluating *who is creating* the ideas contained in cloaked websites, then they may have an advantage over those steeped in the epistemology of a white supremacy that reinforces illiteracy about racism.[19]

Conclusion

Understanding any element of culture, as Wendy Griswold reminds us, must involve an investigation into how people use it and attempt to make sense of it. This is no less true with the Internet, and here I have attempted to examine how people, particularly young people who often rely heavily on the Internet in their knowledge gathering, make sense of cloaked sites. What I find is that the young people who participated in this study were, in fact, fooled by cloaked sites. Using a popular search engine to look for information about an important civil-rights leader, the young people I observed moved quickly and seamlessly from legitimate sources of information, such as Stanford University and *The Seattle Times*, to the cloaked site hosted by Don Black without realizing it. Therefore, I conclude that cloaked white supremacist sites are accessible and easily within the knowledge landscape of young people using search engines to find information about civil rights. The threat posed is not the shrill panic over possible recruitment but rather is an epistemological hazard—that is, danger that the ideas and values of racial equality will be undermined and eroded. Cloaked websites are an attempt at the discursive production of uncertainty[20] about racial equality.

Assessing the relative merit of online content within this landscape requires more than Internet literacy. In a skills-based approach to Internet literacy, we often learn to "look at the URL" or domain name as an initial step for evaluating whether the content at a particular site is worthwhile. Yet this way of knowing whether or not a site contains legitimate civil-rights information leads to more confusion rather than less. In this way, the domain names themselves are part of the epistemology of white supremacy online. And in order to evaluate these with a discerning eye, one must incorporate a critical understanding of racial inequality alongside other skills for assessing content online.

This research is limited because it is a small, qualitative study drawing on a nonrandom sample of urban adolescents in New York City who responded to an Internet advertisement for the study. Future research should include a randomly selected sample not drawn from those who are likely to respond to an ad on the Internet. A more comprehensive study would include a larger sample size and perhaps a purposive sampling of specific populations by age. In addition, teen girls were overrepresented in this sample, and more research is needed on teen boys and their use of the Internet. The focus here is on urban young people from New York City who have grown up using digital media. Future studies would do well to expand beyond this demographic and examine the way that Web users from rural areas, from other cities and other countries, and from a range of age groups make sense of cloaked sites. Even with these limitations, the findings from this small study are an initial step toward understanding how people make sense of cloaked sites.

For those readers primarily interested in race, the findings suggest that it is important to understand digital media and its relationship to the contested terrain of race, racism, and civil rights. For those readers primarily interested in Internet technologies and digital media, these findings suggest that it is important to think critically about race, racism, and racial equality in trying to understand emerging online worlds. This research also has implications for those readers who are in the classroom and increasingly faced with issues of digital literacy as we all rely more heavily on the Internet. These issues are particularly urgent when we rely on the Internet as a source of information about race, racism, and civil rights. Given the context of cloaked white supremacy online, it is imperative that we move beyond a skills-based approach to Internet literacy that would have us assume that "looking at the URL" is a sufficient filter in determining the credibility of the site. Trying to understand a cloaked website exclusively in terms of a skills-based Internet literacy, which lacks critical thinking about race and racism, is doomed to fail. The emergence of cloaked white supremacist websites calls for different and multiple kinds of literacies: a literacy of digital media and new literacies not merely of tolerance but also of social justice that offer a depth of understanding about race, racism, and multiple, intersecting forms of oppression. At stake in this shifting digital terrain is our vision for racial and social justice in a democratic society. Since both the Internet and white supremacy online are global in the Information Age, our understanding of racial and social justice must be globally informed. It is to global efforts to combat white supremacy online that I turn in the next chapter.

Notes

1. *The Fine Art of Propaganda; A Study of Father Coughlin's Speeches.*
2. Stern 1996, discussed at length in chapter 2. This anecdote is used with permission of the author given via e-mail, August 9, 2007.
3. Prensky 2001.
4. Green 2006. See also Green 2005 and Resnick 2002.
5. See, for example, Adams and Roscigno 2005. See also Atton 2006 and Back, Keith, and Solomos 1996, Bostdorff 2004, Gerstenfeld, Grant, and Chiang 2003, Kaplan, Weinberg, and Oleson 2003, and Levin 2002.
6. Burris, Smith, and Strahm 2000. See Hara and Estrada 2003 and Tateo 2005.
7. Becker 2002. Livingstone 2004b.
8. Lee and Leets 2002.
9. Rheingold 2006.
10. See the MacArthur Foundation initiative on Digital Media and Learning, at http://digitallearning.macfound.org/.

11. For a thorough discussion of the methodology I use in this chapter and throughout the book see the methods appendix.

12. Sherman and Price 2001.

13. Byrne 2004. Kahn and Kellner 2004.

14. Aronowitz and Girou 1993.

15. Feagin 2006b.

16. Smith and Chang 1997.

17. Mitchell 1992.

18. Hunt 1999.

19. Mills 1997.

20. Lynch 1998. The Discursive Production of Uncertainty: The OJ Simpson "Dream Team" and the Sociology of Knowledge Machine. Social Studies of Science 28 (5–6): 829–68.

PART FOUR

FIGHTING WHITE SUPREMACY
IN THE DIGITAL ERA

~

CHAPTER NINE

Combating Global White Supremacy in the Digital Era

In cyberspace the First Amendment is a local ordinance.

—John Perry Barlow

In 2002 Tore W. Tvedt, founder of the hate group Vigrid and a Norwegian citizen, was sentenced to time in prison for posting racist and anti-Semitic propaganda on a website. The Anti-Racism Center in Oslo filed a police complaint
against Tvedt. On Vigrid's website, Tvedt puts forward an ideology that mixes
neo-Nazism, racism, and religion. Tvedt was tried and convicted in the Asker
and Baerum District Court on the outskirts of Oslo. The charges were six counts
of violating Norway's antiracism law and one count each of a weapons violation
and interfering with police. He was sentenced to seventy-five days in prison,
with forty-five days suspended, and two years' probation. Activists welcomed
this as the first conviction for racism on the Internet in Norway. Following
Tvedt's release from prison, his Vigrid website is once again online.[1]

In contrast to the Norwegian response, many Americans seem to view
white supremacy online as speech obviously protected under the First
Amendment. Senator Orrin Hatch (R-Utah) articulated this view following
congressional hearings about hate crime on the Internet in September 1999:

> We must be vigilant and prompt in our efforts to begin eliminating hate on the
> Internet, but we must also do so with exactitude. From this complicated maze

of issues, there is simply no simple answer, and with the First Amendment as our country's first premise, we know that any solutions that we endorse must recognize that the surest way to defeat the message of hate is to hold it under the harsh light of public scrutiny.[2]

The U.S. Senate's legislative response to those hearings was to adopt a series of technical approaches, such as filtering software, to block particular websites.[3]

Both the Norwegian and the American responses to online hate are notably from democratic nations theoretically committed to egalitarian ideals. In Norway, a man is arrested for creating a website filled with racist and anti-Semitic propaganda, even though the server for that website is located in the United States; ultimately, the man is released from jail and the website goes back online. In the United States, citing the protection of hate on the Internet as the country's "first premise," senators take a narrowly focused technolegal view of white supremacy online by attempting to mandate the use of software filters in public schools and libraries. These examples well illustrate John Perry Barlow's point (and this chapter's epigraph) that in the Information Age the First Amendment, which protects free speech, is a "local ordinance"—that is, one specific to the U.S. context. Barlow's views about Internet regulation, as well as critiques of his views from outside the United States and oppositional views from U.S.-based critical race theorists, can shed some light on these disparate democratic responses to white supremacy online.

John Perry Barlow, retired Wyoming cattle rancher, former lyricist for the Grateful Dead, and cofounder of the Electronic Frontier Foundation, is a widely known critic of Internet regulation. Barlow authored *A Declaration of the Independence of Cyberspace*,[4] an influential essay written in the polemical style of a manifesto and declaring the Internet a place that should remain free from control by "governments of the industrial world," which he refers to as "weary giants of flesh and steel." In that essay Barlow also writes that "we" (those people online in 1996) would "create a civilization of the mind in cyberspace. May it be more humane and fair than the world your governments have made before." Barlow variously describes himself as an anarchist[5] or cyberlibertarian[6] and believes that government should have no power over the Internet and that the "only thing that is dangerous is the one that is designed to stop the free flow of information." Barlow's views are acclaimed[7] and shared by most of cyberculture's leading writers and thinkers[8] in the United States. In fact, it could even reasonably be argued that within the United States the cyberlibertarian view of the absolute protection of free speech online is one that is hegemonic—an idea so pervasive as to be taken for granted as a fundamental, unquestionable truth. In contrast to the cyberlibertarian view, critical race theorists have argued that interpretations of the First Amendment that categorize hate speech as protected speech effectively arm "conscious and unconscious racists—Nazis and liberals alike—with a constitutional right to be racist."[9] My purpose here is to complicate both views in light of the research presented in the rest of this book about white supremacy online.

These two opposing views—one focusing on the Internet, the other on race—reflect the point I made earlier (chapter 2) that most theories about race do not take the Internet into account and most theories about the Internet do not take race into account. However, I can now add one small exception to that overarching observation: when it comes to hate speech online a number of critical race theorists have begun to explore the implications of this theoretical perspective for the Information Age,[10] and some cyberculture writers have thoughtfully considered hate speech in digital media. The discussion here is intended to contribute to this emerging literature by using a comparative, transnational perspective to understand the global response to white supremacy online.

In this comparative analysis I first take up a number of illustrative examples of responses to white supremacy online outside the United States and then contrast them with analogous responses inside the United States, returning to two cases discussed earlier in the book (e.g., Machado and Jouhari). The United States' response to white supremacy online is markedly different from that of other democratic nations and has been referred to as the *cyberhate divide*. I explore the significance of this divide by examining the case of *France v. Yahoo! Inc.*, the California-based international Internet company. While others have focused on the case's implication for American notions of free speech, what it reveals about transnational responses to white supremacy online is equally interesting.

I then shift from this comparative analysis using selected case studies and offer a more theoretical analysis. I locate the different responses between the United States and other democratic nations within the conceptually opposing views of cyberlibertarians and critical race theorists. In the last section, I analyze the connection between online extremist white supremacy and mainstream white supremacy through the lens of interpretation and implementation of the First Amendment and the Patriot Act in the United States. I place this comparison within the theoretical tradition of critical theory, drawing on Marcuse's notion of *repressive tolerance* to clarify the links. Namely, the American absolutist interpretation of the First Amendment, which views of white supremacy online as protected speech, is an interpretation born out of a white racial frame, rooted in colonialism, and stands at odds with the wider democratic global community.

Responses to White Supremacy Online in Transnational Perspective

Efforts to combat white supremacy online extend across national boundaries.[11] In fact, according to one scholarly assessment there has been a "nearly unanimous international institution of regulations restricting online hate speech."[12] While in the earliest days of the Internet many people imagined a borderless world in which the regulation of nation-states no longer mattered,[13] now that expectation is beginning to fade away.[14] Instead of a truly *global* network, the Internet is increasingly a collection of nation-state networks—networks still linked by the Internet protocol, but for many purposes separate.[15] Today national governments around the world can and do make laws that govern the content posted on the Internet (or sent via e-mail). Australia, Canada, Denmark, England, France, Germany, Israel, Italy, Norway, and Sweden are among the long list of nation-states that have taken such action.[16]

Governments in democratic societies are supposed to be responsive to their citizens, and this responsiveness should extend to considering white supremacy online. In the Norwegian case described at the beginning of this chapter, a citizen-led nongovernmental organization (NGO) prompted the government to take action against Tore W. Tvedt's online white supremacy. The Anti-Racism Center in Oslo filed a complaint against Tvedt, citing his racist website, and since the Norwegian government had an existing antiracism law on the books that extended to white supremacy online, they honored their law and responded swiftly.

Individual citizens acting apart from any institutional or governmental affiliation can elicit government response. For example, Canadian citizen Richard Warman has, over the past six years or so, lodged fifteen different complaints with the Canadian Human Rights Commission against white supremacists who use the Internet to persecute Jews, blacks, and gays and lesbians, among others.[17] As with the Norwegian NGO, Warman's complaints find traction in Canada, where antiracism laws, including prohibitions against white supremacy online, are already enacted. Such individual actions by citizens like Warman do not occur in a vacuum; they take place within specific national contexts with particular cultural and social histories, and of course, these contexts vary tremendously.

In Germany freedom of speech is a central tenet of their view of democracy, and their interpretation of this right includes bans on certain forms of white supremacy online. For example, the German ban on Nazi emblems, like the swastika, extends to the prohibition of the sale of such items on the Internet. To enforce this law, in March 2008 police in eight German states raided the homes of twenty-three suspects as part of a lengthy probe into the illegal sale of right-wing extremist literature and audio material. Another seventy suspects were identified in the investigation, which had begun in August of 2006 after the German unit of the U.S. online-auction company eBay Inc. reported the online sale of far-right material. Among the items seized were twenty-four computers, some fifty memory devices, and approximately 3,500 right-wing extremist CDs and LPs. According to a spokesperson for the Federal Crime Office (BKA), the raids were part of the ongoing "fight against right-wing extremism on the Internet. These raids demonstrate that the Internet is not a law-free zone."[18] (Adjudication of this case is still pending as of this writing.) The Germany Constitutional Framework, embodied in the *Grundgesetz*, or Basic Law, became the foundation for the German constitutional system in the aftermath of World War II. Drafters of the Basic Law were careful to include broad guarantees of freedom of expression in order to prevent any recurrence of Nazi-style totalitarianism, with the Basic Law specifically noting that "there shall be no censorship."[19] The *Grundgesetz* conditions all rights and guarantees to free speech on preservation of the right to "human dignity," that constitution's most highly prized value. It is within this framework that German legislators have established severe penalties for hate speech on the Internet. Even before the emergence of the Internet, German law prohibited speech that incited racial hatred,[20] so with the dawn of the Information Age, lawmakers extended the prohibitions to the Internet. Germany was the first among Western democratic nations to regulate white supremacy online with the 1995 passage of its Information and Communications Services Act (ICSA). The ICSA holds ISPs liable for knowingly making illegal content available, has established a cybersheriff who monitors the Internet for objectionable content, and makes it a crime to disseminate or make accessible materials deemed harmful to children.[21] In 1998 the general manager of California-based CompuServe Germany, Felix Somm, was prosecuted and convicted under the ICSA as an accessory to the dissemination of Hitler images and Nazi symbols. Somm's conviction was overturned in 1999, but the case sent a powerful message to all ISPs that they can and will be held liable in Germany for the content on their servers.[22] Although the outcome of this one case remains unknown, it reflects a wider pattern of response from the German government. In 2002 the

German government adopted a broad strategy to combat right-wing extremism. The "four pillars," as they are called, aim to educate all citizens of their human rights, strengthen civil society and promote civil courage, help integrate foreign nationals into society, and target suspected far-right extremists.[23] This approach acknowledges that it is important and possible to strike a balance between safeguarding human dignity and protecting freedom of expression in a democratic civil society. Germany embraces democratic ideals while seriously addressing the racist, anti-Semitic propaganda that threatens them. Other Western industrialized democratic nations take similar approaches, broadening the scope of their existing antiracism laws to address online racism.

In 2001 the Council of Europe (COE)'s Committee on Legal Affairs and Human Rights submitted a report titled "Racism and Xenophobia in Cyberspace."[24] The COE (comprised of forty-seven nations) was founded in 1949 with the ideals of the European Convention on Human Rights as its basis. The report recommended the COE adopt a protocol that would define and criminalize the "dissemination of racist propaganda and abusive storage of hateful message(s)." In 2003 the COE passed the Additional Protocol to the Convention on Cybercrime, an agreement between member states "to ensure a proper balance between freedom of expression and effective fight against acts of a racist and xenophobic nature."[25] There is disagreement among European nations as to how and when white supremacy online should be addressed at a governmental level (e.g., a Nazi symbol is illegal in Germany but not in Denmark). Still, transnational agreements between European Union (EU)[26] member nations address expressions of white supremacy and racism. In a 2007 vote EU ministers passed a broad antiracism law applying mainly to racist expressions offline. It took six long years to finalize the wording of the motion, and in the end some NGOs, like the European Network Against Racism, complained that the language was too weak.[27] The transnational dialogue is not perfect, but it is vital, and the cross-border work of such NGOs is critical to moving the discussion forward.

The Amsterdam-based International Network Against Cyberhate (INACH) is an NGO that organizes transnational efforts to fight online white supremacy (www.inach.net). Established in 2002 as a foundation under Dutch law, INACH's original mission was to connect online complaint bureaus in a number of different nation-states that were actively monitoring white supremacy online. INACH has since evolved to include a cross-national network with fourteen participating states called by one leading activist a "model for international cooperation in the fight against cyberhate."[28] Since 2005 INACH has been administered by American Chris Wolf, known as a leader in the practice of Internet law and as chair of the ADL's Internet Task Force. Each year INACH convenes an international conference of legal, academic, nongovernmental, and antiracism activist-leaders to address the issue of white supremacy online. Throughout the year, INACH connects the network nodes—or members—who actively monitor white supremacy online from Austria, Canada, Denmark, France, Germany, Latvia, Moldova, The Netherlands, Poland, Russia, Slovakia, Spain, Sweden, United Kingdom, and the United States (represented by the ADL). Within this coalition of nation-states, the United States represents something of an anomaly. While other democratic nations enshrine free speech as a fundamental right for each of their citizens, they have found ways to simultaneously preserve their citizens' right to human dignity.[29] The American view is quite different.

Responses to White Supremacy Online within the United States

In 1999 Richard Machado was the first person to be convicted of using the Internet to commit a hate crime (discussed in chapter 3). Unlike Tvedt, the man in the Norwegian case, Machado did not publish a white supremacist website but rather sent threatening e-mails. White supremacy online forfeits its First Amendment protection in the United States only when it is joined with conduct that threatens, harasses, or incites illegality.[30] Yet even when this narrow prosecutorial standard is legitimately met, the law fails to be consistently applied.

Uneven prosecution of hate speech is rooted in racial inequality. The only individual prosecuted to date for white supremacy online is a Mexican American, which is disturbingly consistent with racial trends in the rest of the U.S. criminal justice system. There minority men are suspected, arrested, prosecuted, and incarcerated differently than are whites. In the lone conviction for Internet hate speech the victims were Asian and Asian American, who, because they are often stereotyped as *model minorities*, might be less likely to interpret and then condemn their harassment as part of systemic discrimination. The victims' lack of public recrimination only made it easier for those outside the case to ignore any connection it had to white supremacy.

When Bonnie Jouhari reported that she and her daughter were being targeted by Roy E. Frankhouser's online threats, local authorities in Reading, Pennsylvania, neglected to enforce the law, believing that to do so violated Frankhouser's right to free speech. Jouhari's biracial daughter and work at HUD assisting minorities made their household a target for white supremacist harassment, and her gender situated her as a comparatively powerless member of society, thus rendering her initial attempts to get protection from the legal system ineffectual because her complaints were given less legitimacy. Interpretation of the First Amendment and what speech it protects is often in the hands of local law-enforcement officials, and so Jouhari was powerless when they refused to assist her. Eventually Frankhouser was prosecuted only after additional legislation was passed by Jouhari's employer, the Department of Housing and Urban Development (HUD), which moved to create new legislation to protect employees from racially-motivated harassment.

And though William A. White posted to his website threatening messages along with the names, addresses, and telephone numbers of the African American youth involved in the Jena 6 case, as of this writing he has not been prosecuted. Why White remains free is troubling, as he is well known to local and federal law-enforcement officials.[31]

The prosecution of white supremacy online[32] seems to rely on racialized notions of whose speech is protected (white supremacists Frankhouser and White) and whose is not (Mexican American Machado). Sadly, rather than prosecuting online white supremacy, the United States prefers to hide behind a technolegal stance and advocate filtering software.

Technolegal Responses

In fall of 1999 the U.S. Congress held hearings on hate crime on the Internet (mentioned in the opening of this chapter). Following the hearings, legislators decided that mandating Internet-filtering software was the best way to deal with white supremacy online. Filtering software uses key themes or words (e.g., racial epithets) to block some websites from appearing in searches. With filtering software installed, a search-engine query for information that is on the blocked list will trigger a pop-up window to appear that informs the user that the site they are searching for is prohibited; none of the text or images from that site load into the user's browser. In 1999 Congress attempted to require public libraries to use filtering software capable of screening out white supremacist (and pornographic) sites on computers used by children. The proposed legislation would also have required Internet service providers (ISPs) to offer the necessary software to their customers free or at cost. The legislation also made teaching and demonstrating how to make explosives a crime. This bill failed to pass into law, largely opposed due to concerns about the First Amendment and protection of free speech. While national efforts have been unsuccessful, one state, Arizona, passed a law in 1999 that mandates public schools and libraries use filtering software. In practice, even without that legislative requirement, most public libraries and schools in the United States frequented by children do use filtering software. Since 1999 the issue of white supremacy online has failed to receive national legislative attention,[33] an approach both deeply flawed and characteristically American.

For a number of reasons filtering software is grossly inadequate to addressing white supremacy online. First, it offers a technological solution to what is an inherently social problem, and such solutions are doomed to failure. Also, the software typically blocks only certain predetermined words and themes, which the deceptive cloaked sites will have no trouble sidestepping. Furthermore, filters frequently block sites not intended for censorship. For instance, a block programmed to exclude any sex-related sites will include terms that also appear on legitimate sites, filtering out any websites about breast cancer or other medical concerns in addition to pornographic sites. In a related issue, the filtering software infringes on the First Amendment rights of children. Chris Hansen, a senior lawyer with the ACLU who specializes in Internet matters, argues that children have the right to obtain material, such as sexual- and reproductive-health information—even if some adults find the information offensive. In addition, children who may be wondering about their own gender or sexual identity are usually blocked from exploring LGBTQ sites because gay civil rights organizations are included under the filtering umbrella of pornography.[34]

In the early days of the Internet, when Congress first held the hearings on hate crime and the Internet, anything associated with the online world elicited an air of panicked moralizing; managing online white supremacy with filtering software was a quintessentially American response. The decision was premised on an unwavering faith in American ingenuity to conquer all obstacles, completely ignored race as central to the problem, and included a market-based approach that relied on software companies to produce and sell filtering programs as the centerpiece in combating white supremacy online. If the proposed legislation had passed, it would have required *all* public schools and libraries to install filtering software. The one or few private companies who won those contracts would have enjoyed an economic windfall, yet white supremacist content online would have continued to proliferate, unchecked. And so passing legislation to mandate filtering software would have profited the few, confirmed the American can-do mythology, and entirely ignored white supremacy's racial component. Online white supremacy can be addressed, but not through a solution that relies exclusively on market-based strategies and benefits an elite few while discounting a racial analysis.

Market-Economy Responses

The American approach to handling white supremacy online has routinely featured market-economy responses from leading companies in the Internet industry, most notably AOL (America Online) and Google. AOL, the Internet division of Time Warner, has emerged as the world's largest Internet service provider (ISP), with some 21.7 million subscribers in the United States and Europe as of 2005.[35] Unlike other ISPs, AOL's original business model was known as a walled-garden model—that is, they offered a proprietary network of content, online shopping, and other services to AOL paid subscribers only. This changed in June 2005 when AOL began offering free access to certain features and content. Even after this shift, AOL continues to advertise itself as a safe Internet environment. Jonathan Miller, the company's CEO, was asked in an interview whether or not there was still reason to subscribe. He said, "Yes, because AOL in part—in particular for kids—is very much tied up in providing a safe environment."[36] AOL has fairly aggressively marketed itself as a safe online space because of its vigilance against pornography, though they have paid comparatively little attention to racism online. The Rules of the Road, or Terms of Service (TOS) agreement, used by AOL prohibits attacks based on personal characteristics like race, national origin, ethnicity, or religion. Yet AOL provided hosting for the website of a KKK group, The Knights of the Ku Klux Klan–Realm of Texas, and did not regard the site as violating its terms of service. It was in this context that the Anti-Defamation League (the ADL) challenged AOL to adhere to its own TOS agreement, which states that AOL has the right to "remove content they deem harmful or offensive," and remove the Klan website.[37] AOL declined, arguing that even the KKK's racism is protected under the First Amendment, and pointed out that the AOL search engine does block the use of some terms. AOL prohibits the search of terms like *nigger*, *kike*, *slut*, and *whore* in their Member's Directory and its site. Nor can member profiles include such words.[38] While AOL has been criticized by activist groups like the ADL for its inconsistent enforcement of its own TOS agreement, white supremacists like David Duke see such enforcement as infringing on their constitutional right to free speech. Duke posted the following to his personal website in 2002:

> The ADL works to ensure that commercial ISPs create terms of service that limit what their users can read or say. By lobbying commercial carriers to censor their users, the ADL achieves [sic] their aim of outlawing free speech

and expression without the contraints [sic] of the First Amendment's protections.[39]

Here Duke sounds like any other American concerned about encroach-
ment on his civil liberties. Duke's rhetoric, when separated from the anti-
Semitism in the rest of his post, fits seamlessly with that of others who would
argue that the First Amendment is intended to protect his speech. Nongovernmental organizations like the ADL can bring political pressure to bear
on Internet-industry companies, like AOL, to get them to enforce their own
TOS agreements. But when the First Amendment is popularly seen to protect white supremacy online, Internet companies are put in a difficult position. From the perspective of AOL, they are caught between upholding a
constitutional right and removing content that is clearly offensive and in violation of their TOS agreement.

Google, the search engine company whose motto is "Don't be evil," has
had its own encounters with white supremacy online. In 2004 Steven Weinstock (described in press accounts as "a real estate investor and former
yeshiva student") did a Google search using the term *Jew* and was shocked to
find that Frank Weltner's anti-Semitic website JewWatch.com appeared first
in the Google search results. Weltner, you will recall, is the white supremacist who also published the cloaked sites soliciting donations for victims of
Hurricane Katrina and maintains the cloaked American Civil Rights Review
site (discussed in chapter 7). Weinstock began an online petition in an effort
to get Weltner's site removed from the Google index that produces search
results. He hoped that if he could amass fifty thousand requests to remove
the site, Google would comply. Although his petition fell far short of this
goal (he got about 2,800 signatures), it would not have mattered. According
to Google spokesperson David Krane, the company "can't and won't change"
the ranking for Jew Watch, regardless of how many signatures the petition at-
tracts. Krane went on to say that "Google's search results are solely determined by computer algorithms that essentially reflect the popular opinion of
the Web. Our search results are not manipulated by hand. We're not able to
make any manual changes to the results."[40]

This is both true and not true. Google receives about thirty requests per
month to remove specific pages from its search results, usually because of alleged copyright or trademark infringement, and Google complies with most
of these requests, even though many of those pages are located on servers
outside the United States.[41] When Google issued the statement through
Krane, it was true that Google was not in the habit of altering the results of

their algorithm based on political content, but by 2006 Google had followed chief competitor Yahoo! Inc. into China. In order to receive permission from the Chinese government to gain access to its enormous market, Google would first have to restrict the results of their algorithm to block any sites about human rights, democracy, Tibet, Taiwan, and the Tiananmen Square uprising. At the World Economic Forum in Switzerland, Google CEO Eric Schmidt explained the decision-making process this way: "We concluded that, although we weren't wild about the restrictions, it was even worse to not try to server those users at all. We actually did an evil scale."[42] Google executives said that its approach in China would be to notify users when results had been blocked by the government.

Google applied a similar strategy to search results for *Jew*. Weltner's Jew Watch site is still first in Google's search-engine results, but in response to protests by Weinstock and intervention by the ADL,[43] above the result for Jew Watch is a message from Google warning of "offensive search results" (google.com/explanation), with small text on that page that reads "We're disturbed by these results as well," followed by an invitation to "Please read our note here." For those who follow the link, Google offers a lengthy explanation with this central argument:

> A site's ranking in Google's search results relies heavily on computer algorithms using thousands of factors to calculate a page's relevance to a given query. Sometimes subtleties of language cause anomalies to appear that cannot be predicted. A search for *Jew* brings up one such unexpected result.[44]

The "subtleties of language" that Google attributes causality to here are the distinction between *Jew* and *Jewish* in common usage. Google's explanation page points out the social and political context of the usage of these two words in which the former is "often used in an anti-Semitic context" and the latter is more likely used by members of the community talking about their faith. This acknowledgment of the anti-Semitic context marks a curious and impartial departure from the usual business of search engines in which information is presumed to be free of social and political context. It is curious, because there is no similar disclaimer above the search-engine results for a search for other common racial (or sexual) epithets, such as a common racial epithet for African Americans. And it is impartial because, along with Google's disclaimer about anti-Semitism, the Google algorithm also returns related searches, including Jew jokes.

The responses to white supremacy online from Internet-industry giants AOL and Google may seem contradictory at first. AOL wants to provide a

safe environment yet allows KKK websites. Google claims the company operates according to its motto "Don't be evil" though Jew Watch remains at
the top of the search returns and the company blocks prodemocracy websites
for users in China. These responses are not all contradictory when viewed
through the lens of a cyberlibertarian interpretation of the First Amendment
and neoliberal capitalism. The cyberlibertarian ethos that information exists
apart from social and political context (e.g., information wants to be free) allows white supremacy online to continue unchecked and is beneficial to the
Internet industry as a whole.[45] For Internet companies operating within the
framework of a cyberlibertarian ethos and neoliberal capitalism, matters of
race are always viewed as irrelevant unless and until they are seen to be interfering with the smooth operation of the market system. Of course, the supposedly free-market approach of neoliberal capitalism relies heavily on nation-states to operate. Nation-states, by maintaining the rule of law, provide
the infrastructure necessary for companies like AOL and Google to operate.
AOL and Google could not exist in the anarchy that prevailed in Russia in
the 1990s or in the failed states of Africa, where the lack of basic public
goods would make thriving Internet businesses impossible.[46] As long as the
status quo of white supremacy online does not threaten the profits for those
in charge of large corporations and their shareholders, racism will continue
to be regarded as irrelevant.

If someone posted online their clear intention to violate the prohibition
against discrimination in housing, guaranteed by the Civil Rights Act of
1964, then surely *that* would constitute a form of white supremacy online
that the courts would address. Or so thought some activist lawyers in
Chicago. It was this logic that prompted the Chicago Lawyers' Committee
for Civil Rights Under Law to file suit against the online classified advertising site Craigslist.org, arguing it violated the Fair Housing Act when real estate ads displayed racially discriminatory statements like "no minorities." A
judge in the Seventh Circuit Court of Appeals ruled that Craigslist.org was
not responsible for the listings, as they were simply a messenger and should
not be liable for the content of the ad. Furthermore, the judge in this case
ruled that monitoring the ads for discriminatory language was "impractical,"
due to the "complexity of the task." And, indeed, the model developed by
Craigslist founder Craig Newmark relies on an extremely small staff of people to run the site (fewer than twenty people), while users throughout the
world do the bulk of the work of posting and responding to ads. Any user on
any Craigslist can flag a post as inappropriate, but this is a far cry from the
site itself eliminating racist ads in clear violation of the Fair Housing Act. In
effect, the judge in this case ruled in favor of the market economy, giving

Craigslist a free pass because to do otherwise would be "impractical" and "complex."[47] Given the expansion of white supremacy online, the simultaneous unwillingness of U.S. courts to address it, and the ineffectiveness of technolegal and market-economy responses, the task of responding to white supremacy online in the United States is left principally to three NGOs and the rare individual.

NGOs in the United States Fighting White Supremacy Online

The effort to combat white supremacy online in the United States is led by three nongovernmental organizations: the Anti-Defamation League (ADL), the Simon Wiesenthal Center, and the Southern Poverty Law Center (SPLC). The ADL (adl.org) is the oldest of these, founded in 1913 to "stop, by appeals to reason and conscience and, if necessary, by appeals to law, the defamation of the Jewish people." Their mission includes monitoring and taking action against white supremacy online. Currently led by Abraham Foxman and headquartered in New York City (with twenty-nine offices across the United States), the ADL has an annual budget of over $50 million.[48] Brian Marcus, a scholar and activist, serves as director of the ADL's Internet Monitoring Unit, comprised of a team of investigative researchers and analysts who, since 1985, have gathered information about white supremacy online from their New York offices. Over the last twenty years the ADL has expanded their Internet monitoring to include the monitoring of extremists of all types, including Islamic terrorists. The ADL shares the information collected with law enforcement via a number of mechanisms, including published reports, e-mail newsletters, and professional trainings. A valuable source for law enforcement is the ADL Law Enforcement Agency Resource Network (adl.org/LEARN), an online resource that receives over a million visitors per year. The ADL is also the only NGO in the United States that is part of the International Network Against Cyberhate (inach.net).

A major resource in the effort to combat white supremacy online and offline is the Simon Wiesenthal Center (wiesenthal.com). The Wiesenthal Center is an international Jewish human-rights organization with a major presence in the United States, primarily in Los Angeles and New York, and an operating budget of just over $35 million. The center includes a values-based educational effort aimed at confronting anti-Semitism, racism, and hate; teaching the lessons of the Holocaust for future generations; and confronting Islamic terrorism, a relatively new emphasis. The center's educational efforts are administered primarily through the Museum of Tolerance in Los Angeles and the New York Tolerance Center. *Digital Terrorism and Hate*, the annual interactive report (CD-ROM) produced by the center, analyzes over six thousand problematic website portals, terrorist manuals, blogs, chat rooms, videos, and hate games on the Internet that promote racial violence, anti-Semitism, homophobia, hate music, and terrorism. The report is based on data collected by a team of researchers led by scholar-activist Mark Weitzman, the director of Task Force Against Hate and Terrorism (Weitzman also serves as director of the New York Tolerance Center), and Rabbi Abraham Cooper, associate dean of the center. Translated into multiple languages, the report is distributed to government agencies, community activists, educators, and members of the media as part of the center's broader educational efforts to teach tolerance.

The Southern Poverty Law Center (splcenter.org) based in Montgomery, Alabama, has an annual operating budget of around $37 million and an endowment of approximately $200 million. When founded in 1971, the SPLC was originally the small civil rights law firm of Morris Dees and Joe Levin, two lawyers committed to fighting for racial equality through the courts. Since 1981 the SPLC has been monitoring extremist white supremacist activity throughout the United States. Additionally, the SPLC has developed a K–12 curriculum for teaching tolerance and respect in U.S. schools. Dees and Levin pioneered the legal strategy of filing civil suits against white supremacists for activities offline that escaped the reach of criminal prosecution. One of the SPLC's notable lawsuits was in response to the murder by skinheads of an Ethiopian immigrant in Portland, Oregon. The skinheads who beat this man to death were acolytes of White Aryan Resistance leader Tom Metzger. In October 1990 attorneys for the SPLC won a civil case on behalf of murdered hate-crime victim Mulugeta Seraw's family against Tom Metzger and his son John Metzger for a total of $12.5 million.[49] The SPLC, through the efforts of Mark Potok, who heads the Intelligence Project, is also actively engaged in monitoring white supremacy online, and they keep an extensive archive of websites, blogs, and chat rooms associated with extremist groups based in the United States.

It is worth briefly mapping out the conceptual differences between these three premier organizations. The ADL is a Jewish organization with a primary focus on anti-Semitism online as well as racism. As the Internet Monitoring division has expanded their work, they have broadened their scope to include all types of political extremism, such as Islamic extremists. Similarly, the Simon Wiesenthal Center is primarily focused on anti-Semitism and casts a wide net when collecting the six thousand "problematic" Web sources for their *Digital Hate and Terrorism* report, which includes white supremacists as well as Islamic terrorists. Of the three organizations, the SPLC is the most narrowly focused on white supremacist groups in the United States. While the SPLC does not actively monitor Islamic extremists, it does include black separatist groups in its tracking data. There is, as far as I can tell,[50] some co-operation between the three organizations but very little, if any, strategically coordinated efforts at addressing white supremacy online. In part, this has to do with the different missions that overlap significantly but not completely or seamlessly. In part, the lack of strategic coordination has to do with the unique histories and constituencies of each organization. These divergent backgrounds mean that, for each organization, there is a slightly different definition of the problem that overlaps or diverges from the organizations' missions in various ways. In an ironic turn, the widening focus of the ADL and the Simon Wiesenthal Center to include Islamic extremists converges with the U.S. government's interest in fighting terrorism in the post-9/11 era. Similarly, the SPLC's widening scope to include black separatist groups converges with the long history of the U.S. government's interest in monitoring domestic black-nationalist groups. While Islamic extremists are certainly a source of violent anti-Semitism, it is difficult to see how black-nationalist groups pose a serious threat to a democratic society within the context of decades of targeted violence and harassment by the U.S. government itself. My point here in mapping out these areas of similarities and differences in strategies between and among these organizations is to illustrate how the understanding shifts depending on the lens: if the lens is extremists world-wide, with an emphasis on anti-Semitism, then Islamic extremists are included with white supremacists. If the lens is extremists solely in the United States with a focus on race, then black separatists are included. When mapped in this way, the efforts the ADL, Simon Wiesenthal Center, and SPLC set in sharp relief a broader failure within American society as a whole to address embedded white supremacy in a meaningful way within its cultural and social institutions.

Individual Efforts within the United States

Some have argued that the most appropriate response to white supremacy online is for individual computer users to infiltrate white supremacist web-sites to try and change the discursive subculture.[51] Others have hacked hate websites to disrupt their Internet service.[52] Perhaps the most significant re-sponse from an individual activist in the United States to white supremacy online was that of David Goldman. Goldman, a Harvard Law School librar-ian, created a website in 1995 called Hatewatch, the first site to track white supremacy online. Goldman's Hatewatch attracted incredible media coverage and Web traffic, at one point attracting one million visitors a year.[53] It also attracted controversy. In 2000 film critic Roger Ebert launched a scathing public attack on Goldman at the Conference on World Affairs for linking to hate sites. Ebert argued that Hatewatch gave free publicity to haters, providing a "virtual supermarket" for those interested in finding white supremacy online. Ebert also criticized Goldman for his failure to offer any critical analysis of the racist propaganda at these sites (unlike the ADL and Simon Wiesenthal Center that point out the lies and distortions).[54] A year later, in 2001, Goldman stopped maintaining the site.[55] He said it was not because of the criticisms he had received but because he felt that the site had done its job. "We have succeeded in fulfilling the mission we set for ourselves," he wrote in a farewell message posted on the site. Goldman was bolstered by news that "hate sites simply weren't proving to be such powerful recruitment tools as many had feared."[56] Goldman's assessment is interesting in light of the earlier discussion about social-movement recruitment and the Internet. His view coincides with my own analysis that brochure sites with static displays of information are not effective mechanisms for social-movement recruitment. However, Goldman disbanded Hatewatch in 2001 just prior to the phenomenal increase in participation at Stormfront. Still, no one can blame Goldman for wanting to stop monitoring white supremacist websites after six years; it is difficult, sometimes courageous, and often thankless work. Individual approaches such as Goldman's brave (if perhaps a bit misguided) actions ultimately offer limited effectiveness on a broad scale (and tend to be site-specific and small scale).

Valuing Free Speech Differently

Free speech is among the most highly valued ideals in mainstream American culture. This ideal is tied to Enlightenment philosophical traditions of reason and tolerance. Yet this supposedly shared American value of free speech seems less than ideal when viewed by those who are targets of hate speech. For example, a 2005 Knight Foundation study of U.S. high school-aged students found that African American students (43 percent) and Hispanic students (41 percent) were more likely than white students (31 percent) to think the First Amendment "goes too far" in the rights it guarantees.[57] Such findings from public-opinion polling suggest that at an early age young African American and Hispanic people realize that the ideal of free speech does not apply to them equally; thus they evaluate the First Amendment less favorably than white youths. The findings also suggest an epistemology that begins with an understanding of racial inequality and an ethic of caring (about the victims of hate speech) at the center of analysis. When divorced from this analysis of racial inequality and ethic of caring, however, it is clear that in the United States white supremacy online benefits from near absolute First Amendment protection.[58]

The Cyberhate Divide: How the U.S. Response Affects Global Response to White Supremacy Online

Given the nearly unanimous international adoption of regulations restricting online hate speech, the United States stands alone in its support of free speech—including white supremacy online.[59] One scholar has called these divergent approaches to white supremacy online the *U.S./Europe cyberhate divide*.[60] Global efforts to combat white supremacy online are seriously undermined by the U.S. position in a number of ways.

The cyberhate divide also means that the United States becomes the location of choice for white supremacists worldwide who wish to post their hate speech online without fear of prosecution. This practice is what another scholar has referred to as "importing" hate.[61] It is possible to prosecute someone within one national jurisdiction for material on the Web that is hosted on a server in the United States, and this is what happened in the Norwegian case. Tvedt's Vigrid website was hosted on a U.S. server, yet he was successfully prosecuted. Even so, because U.S.-based servers allow for such content, fighting white supremacy becomes an international game of whack-a-mole: hate material is quashed in one jurisdiction only to pop up in another. And this is exactly what happened in Tvedt's case: after serving one year in prison and denied a Web presence for one year, Tvedt was released from jail and put his site back online.

In addition, the United States exports white supremacy via the Internet. The majority of white supremacist sites online are created by Americans and hosted in the United States. Given the global nature of the Web, these sites made in the United States are, then, available anywhere in the world, even in countries where the material is illegal.

An important example of the very literal way that U.S.-based understandings of First Amendment protections for white supremacy online get exported around the world is the *France v. Yahoo! Inc.* case.[62] In 2000 two French NGOs, the International League Against Racism and Anti-Semitism (LICRA) and the Union of Jewish Students, filed a complaint in the French courts against Yahoo! Inc., the Cupertino, California–based Internet company. LICRA and the Union of Jewish Students charged that Yahoo's auction sites, available through the company's French-based affiliate Yahoo.fr, allowed Nazi memorabilia to be sold in France where such materials are illegal. The French courts ruled in May 2000 that Yahoo! Inc. was in violation of French law and must therefore "make it impossible" for Internet users in France to access any Yahoo! websites that auction anti-Semitic material. CEO Jerry Yang refused to comply with the judge's decision, saying, "We are not going to change the content of our sites in the United States just because someone in France is asking us to do so."[63] When Yang failed to comply, the French courts began levying fines against Yahoo! Inc., costing the company estimated millions.

What followed was a years-long legal battle between France and Yahoo! Inc. fought in both French and U.S. courts that hinged in a very central way on the ability of individual nation-states to control white supremacy online in a global context. On the one side were the antiracism activists who argued that French laws applied to Internet content. One lawyer representing the French groups said, "There is this naïve idea that the Internet changes everything. It doesn't change everything. It doesn't change the laws in France."[64] On the other side were leading figures in the United States who adopted a cyberlibertarian approach, such as MIT's Nicholas Negroponte, who said, "It's not that the laws aren't relevant; it's that the nation-state's not relevant. The Internet cannot be regulated."[65] This "impossibility" argument was the main tenet of Yahoo! Inc.'s defense; they argued that to limit what Internet content users in one geographic location (e.g., France) could access on the Internet was an impossible technological request.[66] Yet this claim was at odds with the shifting technological and political reality of the Internet. A key turning point in the case was evidence introduced about new technology, referred to as geo-ID, that could identify and screen Internet content on the basis of geographical source.

In 2001 Yahoo! Inc. seemed to change course and embrace the geo-ID and governmental control of the Internet. Early in that year the company issued a statement that it would stop selling Nazi memorabilia on sites available in France, citing bad publicity rather than the judge's ruling. Later in 2001 Yahoo! Inc. contracted with a geo-ID firm to target advertising to Web visitors in geographically specific locations. Then in the summer of 2002 they signed an agreement with China called the Public Pledge on Self-discipline for the Chinese Internet Industry. By signing this pledge Yahoo! Inc. won a lucrative contract to provide Internet services for China with the condition that it would block any content the Chinese government deemed objectionable, such as prodemocracy websites. Despite this seeming shift toward embracing the possibility of government control of the Internet, in 2005 Yahoo! Inc. filed a countersuit in California against the French government for the decision in the Nazi memorabilia case, and the 9th U.S. Circuit Court of Appeals said it would rehear some arguments in the case.[67] As of this writing, there has been no decision in this case, but the lengthy court battle and Yahoo! Inc.'s conflicting stance on whether and when to cooperate with nation-states who want to control Internet content is telling. In the French case, Yahoo! Inc. resisted the French government's efforts to protect its citizens from Nazi memorabilia; in the Chinese case, Yahoo! Inc. was complicit in the antidemocratic wishes of the Chinese government to prevent its citizens from accessing texts about democracy. The decisions by U.S.-based Internet companies that operate globally have an impact well beyond the geographic borders of their home country.

The United States holds a disproportionate amount of economic resources and wields an extraordinary amount of cultural and military power in the global context. Therefore U.S. policies exert an enormous amount of influence over the rest of the world. In protecting white supremacy online the United States dramatically reduces the likelihood that nations who wish to regulate it will be able to do so.[68] For other democratic nations white supremacy online is viewed as an important human-rights issue, based on a collective awareness of historical inequality. Reflecting on past confrontations with Nazis and other extremists, most Europeans feel that their concerns about white supremacy online are more than justified.[69] In contrast, the prevailing view in the United States is one of intentional disregard and indifference, in which U.S. policymakers are virtually absent from the international scene. For example, in 2000 the United States failed to send any representatives to an international conference on Internet extremism hosted by the German justice minister.[70] This is not the first time that the United States has stood apart from the international democratic community on issues of human rights.

The United States hesitated for forty years before ratifying and implementing a key international UN human-rights convention. For years the U.S. Senate rejected human-rights treaties on the grounds that they diminish basic rights—including the First Amendment right to free speech—guaranteed under the U.S. Constitution. Among the other justifications for not ratifying the terms of the 1948 Genocide Convention was an assertion that the treaty would violate states' rights, promote world government, enhance communist influence, subject citizens to trial abroad, threaten the United States' form of government, and increase international entanglements. In 1988, after decades of work by Senator William Proxmire, the United States finally ratified and enacted into national law the Genocide Convention Implementation Act. At that point it became illegal under U.S.

law for any group or individual to "directly and publicly incite another" to violate the 1948 Genocide Convention, including inciting racial or ethnic hatred. To date, this is the only international human-rights norm with media consequences to be incorporated into U.S. law.[71] And it seems reasonable to suggest that this international law be leveraged to effectively fight white supremacy online transnationally. The biggest barrier to this is the United States, for not only is it indifferent to addressing this issue within the global democratic community, but it also simultaneously undermines such efforts abroad by operating as a safe haven for white supremacy online and serving as the primary creator of this content available globally.

The resistance to restricting white supremacy online betrays an ignorance about both the history and contemporary reality of racial inequality in the United States. Often the embrace of restrictions for white supremacy online in other countries is contextualized by reference to specific histories of oppression, from which the United States is presumably free. For example, in Goldsmith and Wu's *Who Controls the Internet?*, the authors briefly offer an explanation for why some countries ban hate speech online. They write, "Germany bans Nazi speech for yet a different reason, the same reason that Japan's Constitution outlaws aggressive war: it is a nation still coming to grips with the horrors it committed in its past, and it is terrified that they could happen again."[72]

Here Goldsmith and Wu locate aggression, war, and "horrors" within *other* countries and within a distant past, far removed in time, distance, and political reality from the contemporary American context. The authors here also read a kind of neurosis into these national responses, saying Germany and Japan are *terrified* that this could happen again, not, say, that they are "taking reasonable precautions" or "learning the lessons of history." Thus, while the history of fascism and totalitarianism is seen as relevant for understanding restrictions on white supremacy online in Germany and Japan, there is a tendency in the United States to ignore or downplay the formative effects of colonialism, slavery, ongoing and systemic racism, and the white racial frame on the acceptance of white supremacy online.

Free Speech, Freedom from Hate:
Cyberlibertarians vs. Critical Race Theory

Cyberlibertarians like John Perry Barlow view Internet regulation as antithetical to principles of freedom in cyberspace and in the U.S. Constitution. The cyberlibertarian view holds that "a select number of essential freedoms—including freedom of speech—are understood to be absolute and not negotiable or subject to being balanced."[73] For cyberlibertarians, white supremacy online is a trivial concern compared to the *regulation* of white supremacy online, which is viewed as a more serious threat. For those who adopt this view, the stories of the Norwegian man arrested for authoring a white supremacist website or the raid on Germans who used eBay to trade in Nazi memorabilia are cautionary tales about what happens when free speech gets trampled. Indeed, they view the regulation of the Internet as perhaps *the* most important threat to the civil rights in the digital age, to the exclusion of all other threats.

Mike Godwin,[74] author of *Cyber Rights: Defending Free Speech in the Digital Age*,[75] argues convincingly for the need to protect freedom of expression as a fundamental right for ensuring individual liberty in a democracy. In a chapter of his book called "When Words Hurt: Two Hard Cases about Online Speech," Godwin takes on the critique of feminist legal scholar Catherine MacKinnon, who argues that words have power to harm.[76] Her argument, consistent with that made by critical race theorists, claims that beyond instances in which words *incite* people to act in violent ways, some words *enact* domination and oppression. Godwin takes this claim and uses it to shore up his assessment that free speech is to be valued above all other rights:

> The reason freedom of speech matters is that words do have power—they can inspire both pleasant and unpleasant thoughts and feelings in the minds of others. If speech and expression didn't matter—if they weren't able to have such a strong effect on us much of the time—far fewer of us would feel the impulse to ban or restrict what other people say. But neither would so many of us defend free speech as vehemently as we do.[77]

Here Godwin acknowledges the power of words and reaffirms the need to protect free speech. Yet Godwin frames his analysis in this chapter in such a way as to trivialize[78] the power of words and the critique of that power offered by MacKinnon.[79] Godwin's assessment of the importance of free speech rests on an analysis of the Internet, and the exchange of information it facilitates as existing apart from political and social context. Such an analysis does not take race into consideration and offers no mechanism for evaluating claims for racial or social justice against the protection of free speech.

Godwin's cyberlibertarian frame of free speech as separate from a social and political context systematically disadvantages some members of society while it privileges others. For example, the lived experience of Bonnie Jouhari and her daughter illustrates the way this interpretation of free speech online can have real consequences for people's lives. The ethos that "information wants to be free" means that Bonnie Jouhari and her daughter are *less* free. Framing white supremacy online exclusively as a free-speech issue simultaneously enables the formation of a translocal white identity through the Internet and shifts focus away from any analysis of the human rights of those targeted by violent white supremacy online, people who are members of already marginalized groups. Arguments in favor of an absolutist interpretation of the First Amendment are the product of historically, socially, and culturally situated knowledge.

Many of the first-developed technological advances that gave rise to the Internet were created in Northern California, much of it in and around Palo Alto Research Center (PARC).[80] Following those technological innovations were a remarkable series of innovations in business that gave rise to a new industrial sector centered in San Jose, California, just south of San Francisco, in an area dubbed *Silicon Valley*. The inequalities of race, class, and gender of the broader social context were reinscribed within this newly developed industrial sector.[81] Given this confluence of cybertechnology and Internet industry in one geographic region, it is not surprising that a particular set of social and cultural commentators emerged alongside these milieux and shaped our view of cyberculture. Cyberlibertarians Barlow and Godwin are part of this cultural milieu, and their view of free speech is a product of this setting. Critics outside the United States, such as Richard Barbrook, have argued that beyond the "techno-mysticism" (for example, in Barlow's *Manifesto*) is a legitimating ideology for a nineteenth-century form of nasty, brutish capitalism. Barbrook argues that those who share this perspective envision the Internet as a sort of unregulated marketplace usually found only in economics textbooks. Barbrook (with Cameron) writes, "Instead of supporting a caring society, they hope that technological progress into the twenty-first century will inevitably lead back to nineteenth-century 'tooth-and-claw' capitalism."[82] While Barbrook's critique errs in its hyperbole, the cyberlibertarian view of free speech does support an analogous cyberlibertarian model of business that is peculiar to a specific geographic, temporal, social, and cultural context. The cyberlibertarian view of the Internet is one rooted in a particular American geography imbued with a frontier ethos, tied to both a free-market analysis of the Internet and a very recent (mis)reading of the First Amendment as an absolute protection of all speech. Barlow's pithy aphorism that in cyberspace the First Amendment is a "local ordinance" takes on new meaning when we consider the specific context of the emergence of an absolutist defense of free speech online. Of course, this is not a view of the First Amendment that is universally shared, even within the United States.

Critical race theorists take a different approach to the First Amendment. Writing from a critical-race perspective in the introduction to their volume *Words that Wound*, legal scholars Mari J. Matsuda, Charles R. Lawrence III, Richard Delgado, and Kimberle Crenshaw address those who defend an absolutist view of the free speech in the following:

> Words like *intolerant, silencing, McCarthyism, censors*, and *orthodoxy* are used to portray women and people of color as oppressors and to pretend that the powerful have become powerless. . . . Stripped of its context, this is a seductive argument. The privilege and power of white male elites is wrapped in the rhetoric of politically unpopular speech.[83]

At the same time that critical race theorists argue that we should entertain the absolutist free-speech arguments, they also contend that we should place the stories of the victims, those on the receiving end of hate speech, at the center of our analysis. Indeed, when we reframe white supremacy online such that at the center of our analysis is the damage to the dignity of human beings, the issue looks quite different than when framed exclusively as an issue of free speech. This may be a more challenging task within the Information Age in which there is a plethora of multivocal stories to be heard; it is not impossible.

Critical race theory faces other, very real, challenges in the digital era. One particularly strenuous critique of the speech act perspective (the notion that speech constitutes action and a central feature of critical race theory) is Judith Butler's critique.[84] Butler incorporates MacKinnon's argument about speech *enacting* gender oppression with the critical race theorists' argument that *words wound* in the realm of racial oppression. Butler argues that when race and gender scholars emphasize the damage that words can do, they often fail to fully take into account the state's ability to powerfully enact words in a way that has the potential to harm real people in life-altering ways. In an analysis of white supremacy, such as the one at hand, it seems that the racist state, as David Theo Goldberg argues, is a powerful force for maintaining racial inequality.[85] Given that the racist state implements systemic racism, most notably through the criminal-justice system, the notion that the state might be an effective arbiter of white supremacy online seems deeply flawed. This is a different argument than the content-free version offered by cyberlibertarians. Furthermore, while critical race theory offers a powerful critique of racist hate speech, it inadequately addresses the more sophisticated forms of white supremacy online, such as cloaked sites and the vast number of posts at Stormfront, many of which do not meet the legal standard of hate speech.

Conclusion

The move from print to digital media marks a new, global and Internet-worked era of white supremacy online that requires global responses. Freedom of speech and the protection of equality are both fundamental to the preservation of human dignity. Within a global context, there is near-universal agreement among democratic nations that these human rights should be weighed against one another. The United States stands in stark relief against this global community, functioning as a haven and importer-exporter for white supremacy online. Yet even the type of antiracism legislation adopted in the rest of the world would be inadequate to address the kind of cloaked sites developed by white supremacists in the United States. In order to engage in a meaningful fight against white supremacy online and offline in a global context, we need a new strategy. In the Information Age old- and new-media white supremacy converge to undermine civil rights, meaning that we need better and more ways to think critically about the Internet, race, and multiple, intersecting forms of oppression. And it is to that need for an alternative that I turn in the next, last, chapter.

Notes

1. Associated Press 2002. Also discussed in Goldsmith and Wu (2006).
2. U.S. Congress, Senate, Committee on the Judiciary 1999, 2.
3. There is mention of anti-Semitism online in a report made by the U.S. Department of State (2008). More about this report toward the end of this chapter.
4. Barlow 1996.
5. Jayakar 2000.
6. Goldsmith and Wu 2006, 17.
7. The acclaim for his views is evident in his recent appointment as a fellow at one of the nation's most prestigious institutions, Harvard Law School's Berkman Center for Internet and Society.
8. There is a long list of names that could go here, but most notable critics of the regulation of the Internet include Mike Godwin, Lawrence Lessing, and Howard Rheingold.
9. Matsuda et al. 1993, 13–14.
10. Esteban 2001. Ramasastry 2003. Smith 2002.

11. I leave out of this analysis many, many nations and parts of the world simply for lack of adequate space and time. In that sense, then, this is more accurately a transnational and comparative analysis than a truly global one.

12. Breckheimer 2002.

13. See Sassen (1996); and, perhaps more colloquially, John Perry Barlow (1996), who famously wrote, "We will create a civilization of the mind in cyberspace. May it be more humane and fair than the world your governments have made before."

14. Goldsmith and Wu 2006.

15. Goldsmith and Wu 2006, 149.

16. Siegel 1999. Banton 1996. Heintze 2007, 51–63. Erel 2007, 359–75.

17. Butler 2007.

18. Reuters 2008.

19. Breckheimer 2002, 9.

20. Article 131 of the German Penal Code makes it illegal to write or broadcast anything that incites racial hatred or describes "cruel or otherwise inhuman acts of violence against humans in a manner that glorifies or minimizes such acts." Furthermore, the publication or distribution of neo-Nazi or Holocaust–denial literature is a criminal offense (Breckheimer 2002, 10).

21. Breckheimer 2002, 10.

22. Breckheimer 2002, 10–11.

23. Reuters 2008.

24. Council of Europe (COE) 2001.

25. Council of Europe (COE) 2003.

26. The European Union (EU) and the COE are separate bodies with different mandates. The EU is a governing body of the nation-states within Europe; the COE is an institutionalized watchdog. For American readers, there is no U.S. equivalent of the COE. Although separate, the EU and the COE engage in joint initiatives, such as country-specific efforts aimed at facilitating institutional and legal reform. For more information, see the EU's website: http://ec.europa.eu/external_relations/coe/index.htm#join.

27. Spiegel Online 2007.

28. Marcus 2006.

29. Breckheimer 2002, 13.

30. Breckheimer 2002, 8.

31. White also maintains a public Web presence through a blogger account hosted by Google, yet no one at Google has acted to remove the site.

32. For a similar analysis of the disproportionate enforcement of bias crimes, see Lawrence (2003).

33. There is one mention of anti-Semitism online in the U.S. Department of State's *Contemporary Global Anti-Semitism Report* (2008).

34. Kaplan 1998.

35. Richardson 2005.

36. Szalai 2005.

37. Anti-Defamation League 1997.

38. Chaudry 1999.

39. Duke 2002.

40. Becker 2004.

41. Goldsmith and Wu 2006, 75.

42. Vise and Malseed 2006, 278.

43. Anti-Defamation League 2004.

44. Google. *An explanation of our search results.* http://www.google.com/explanation.html.

45. Castells 2001.

46. Goldsmith and Wu 2006, 145.

47. International Network Against Cyberhate 2008.

48. Traub 2007.

49. See Dees and Fiffer (1993). The Metzgers did not have millions, thus the Seraw family only received assets from Metzger's $125,000 house and a few thousand dollars. Metzger declared bankruptcy and stopped publishing his newspaper for the White Aryan Resistance. However, partly because of the relatively low cost of the Internet—and partly because of Metzger's tenacious commitment to white supremacy—Metzger's White Aryan Resistance became Resist.com (as discussed in chapter 6).

50. I have worked with all three organizations in doing research for both this book and my previous one.

51. Zickmund 1997, 185–205.

52. Marcus 2000.

53. Dixit 2001.

54. Ladd 2000.

55. The Hatewatch.com domain name is now owned by SPLC, and they use it in their work against white supremacy online and off.

56. Ladd 2000.

57. John S. and James L. Knight Foundation 2005.

58. Breckheimer 2002, 8.

59. Breckheimer 2002, 1.

60. Ramasastry 2003.

61. Breckheimer 2002, 13.

62. This account of *France v. Yahoo! Inc.* is drawn from reports published at the time the case was in court and draws on the excellent synthesis of the case by Goldsmith and Wu (2006, 1–10 and 183).

63. Goldsmith and Wu 2006, 5.

64. Goldsmith and Wu 2006, 2.

65. Goldsmith and Wu 2006, 3.

66. At the time, Yang was quoted as saying, "Asking us to filter access to our sites according to the nationality of Web surfers is very naïve" (Goldsmith and Wu 2006, 6).

67. Wired News Report 2005.

68. Breckheimer 2002, 14.
69. Breckheimer 2002, 14.
70. Breckheimer 2002, 14.
71. Facing History and Ourselves (*Raphael Lemkin: International law in the age of genocide*).
72. Goldsmith and Wu 2006, 150.
73. Nemes 2002, 193. See also Godwin (2003), Jordan and Taylor (1998, 2004), and Killick and Starr (2000, 2003).
74. Godwin is counsel to the Electronic Frontier Foundation (EFF), the organization Barlow helped found. The EFF is the leading organization that fights regulation of the Internet and advocates speech rights online.
75. Godwin 1998.
76. MacKinnon 1993. Matsuda et al. 1993.
77. Godwin 1998, 102.
78. This trivialization is evident in the opening and close of the chapter: In the opening, Godwin relates a story from his childhood in which he was hurt by words and goes on to offer the sticks-and-stones nursery rhyme; this situates the argument as being worthy of the concerns of a kindergartener. He later concludes the chapter by saying, "We have to learn as a society what we learned as children: words *do* hurt, yes, but learning to cope with those words rationally and without fear is part of what it means to reach maturity" (1998). Godwin uses this story to frame his discussion of hate speech, suggesting that once we "reach maturity" we will outgrow any silly insistence that words have the power to harm.
79. In a curious omission, Godwin's book *Cyber Rights* (1998) never explicitly addresses race or white supremacy online its chapter on hate speech. Instead, MacKinnon's feminist analysis stands in for all others who make this type of argument, including critical race theorists.
80. Mowery and Simcoe 2002.
81. Park 1999. Hossfeld 2001. Matthews 2003. Pitti 2003.
82. Barbrook and Cameron 1996.
83. Matsuda et al. 1993, 14–15.
84. Butler 1997.
85. Goldberg 2002.

CHAPTER TEN

Conclusion: Racial Justice and Civic Engagement in the Digital Era

> I refuse to accept the view that mankind is so tragically bound to the starless midnight of racism and war that the bright daybreak of peace . . . can never become reality.
>
> —Martin Luther King Jr.

White supremacy in the digital era raises important new questions about racism, racial equality, and civil rights. It also raises questions about the transformation of social-movement discourse on the Internet. The centerpiece in this book is an empirical investigation into white supremacist movement discourse across print and digital media that is meant to make a contribution to our understanding of the way five organizations within one particular social movement changed their communication strategies to accommodate the Information Age. The five organizations I studied varied in their relative success or failure in making the transition from print to digital media as the result of a number of different variables (resources, group cohesion, and savvy use of interactive Web features). These five organizations and their transition from print to digital media constitute only part of the investigation offered here.

White supremacy online is a complicated social phenomenon that poses real threats but not necessarily the threats that receive the most attention. The perceived threat of recruitment into organized racism via the Internet belies a more complex reality and calls into question the definition of a *social movement member* in the era of registered users. White supremacists are often regarded as ignorant, poor, and marginal to mainstream culture in various ways, but the manifestation of white supremacy online suggests a different reality in which the Internet offers the opportunity for a racialized, gendered, and global white supremacy. This new media form of white supremacy collides with old media and white supremacy in various ways as it constructs a unified white male heteronormative subject that remains embedded in a relatively privileged position in the material, offline world. The emergence of global white supremacy online supports the formation of a translocal whiteness that is simultaneously rooted in American culture and transcends national geographic borders.

Digital media is neither a raceless panacea nor a dangerous place where people (particularly young people) are unsuspectingly lured into hate groups. Old forms of overt white supremacy (e.g., racist hate speech) have moved into the Information Age alongside new, emergent forms of white supremacy that include searchable databases of (racially identifiable) user names easily exported for use in mass e-mails, along with new forms of covert white supremacy at cloaked sites, whose goal is to undermine the very idea of racial equality. Domain-name registration, GoogleRank, and Graphic User Interface (GUI) are the new terrain of racial politics. Gender and sexuality are key here, and, as in the old print-only era of white supremacy, masculinity is constitutive of white supremacy. Yet, there are important new dimensions as well. More women participate in white supremacy online, and they redraw the boundaries of whiteness and question white supremacist orthodoxy and male dominance in ways that include significant elements of (white) liberal feminism. Even so, these women remain marginalized within white supremacy online and within larger society because of structural gender inequality.

White supremacy online matters to democratic societies committed to equality for all of its citizens. It matters because the increased ease of access to white supremacist discourse and the global linkages between groups and individuals in virtual communities like Stormfront.org hold the potential for harm in real life. In addition to this potential harm, the emergence and increasing popularity of white supremacy online undermines cultural values of racial equality and inclusion. Cloaked sites that challenge the advances of the civil rights movement and even question whether the end of slavery was necessary given that it was a "humane" institution shift the ground beneath taken-for-granted and supposedly shared values about racial equality.

White supremacy online challenges the notion that we who live in the United States have a shared culture that values all our citizens equally. Indeed, the popularity of online communities like Stormfront, which features a rotating banner of Thomas Jefferson reiterating for the digital age his colonial-era belief that "distinct races" are unable to live together under one government, suggests that the white racial frame is one that resonates broadly within American culture. And epistemologies that ignore the lived experience of racial and gender inequality seem inadequate to the task of either understanding or fighting white supremacy online.

The Epistemology of White Supremacy Online

Epistemologies of race, how we know what we say we know about race and racism, are rooted in profoundly different experiences for whites and people of color living in a social context of racial inequality. Within such a context, some people experience the constant drumbeat of racism as part of everyday life,[1] while others enjoy the privilege[2] of ignoring it on a daily basis. The epistemological peril of white supremacy online lies in its ability to change how we know what we say we know about issues that have been politically hard won, issues such as civil rights.

Both forms of online hate speech discussed here, overt and cloaked, are grounded in an epistemology of white supremacy. The presence of overt hate speech online reinforces this epistemology by allowing white racists to retreat from civic engagement into a whites-only fantasy of superiority and victimhood. For those who create overtly white supremacist content, the Internet provides a forum for amplifying racist propaganda. For those who seek it out, overt hate speech online validates essentialist notions of white racial purity, privilege, and entitlement by rearticulating white supremacy using the rhetoric of civil rights. Such a rearticulation rests on a disavowal of everyday racism and blindness to the myriad ways in which whites are privileged by race. Within a context filled with like-minded individuals and absent gatekeepers, these rearticulations set up an infinite loop within the technology, reinforcing white supremacy by design. Even for nonracist whites, the Internet and white supremacy work as reinforcing mechanisms. For well-meaning white liberals, extremists often represent an Other, which signifies racism and undermines any examination of the ways white supremacy is embedded in the broader culture and institutions of the United States.[3] For some white liberals hate speech online is a reliable target for focusing attention on issues of racism, because it is easy to point to distinctions between liberals and extremists. Yet this focus often obfuscates the more difficult investigation into the ways that white supremacy is built into the mechanisms of the dominant culture, institutions, even the technology itself, administered by those with no ties to extremist groups.

Multiple Literacies:
Digital Media, Antiracism, and Social Justice

To fight white supremacy online, we need multiple literacies, including literacies of digital media, antiracism and social justice. We live in an era in which education is under siege,[4] and so I recognize how daunting calling for multiple literacies may seem in the face of these other challenges. However, one of the reasons that digital media is so compelling and part of the reason that it has sparked innovation is because it opens people's minds to new possibilities and reminds us that we are, in fact, designers of our own social futures.[5] New ways of thinking and learning have emerged. Among those leading the way in thinking about these issues are Richard Kahn and Doug Kellner, who have called for a *multiple-literacies* approach.[6] A multiple-literacies approach combines traditional print literacy with critical media literacy and new forms of literacies about how to access, navigate, create, and participate in digital media.[7] Digital media also pose new challenges and opportunities for parents, educators, activists, and scholars for understanding racism, antiracism, and social justice.

Ten years into the digital-media revolution, our initial ways of educating young people about digital-media literacy are ineffectual at best and misleading at worst. For example, one strategy widely used in Internet-literacy curricula is instructing students to "look at the URL," especially the three-letter suffix (.com, .edu, .org). In the case of the cloaked websites, following this advice only serves to make the cloaked site appear *more* legitimate rather than less so. Another response popular with some parents and youth-oriented organizations is to install "hate filters," software programs designed to filter out hate sites encountered through search engines. These filters are woefully inadequate for addressing anything but the most overt forms of hate speech online, and, even when they work as intended, they disable the critical thinking in the person using the technology, which is the central feature needed in our approach to digital-media literacy. The direction that digital-media literacy must take is one that promotes reading text, URL, and external and incoming links closely and carefully, as well as the skills necessary to critically interpret visual imagery and graphic design in relation to the text.

As they exist at this moment, many of the white supremacist sites contain clearly amateurish graphic design and layout; when these sites grow in visual sophistication (and I think it is inevitable that they will), it will be even more difficult to detect racist propaganda. Along with visual and textual literacy, the critical-thinking skills required to decipher Web authorship, intended audience, and cloaked political agendas in making knowledge claims must be combined with at least some understanding of how domain-name registration works. At a minimum, this is what is required to be a fully engaged, thoughtful user of the Web. In my view, it is especially important for young people to become content creators actively engaged in authoring their own digital media, which helps demystify the medium in significant ways. And introducing young people to the regular use of a range of free online tools for Web analysis is important as well. Technology such as the Who Is Registry (internic.net/whois.html) can sometimes help determine the author of a website in the absence of clear information. Alexa (alexa.com) Web-trafficking service shows how many visitors a particular site gets and provides some analysis about how that site relates to other sites (by showing which sites link to it). The free software Touch Graph (touchgraph.com) uses a Java applet to visually display the relationship between links leading to and from a site. Even though many youth are fluent in the use of digital media, they are not necessarily adept at thinking critically about digital media, and this is where adults, whether parents, teachers, activists, or scholars, can play a role in connecting them to technology that facilitates this critical thinking. However, simply being literate and even fluent in digital media is not enough for addressing the challenges of white supremacy online.

Critical-media literacy needs to be added to the technical skills of digital fluency. Among the advantages of incorporating principles of critical-media literacy is that it calls for valuing multiple voices as well as deconstructing images produced by corporate-owned media. Understanding multiple perspectives is an important corrective to the racism, sexism, and homophobia generated by corporate-owned media outlets, and as Henry Jenkins has rightly pointed out, this is a vital contribution of participatory media.[8] However, I want to add a small but significant corrective to the idea of valuing multiple perspectives, by suggesting that not all perspectives are to be valued equally. If "valuing multiple perspectives" is our only standard, then we have no basis on which to critically distinguish between a cloaked website and a legitimate civil rights website, no way to evaluate the content generated by The King Center over that produced by the cloaked site martinlutherking.org. The usual approach within critical-media literacy of "understanding multiple perspectives" is simply not adequate to the task of resisting white supremacy online. If we merely advocate valuing multiple perspectives without regard to content, there is no way to distinguish between different perspectives, no basis for a vision of social justice.

Alongside digital-media literacy and critical-media literacy, we need to develop literacies of racism, antiracism, and social justice. Most whites in the United States have very little understanding of the historical context of racial oppression, and very few have a depth of understanding that might fairly be termed racial literacy. These issues are particularly relevant for youth. Part of the empirical investigation in this book focused on interviews with young people, and it is young people who are often seen as holding the promise of transforming the intergenerational transmission of white supremacy. However, disrupting the inheritance of white supremacy does not happen on its own, inevitably nor automatically; it requires thoughtful, engaged, and ethically informed education joined with political action to transform structured inequality. Young people of all racial and ethnic backgrounds need to read histories of the United States that include critical-race perspectives and critiques of entrenched power elites. Youth of color need critical consciousness to go with lived experiences of everyday racism, and white youth need to begin the lifelong process of unlearning the epistemology of white supremacy, which hobbles them by blinding them to racial inequality. Bringing these multiple literacies together—visual and textual literacy, critical-media literacy, and a racial literacy informed by an ethic of social justice—will empower young people to resist white supremacy, whether overt or cloaked, whether online in digital media, or offline in culture and institutions.

The possibilities of these multiple literacies should give us tremendous hope for the future when it comes to fighting white supremacy online. None of the small sample of young people I interviewed for this study, nor indeed any of the students I have met teaching in the urban, northeastern United States, are, in my view, in any serious danger of being recruited into organized white supremacist movement organizations. But I do see some convincing evidence that, for young people who are often fluent in digital media but not in critical-media literacy or who do not have an understanding of racial inequality, the cloaked white supremacist sites do pose a serious threat to how they understand the history of civil rights in this country, how they view civil rights in the present, and how they value racial equality and human rights in a global society. The good news is that those who already possess those multiple literacies and have an ethic of caring can pass that on intergenerationally, and some are doing that well already.[9] What we have not done particularly well in the United States after the civil rights movement is to engage in civic life in a way that meaningfully transforms the core elements of white supremacy built into our culture and institutions. Even as the United States has elected its first African American president in its history and many point to this as a harbinger of a new, "postracial" era, the stark facts of racial inequality remain grimly in place. Some forty percent of black children still grow up in poverty; black women are more likely to give birth to low-birth-weight babies, regardless of income or education; and young black men remain more likely to go to prison than to college. The fact that one black family has moved into the White House certainly signifies a blow to white supremacy but not the end of the struggle against it. In order to change the deeply embedded white supremacy in our culture and institutions, we have to first acknowledge that it exists, and then we must become more engaged in civic life.

Civic Engagement

Given the presence of white supremacy online, those who are neophytes to digital media may express trepidation about going online at all. Yet I contend that we should engage in civic activism online not in spite of the presence of white supremacy online but precisely because of it. For those of us who are concerned with racial equality, civil rights, and democratic ideals, then civic engagement[10] via the Internet offers a tremendous opportunity for speaking out against injustice. C. Wright Mills recognized this urgent need to speak out against injustice when he wrote that "Everytime intellectuals have the chance to speak yet do not speak they join the forces that train [people] . . . not to be able to think and imagine and feel in morally and politically adequate ways."[11] In this passage Mills was challenging his fellow academics to speak out against the increasing militarization of global politics, and his analysis is as cogent and relevant today as when it was written in 1958. I agree with Mills and his sociological heirs like Stanley Aronowitz,[12] who argue that a new democratic public needs a reinvigorated civic life. Part of what is necessary for that to be realized is an impassioned, radical critique of a hegemonic American elite that threatens democratic institutions in the United States and around the world through an increasingly militarized presence and by promoting a locked-down global society that systematically and efficiently reproduces racial inequality.[13] One of the differences between when Mills was writing and now is that the "chance to speak" in the digital era is ever-present. For example, when people wanted to mobilize a protest against the racial injustices of the criminal prosecution and incarceration of six African American teens in Jena, Louisiana, they organized that protest almost entirely through digital media, including e-mail, blogs, Facebook, MySpace, and YouTube. One young man who joined the protest of almost ten thousand people said, "One of the things about it that inspired me and a lot of other students was the online-activism component."[14] A proliferation of on-line activists such as Afro-Netizen (www.afro-netizen.com) are leading the way in digital civil rights activism and civic engagement. And African American women have long been engaged in civic activism online, organizing the Million Woman March using digital media back in 1999.[15] Today it is black women bloggers that continue to focus attention and activism on the Dunbar Village atrocity, challenging both white-dominated mainstream media indifference to race and the gender bias male-dominated civil rights activists.[16]

For those of us who share Martin Luther King Jr.'s vision and reject the view that we are all "so tragically bound to the starless midnight of racism" that peace and justice can never become reality, civic engagement online of-fers real hope for organizing political activism to make that vision real. The shifting terrain of race, civil rights, and white supremacy online compels us to think critically about how we make and evaluate knowledge claims within digital media. How we develop and teach multiple literacies, how we articu-late a vision for social justice, and whether or not we become engaged in po-litical struggle for equality in the Information Age will determine whether we will carry forward hard-won civil rights victories and the ideals of demo-cratic society here and abroad or we will relinquish them in the dawn of a new global era of white supremacy.

Notes

Martin Luther King, Nobel Peace Prize Acceptance Speech, December 10, 1964, Oslo, Norway; http://nobelprizes.com/nobel/peace/MLK-nobel.html.

1. Feagin and Sykes 1993.
2. Harris 1998. Lipsitz 1998.
3. Wise 2007. See also Bonilla-Silva (2001).
4. Aronowitz and Giroux 1993.
5. Cope and Kalantzis 2000.
6. Kahn and Kellner 2005.
7. Kahn and Kellner 2005, 242.
8. Jenkins 2006a.
9. Notably, the SPLC, the Simon Wiesenthal Center, and the ADL.
10. Bennett 2007.
11. Mills 1958.
12. Aronowitz 2003.
13. Sudbury and Chinyere Oparah 2005.
14. Krigman 2007.
15. Everett 2004.
16. See, for example, Womensphere 2008.

Methodology Appendix: On the Craft of Sociology in the Digital Era

Sociologists are still deciding which methods are suitable for the task of investigating society in the digital era. The social world is changing because of the Internet, and sociological methods for studying patterned human behavior must change as well. Yet sociologists have been slow to take up the challenge of Internet research, as DiMaggio and colleagues have observed.[1] There are many possible reasons for this including, perhaps, a distrust and anxiety about the new.[2] Ben Agger poses the question, "Does the Internet require that we revise sociology's and social theory's categories?"[3] That can seem a daunting task to those contemplating a study that includes some Internet component. Sociologists of a certain generation may also view the Internet as something for the young or the not-sufficiently serious. A former colleague of mine assured me the Web was a fad and urged me to abandon my interest in it if I wanted to be taken seriously as a scholar. That was in 1997, and he was wrong, as it turns out. Although some of these concerns may explain part of sociology's failure to take up the challenge of Internet research, I think there is another reason still.

One of the main barriers to the sociological study of the Internet has to do with the fact that there is not, as of yet, a well-developed sociological method for studying patterned human behavior involving the Internet. While there are some empirical studies in the sociology of the Internet, including large-scale, quantitative studies of people's Internet skills,[4] content analysis of the Web,[5] ethnographies of online games,[6] studies of community formation among Filipinos in diaspora,[7] and neighborhood-based use of new media[8] as well as some impressive theoretical contributions about understanding the social implications of the Internet by some of the leading figures in sociology,[9] there is comparatively little about the sociological research methods most appropriate for studying the Internet.[10] The field of Internet studies is also widely (even wildly) interdisciplinary, and some sociologists may be daunted by the prospect of venturing beyond disciplinary boundaries. While in the rest of this book I have drawn on a broad range of literature from diverse disciplines, including library science, psychology, cultural studies, and communications, this appendix is intended for my fellow sociologists and those interested in sociological methods. In this appendix my goal is to contribute some notes toward the emerging craft of sociology in the digital era.

The study at hand draws on a range of sociological methods, including ethnographic observation of a white supremacist online forum; qualitative-discourse analysis of Web text and graphic design, layout, and images; secondary analysis of Web analytics; case studies; and autoethnography. In addition, I developed an innovative combination of experiment, usability study, and in-depth interview in which I asked young people who were participants to try and distinguish between legitimate civil rights websites and cloaked white supremacist sites. This appendix, then, is meant to offer much more detail about precisely what I did in conducting this research. The intended audience here includes the graduate student embarking on a sociological study of the Internet and more experienced sociologists who may be considering how to incorporate some aspect of digital media into an existing research agenda. My framework for this discussion is: (1) what other sociologists have to say about a particular methodological problem or issue of Internet research, (2) what I did in my research for this book and how I dealt with that issue, and (3) a suggestion for a general principle that may guide other researchers interested in conducting a qualitative sociological analysis that involves the Internet beyond the specific case of white supremacists or even social movements more generally. I follow this with a discussion about some of the ethical issues involved in doing such research.

Content Analysis of Social-Movement Discourse before and after the Web

There is a strong sociological tradition of analyzing social-movement discourse and framing of issues.[11] And today there is a quickly growing body of literature that examines the use of the Internet by social movements in the form of research on cyberactivism[12] and *Internetworked Social Movements* (ISMs).[13] However, there is no other research that I know of that is taking advantage of the opportunity to use the Web to study social-movement discourse on either side of the advent of the Internet. This strikes me as a lost opportunity for sociologists interested in social movements, particularly those interested in social-movement discourse.

In this research I followed an earlier qualitative content analysis of movement documents in print by looking at how those same groups had translated themselves (or had failed to make the transition) to the Web. To do this I kept a close watch on the Internet for the emergence of websites by white supremacists I had examined in my earlier research. One of the tools I used to do this (more recently) was Google Reader, which I configured to track relevant research terms, such as *white supremacist*, and the names of specific individuals, such as *Matt Hale*. I also used the Internet Archive (archive.org), a.k.a. the way-back machine, a site that provides the general public free access to old versions of websites. I utilized this rich source of data to retrieve older versions of the sites when they were no longer available as live sites on the Web. This was especially useful in the instances in which the groups no longer have a current Web presence. This became particularly important in the case of Matt Hale, who is now incarcerated and whose WCOTC site is no longer active. The Internet Archive also provided me with the opportunity to track the evolution of particular sites' design and content over a number of years (e.g., Thom Robb's KKK-affiliated sites) and also allowed me to see when a site had *not* changed since its creation (e.g., Ed Fields, The Truth at Last).

The principle here is straightforward: sociologists should use the available Internet tools, such as the Internet Archive, to study social-movement discourse on the Web and at different points in time. The Internet Archive is intended for use by researchers and the general public. Sociologists with qualitative interests and skills could use the archive to explore themes in movement websites. And those with more quantitative inclinations could use existing data-mining software to examine statistical patterns in the archive.

(Auto)ethnographic Observation Online and Offline

C. Wright Mills, in his methodological appendix to *The Sociological Imagination*, wrote, "I do not like to do empirical work if I can possibly avoid it. If one has no staff, it is a great deal of trouble; if one does employ staff, then the staff is often even more trouble."[14] And, indeed, it is a great deal of trouble. Research involving the Internet can seem, in contrast, deceptively easy: turn on the computer, log onto the Internet, do some research. While some sociologists may still be under the misguided impression that studying new media is something one does sitting in front of a computer, there is, as Howard Becker has pointed out, a limit to what this method can accomplish.[15] Sociologists who have engaged in ethnographic observation online have written primarily about online ethnography as participant observation,[16] and as such one of the primary dilemmas for researchers so engaged is building rapport with subjects.

Instead of focusing primarily on white supremacists with websites as subjects, per se, I spent time in other online spaces to try to understand white supremacists in comparison to other groups. I was also reflexive about my own encounters with such sites online and, in particular, was interested in the ways that my students encountered white supremacy online both intentionally (by seeking it out) and inadvertently (by stumbling upon it). Thus, the kind of autoethnographic narrative that opens chapter 3, in which I describe my experience of my students' encounters of white supremacy online, is an experience that was part of an ongoing research process in which I formulated and reformulated questions about what I was investigating. I also spent much of the time I was working on this project immersed in Internet technologies (using them for personal connection and knowledge-seeking, teaching with them, reading, writing, and thinking with them, even briefly working in the industry). I systematically spent time and collected data (posts from Web-based discussion forums) at Stormfront. In addition, I kept up with changes in various white supremacist organizations through news reports, their own Web sites, and monitoring organizations such as the ADL, Simon Wiesenthal Center, and the Southern Poverty Law Center. Thus, the form that this (auto)ethnographic investigation took was one that led me down a number of different paths, but all brought me back to my central question about what it means—both for the Internet and for our understandings of race—that white supremacists are online.

There are a number of principles or guidelines to derive from such a methodology, including taking time to pay attention. While some may want to view white supremacy online as a separate, distinct subculture apart from mainstream society, I was interested in understanding how white supremacy online is similar to and part of mainstream American culture. In my methodological approach, online and offline worlds overlap in complex ways. Research that looks only at online worlds suggests a false dichotomy between the Internet and offline interactions and thus limits our understanding of how the Internet and society work in tandem.

Adapting the Cultural Diamond to the Digital Era

In an influential article Wendy Griswold developed the cultural diamond as a methodological framework for the sociological study of culture. Griswold's schema sets out four points for examining any cultural artifact, and in this research, I have adapted this framework for studying the Web. Examining the text of Web pages, discussion forums, and newsgroups is the most straightforward method, and it is also the most common way of studying white supremacy online.[17] Much less common are studies of the *Web user*. In other media, this type of research is called *audience reception* and explores how the listener, viewer, or reader interprets the *text*, whether that text is visual (as in films or television shows) or printed (as in novels or newspaper articles). Sonia Livingstone has suggested that the terms *audience* and *reception* do not work well for digital media for a variety of reasons, such as interactivity (rather than one-to-many, with producer and receiver separate as in broadcast media).[18] When it comes to empirical explorations of how people find, read, and interpret extremist rhetoric on racist websites, there is scant research. An important exception to this is the work of Lee and Leets, who examine how adolescents respond to what they call *persuasive storytelling* online by hate groups.[19] More difficult and less prevalent are investigations into the connections between online interaction and face-to-face social networks among extremists.[20]

Among the questions I wanted to investigate in this study was how young people make sense of white supremacy online. I was much less interested in investigating how avowed white supremacists come to be part of an organized movement or how those in the movement first decided to start using the Internet. My interest in how the young make sense of white supremacy online originated in those classroom lab sessions back in 1997. I struggled for a long time to come up with a way to investigate such an accidental discovery in any sort of systematic way. Then I encountered the work of Dina Borzekowski[21] in 2004 and had the chance to meet her in 2005 at the foundation where I was scholar-in-residence. It was there that Dina suggested I use the talk-aloud method, and this sparked further ideas about how to construct these interviews in conjunction with viewing cloaked sites. In January and February 2006, I asked adolescents (ages fifteen to nineteen) to use the Internet to search for information and to evaluate two preselected pairs of websites about Dr. King and about the civil rights movement. I utilized a mixed-method study design, which included search scenarios, paired website evaluations, and the talk-aloud technique (also referred to as *think aloud*). There were two search scenarios: The first asked participants to "find information on Martin Luther King as if you had a report to write for school." The second scenario asked participants to "find information about the goals of the civil rights movement as if you had a report to write for school." As they reviewed the results of their query returned by the search engine, I asked them questions about what they saw, what looked interesting to them and why, and which websites they would select to read.

After completing the search scenarios task, I asked the participants to evaluate the differences between pairs of websites. The first pair included the legitimate King Center site (thekingcenter.org) and the *cloaked* Martin Luther King site (martinlutherking.org); the second pair included the *cloaked* American Civil Rights Review site (americancivilrightsreview.com) and the legitimate Voices of Civil Rights site (voicesofcivilrights.org). I preselected these sites based on the similarity of content and traffic. For example, the traffic in 2006 to the websites for the King Center and the cloaked Martin Luther King site are nearly identical, with an overall peak in February, which is African American History Month.

I minimized the windows for all four websites on the computer and introduced pairs of sites to each participant. I made sure to change the sequence, introducing a cloaked site first, followed by a legitimate site, and then reversing the order. Some participants had already found these sites during the initial search scenario, and I asked them to look at the sites again, in relation to the paired website and talk aloud about which site they would choose as a source of information if they were forced to select one for a school report.

During both tasks, the search scenarios and the paired-website evaluations, I asked participants to talk aloud about what they were doing. The talk-aloud technique, which is common in usability studies of graphic user interface (GUI) website design and frequently used by marketing firms, asks Web users to describe what they are doing, seeing, thinking, reading, and clicking on—and why they are making those choices—as they navigate a website.[22] Completing both tasks took participants approximately thirty to forty-five minutes. I recorded these sessions using a digital video camera, recording audio of the participants' voices and accounts of their searching and evaluating the Web, and capturing video images of the computer screens as they searched.

To analyze this data I transcribed the audio portion of the interviews and noted in the transcripts what was on the computer screen at the same time so that I could recall to which websites the participants were referring in their interviews. I also noted the sequence of their navigation through the sites, the images on the screen, and the way they responded to these. I then coded the transcripts by theme and analyzed them for similar and discordant themes across interviews and for consistencies or changes in patterns within interviews. This process, although time-consuming, is useful, because it situates the Web user in relation to the visual images, the text, and hypertext of the Web. Reviewing the video portion of the interviews and noting it in the transcripts also provided additional information about the way participants searched, navigated, read, and made meaning of search results or of a particular website.

I used a snowball sampling strategy to find participants for the interviews. Participants for the study were recruited through a variety of means, including through a youth-focused human-rights foundation, word-of-mouth, printed flyers, and online bulletin-board postings. The resulting convenience sample includes ten (N=10) participants. The majority (N=8) were recruited from the online bulletin board, one through word-of-mouth and one from the foundation. Almost all (N=9) were female and came from a variety of racial/ethnic backgrounds (one African American, one Asian-Chinese, two white, two Latina, and three South Asian); the one male respondent was Latino. All indicated that they were born in the United States, and all were enrolled in high school, in the eleventh or twelfth grade, at the time of the study. Participants under age eighteen who participated in the study were required to get parental consent and were guided through the informed assent process. Participants eighteen and over were guided through the informed consent process. Except for the participant at the foundation, all participants were asked to travel to my faculty office at a college campus in the city to complete the interview that lasted less than an hour. Participants usually arrived alone to the interview, although one participant brought her mother, who sat quietly while we completed the interview. Participants who completed the interview received a $20 stipend for their time and were given information about Internet searching during the debriefing following the interview. While I wanted to include a larger sample, constraints of both time and money prohibited more interviews. I hope to continue to develop this methodological approach in future research.

Given that almost all of the participants volunteered for the study via the online bulletin-board postings (newyork.craigslist.org), it is likely that this is a sample of relatively digitally fluent and Internet-savvy teens. Of course, because of the convenience sampling strategy employed, these results are not generalizeable to all teens or even all teens using the Internet in New York City. However, the Pew Internet and American Life Project has conducted large, national, random-sample survey research into the online practices of adolescents that found that of the majority (87 percent) of adolescents ages twelve to seventeen who were online in 2005 51 percent use the Internet on a daily basis and 76 percent get news or information about current events online. This is in contrast to adults, who are less likely to use the Internet, with 66 percent of adults using the Internet.[23] This research also indicates that among older teens (fifteen to seventeen) girls are power users of the Internet and search for information about a variety of subject areas; they are more likely to use a greater variety of digital technology—including e-mail, instant messaging, and text messaging—than are their male peers.[24] It is likely that the sample for this study includes participants who are similar in their Web usage to the national sample. In particular, the fact that I was able to recruit a majority female sample using an online bulletin-board posting suggests that these young women are typical of the power users identified in the Pew research.

There are a number of principles for the sociology of the Internet from this research. The key is that the Internet is a many-to-many medium (rather than a one-to-many medium, such as broadcast or traditional print) and draws an *audience* that is much more interactive than a television audience. For example, *users* are also often *creators* and *producers*. Therefore, our ways of studying Internet audiences need to become more sophisticated as well. Further, one of the key insights I gleaned from talking with the young people in this study is the importance of the Internet as a *visual* as well as text-based medium. Visual cues are important to young people who use the Internet. Our sense of what *reading* means needs to expand to include the *interpretation of the visual*, as long suggested by visual sociologists and cultural-studies scholars. And, finally, a further principle is that sociologists must recognize that text on a website is *contested*, that is read differently by different Web visitors. This is another reason that Internet-only content analysis of websites is a limited methodology at best.

You Never Step in the Same Internet Twice: Doing Sociology on Internet Time

"Sociology is slow journalism," Dale McLemore was fond of saying. And in many ways Dale—a professor of mine at University of Texas—was absolutely correct. Sociology often tackles subjects that have first been brought to light by journalists. We approach the study of the same subject much more slowly, because we like to think of ourselves (as a discipline) as being methodical and systematic. The relative slowness of sociology is a significant factor in keeping pace with the rapidly changing Internet. Manuel Castells has pointed out, "The speed of transformation has made it difficult for scholarly research to follow the pace of change with an adequate supply of empirical studies on the why and wherefores of the Internet-based economy and society."[25]

Even as I write this, the Internet grows and changes every minute of every day as websites are created and abandoned, domain names are reserved and let go. Yet sociology is the study of patterned human behavior, and the challenge is to be able to say something meaningful about those patterns of online behavior before they change again.

In this study I dealt with this problem in a number of ways. Primarily, I used many different research methods over a long period of time. Many times it felt like just as I had figured out what I wanted to say about a particular aspect of white supremacy online something would shift, and my insight into how the Internet worked seemed no longer valid. For example, when I first started writing about white supremacy online, states had not yet figured out how to control Internet content within national borders. That has dramatically changed. But the fact is that it all may change again tomorrow. At some point you have to make an argument and get what you have observed written down and out the door (Becker and Richards 2007).

The principle here for sociologists is to recognize that things change quickly on the Internet and that sociology cannot actually stay ahead of this rapid pace of change. However, it is possible to bring sociology's insights to the study of the Internet, as a number of scholars have already demonstrated. The key, I think, is to try and be part of the phenomenon, to create content and participate in online communities, in order to gain a deep understanding of the medium and the myriad ways it is changing society. This way the data that sociologists systematically collect and the knowledge we create will reflect this deeper understanding and rather than be undermined by the rapid pace of change.

Some Ethical Issues in Doing Online Research

Any research with human subjects carries with it certain ethical concerns, particularly if those subjects are minors. This research was no exception. While I would argue that there was no risk of harm to the young people who were participants in this research, it is possible that participants might find the websites unsettling. Given that possibility, following each interview, I took additional steps to ensure that participants were equipped to think critically about these sites, and others like them, should they encounter them again outside the parameters of the study. Specifically, I took deliberate steps to debrief each participant. I asked each participant if they were upset by anything they saw. I gave each participant a handout that included a tip

sheet for critically evaluating Internet websites. And, finally, I had participants type the URL of one of the cloaked sites into TouchGraph, a free Web-
based software program that graphically and dynamically maps the links to a
site. All these efforts were intended to protect the human subjects participating in the study from any potential harm they may have experienced.
Overall, study participants did not encounter any risk greater than that
which they would have encountered in the course of their usual, everyday
lives. And there were some potential benefits for the participants in terms of
greater awareness about the presence of cloaked sites.

A portion of this research that involved content analysis of the websites
was funded, and because of that, the initial phase of this research had to go
through the Institutional Review Board at my institution. In my view, there
is no reasonable threat of harm to any human subject in a study that involves
a researcher looking at websites. The requirement that such a study undergo
IRB review says more about the iron cage of bureaucracy than it does about
any legitimate ethical concern regarding protecting human subjects.

Some Ethical Issues in Doing Research about White Supremacy

Given that my research questions about white supremacy have always been
about the ideological constructions within movement discourse, interview-
ing individual white supremacists has never been an appropriate or necessary
research method for answering my research questions. In addition, I found it
ethically troubling to interview subjects that I disagreed with so fundamen-
tally, lest I inadvertently lend support to their cause (as I wrote in my earlier
book). This stance is a difficult one to sustain while doing research into
white supremacy online, because, with the advent of discussion-board software that counts the number of users and guests logged on to a particular
website, every visit to a white supremacist website becomes a *de facto* vote of
support. Or, say, to the people who run and maintain those sites. Given this,
I chose to remain an oppositional lurker at Stormfront (and at the other
white supremacist sites, but it was somewhat less of an issue at these sites because of the way the sites counted users). That is, I never registered as a user
at the site but instead read there as a guest. As an online guest I copied and
pasted content from the forums as part of my data collection strategy, but I
never had access to any personal information of anyone at the site and did
not disclose any confidential information about anyone there. Some may
challenge this use of these online forums as ethically questionable; however,
I do not think it violates ethical standards of research. Others have also challenged me on the very enterprise of studying white supremacists because, my

detractors argue, it is a scholarly activity that lends support for the cause of white supremacy and drives interest (and traffic) to their sites. Indeed, one of the ethical dilemmas inherent in writing a book such as this is that I may unintentionally encourage the reader to visit these sites, driving additional traffic there and, thus, unintentionally bolstering the cause of white supremacy by increasing the hits at various sites. I am resigned to the fact that such collateral benefit to white supremacists is beyond my control. It is my sincere hope that the benefits of writing this book will be a sufficient counterbalance and that by offering a critique of white supremacy I will encourage others to look critically at white supremacy online and to think in more complex ways about race, racism, and the Internet.

Notes

1. DiMaggio et al. 2001.
2. Hine 2005.
3. Agger 2004.
4. Hargittai 2001, 2004a.
5. Weare and Lin 2000.
6. Kendall 2004.
7. Ignacio 2005. *Building diaspora: Filipino community formation on the Internet.* New Brunswick, N.J.: Rutgers University Press.
8. Hampton and Wellman 2003. Neighboring in Netville: How the Internet Supports Community and Social Capital in a Wired Suburb. *City and Community* 2 (4): 277–311.
9. Castells, Calhoun, DiMaggio, Healy, Hargittai, Sassen.
10. Notable exceptions here include the work of Hine (2005), Ignacio (2006), and Johns, Chen, and Hall (2004). Still, the fact that there are only a handful of sociologists to list here well into the third age of the Internet makes the point about the relative lack of sociological methods for studying the Internet.
11. To name just a few scholars working in this tradition: Robert Benford, Francesca Polletta, David Snow.
12. McCaughey and Ayers 2003.
13. Langman 2005.
14. Mills 1959, 205.
15. Becker 2002, 342.
16. Kendall 2002. Hine 2000, 2005.
17. For instance, Adams and Roscigno (2005), Atton (2006), Back, Keith, and Solomos (1996), Bostdorff (2004), Gerstenfeld, Grant, and Chiang (2003), Kaplan, Weinberg, and Oleson (2003), and Levin (2002).
18. Livingstone 2004.
19. Lee and Leets 2002.

20. Burris and Strahm 2000. Hara and Estrada 2003. Tateo 2005.
21. Borzekowski 2001a, 2001b, 2006.
22. van Someren, Barnard, and Sandberg 1994.
23. Lenhart, Madden, and Hitlin 2005.
24. Lenhart, Madden, and Hitlin 2005, 6.
25. Castells 2001, 3.

~

References

Abbate, Janet. 1999. *Inventing the Internet*. Cambridge, Mass.: MIT Press.

Abrahamson, Mark. 2004. *Global cities*. New York: Oxford University Press.

Adam, Alison E. 1998. *Artificial knowing: Gender and the thinking machine*. New York: Routledge.

———. 2004. Hacking into hacking: Gender and the hacker phenomenon. *ACM SIGCAS Computers and Society* 32 (7): 0095–2737.

Adams, Josh, and Vincent J. Roscigno. 2005. White supremacists, oppositional culture and the World Wide Web. *Social Forces* 84 (2): 759–78.

Adamson, Greg. 2002. Internet futures: A public good or profit centre? *Science as Culture* 11 (2): 257–75.

Adorno, Theodor W. 1951/2002. Freudian theory and the pattern of fascist propaganda. In *The essential Frankfurt school reader*, eds. Andrew Arato and Eike Gebhardt. Oxford: Blackwell Publishing.

Agger, Ben. 2004. *The virtual self: A contemporary sociology*. Malden, Mass.: Blackwell.

Agre, Philip E. 2002a. Cyberspace as American culture. *Science as Culture* 11 (2): 171–89.

———. 2002b. Introduction: The limits of cyberspace. *Science as Culture* 11 (2): 149–53.

———. 2002c. Real-time politics: The Internet and the political process. *Information Society* 18 (5): 311–31.

Aho, James. 1990. *The politics of righteousness: Idaho Christian patriotism*. Seattle: University of Washington Press.

————. 1994. *This thing of darkness: A sociology of the enemy.* Seattle: University of Washington Press.

Alexander, Jeffery C., ed. 1988. *Durkheimian sociology: Cultural studies.* New York: Columbia University Press.

Alexander, Jonathan. 2002. Queer Webs: Representations of LGBT people and communities on the World Wide Web. *International Journal of Sexuality and Gender* 7: 77–84.

Alexander, Jonathan, and William P. Banks. 2004. Sexualities, technologies, and the teaching of writing: A critical overview. *Computers and Composition* 21 (3): 273–93.

Almaguer, Tomas. 1994. *Racial fault lines: The historical origins of white supremacy in California.* Berkeley: University of California Press.

Amerika, Mark. 2004. Anticipating the present: An artist's intuition. *New Media and Society* 6 (1): 71–76.

Anahita, Sine. 2006. Blogging the borders: Virtual skinheads, hypermasculinity, and heteronormativity. *Journal of Political and Military Sociology* (Summer): 143–64.

Anderson, Benedict, and Richard O'Gorman. 1983. *Imagined communities: Reflections on the origin and spread of nationalism.* London: Verso.

Anderson, Margaret L. 1993. Studying across difference: Race, class, and gender in qualitative research. In *Race and ethnicity in research methods*, J. H. Stanfield II and R. M. Dennis, eds. Newbury Park, CA: Sage.

Anti-Defamation League. 1997. ADL calls on America Online to adhere to own guidelines regarding hate material. Press release, April 7, 1997. www.adl.org/PresRele/DiRaB_41/2945_41.asp.

————. 2001a. Poisoning the Web: Hatred online: Internet bigotry, extremism and violence. http://adl.org/poisoning_web/introduction.asp.

————. 2001b. Don Black: White pride world wide, at http://adl.org/poisoning_web/black.asp (accessed July 25, 2007).

————. 2004. ADL praises Google for responding to concerns about rankings of hate sites. Press release, April 22, 2004. www.adl.org/PresRele/Internet_75/4482_75.htm.

————. 2005a. Neo-Nazi linked to alleged Katrina relief scam. *ADL.org*, September 8, 2005. http://adl.org/learn/extremism_in_the_news/White_Supremacy/weltner_relief_scam_9805.htm (accessed July 17, 2007).

————. 2005b. Matt Hale. http://adl.org/learn/ext_us/Hale.asp?xpicked=2&item=6.

————. 2005c. Edward Fields. http://adl.org/learn/ext_us/Fields.asp?xpicked=2&item=Fields.

Appadurai, Arjun. 1996. *Modernity at large: Cultural dimensions of globalization.* Minneapolis: University of Minnesota Press.

Aronowitz, Stanley, and Henry A. Giroux. 1993. *Education still under siege.* Critical studies in education and culture series, 2nd ed., eds. H. A. Giroux and P. Freire. Westport, Conn.: Praeger/Greenwood.

———. 2003. A Mills revival? *Logos Journal* 2 (3). http://www.logosjournal.com/aronowitz.htm.

Arquilla, Michelle, and Sean J. A. Ronfeldt, eds. 2001. *Networks and netwars: The future of terror, crime and militancy.* Santa Monica, Calif.: RAND.

Associated Press. 2002. Rare case has Norwegian man convicted of racism on the Web. April 24, 2002. www.law.com/jsp/article.jsp?id=900005529498 (accessed June 10, 2005).

Atton, Chris. 2003. Reshaping social movement media for a new millennium. *Social Movement Studies* 2 (1): 3–15.

———. 2006. Far-right media on the Internet: Culture, discourse, and power. *New Media and Society* 8 (4): 573–87.

Austin, J. L. 1962/1994. *How to do things with words.* Cambridge, Mass.: Harvard University Press.

Avisar, I. 1993. The historical significance of Der ewige Jude (1940). *Historical Journal of Film, Radio and Television* 13 (3): 363–65.

Ayers, Michael D. 2003. Comparing collective identity in online and offline feminist activists. In *Cyberactivism*, ed. M. McCaughey and M. D. Ayers. London and New York: Routledge.

Back, Les. 1998. Racism on the Internet: Mapping neo-fascist subcultures in cyberspace. In *Nation and race: The developing Euro-American racist subculture*, eds. Jeffrey Kaplan and Tore Bjørgo. Boston: Northeastern University Press.

———. 2001. Wagner and power chords: Skinheadism, white power music and the Internet. In *Out of whiteness: Color, politics and culture*, eds. Vron Ware and Les Back. Chicago: University of Chicago Press.

———. 2002a. Aryans reading Adorno: Cyber-culture and twenty-first-century racism. *Ethnic and Racial Studies* 25 (4): 628–51.

———. 2002b. The new technologies of racism. In *A companion to racial and ethnic studies*, eds. D. T. Goldberg and J. Solomos. Oxford: Blackwell.

Back, Les, Michael Keith, and John Solomos. 1996. The new modalities of racist culture: Technology, race and neo-fascism in a digital age. *Patterns of Prejudice* 30 (2): 3–28.

Balka, Ellen. 1993. Women's access to on-line discussions about feminism. *Electronic Journal of Communication* 3 (1). www.cios.org/www/ejc/v3n193.htm

Ball, Michael R. 1998. Evil and the American dream. In *American ritual tapestry*, ed. J. Deegan. Westport, Conn.: Greenwood.

Balsamo, Anne. 1996. *Technologies of the gendered body: Reading cyborg women.* Durham, N.C.: Duke University Press.

Banton, Michael. 1996. *International action against racial discrimination.* Oxford: Clarendon Press.

Bar-Ilan, J. 2006. Web links and search engine ranking: The case of Google and the query "jew." *Journal of the American Society for Information Science and Technology* 57 (12): 1581–89.

Barber, Benjamin R. 1996. *Jihad vs. McWorld: How globalism and tribalism are reshaping the world*. New York: Ballantine.

Barbrook, Richard. 2002. The regulation of liberty: Free speech, free trade and free gifts on the Net. *Science as Culture* 11 (2): 155–70.

Barbrook, Richard, and Andy Cameron. 1996. The California ideology: A critique of west coast cyber-libertarianism. Originally published in *Very Cyber* May 1996. http://www.hrc.wmin.ac.uk/theory-californianideology.html.

Barkun, Michael. 1997. *Religion and the racist right: The origins of the Christian Identity movement*. Chapel Hill, N.C.: University of North Carolina Press.

———. 1998. Conspiracy theories as stigmatized knowledge: The basis for a new age of racism. In *Nation and Race*, eds. Jeffrey Kaplan and Tore Bjørgo. Boston, Mass.: Northeastern University Press.

———. 2003. *A culture of conspiracy: Apocalyptic visions in contemporary America*. Berkeley: University of California Press.

Barlow, Andrew L. 2003. *Between fear and hope: Globalization and race in the United States*. New York: Rowman & Littlefield.

Barlow, John Perry. 1996. A declaration of the independence of cyberspace. February 8, 1996. http://homes.eff.org/~barlow/Declaration-Final.html.

Barnes, Susan B. 2000. Bridging the difference between social theory and technological invention in human-computer interface design. *New Media and Society* 2 (3): 353–72.

Baym, Nancy. 1996. Agreements and disagreements in a computer-mediated discussion. Research on Language and Social Interaction 29 (4): 315–45.

Becker, David. 2004. Google caught in anti-Semitism flap. *ZDNet News*, April 7, 2004. http://news.zdnet.com/2100-3513_22-5186012.html.

Becker, Howard S. 2002. Studying the new media. *Qualitative Sociology* 25 (3): 337–43.

Becker, Paul J., Bryan Byers, and Arthur Jipson. 2000. The contentious American debate: The First Amendment and Internet-based hate speech. *International Review of Law, Computers & Technology* 14 (1): 33–41.

Bell, Daniel. 1977. Teletext and technology: New networks of knowledge and information in postindustrial society. In *The winding passage: Essays and sociological journeys, 1960–1980*, ed. Daniel Bell. New York: Basic.

Bell, Derrick. 1993. *Faces at the bottom of the well: The permanence of racism*. New York: Basic Books.

Bennett, W. Lance. 2003. Communicating global activism. *Information, Communication & Society* 6 (2): 143–68.

———. 2007. Changing citizenship in the digital age. In *Civic life online: Learning how digital media can engage youth*, Ito et al., eds. The John D. and Catherine T. MacArthur Foundation series on digital media and learning. Cambridge, Mass.: MIT Press.

Berbrier, Mitch. 1998a. "Half the battle": Cultural resonance, framing processes, and ethnic affectations in contemporary white separatist rhetoric. *Social Problems* 45 (4): 431–50.

————. 1998b. White supremacists and the (pan-)ethnic imperative: On "European-Americans" and "white student unions." *Sociological Inquiry* 68 (4): 498–516.

————. 1999. Impression management for the thinking racist: A case study of intellectualization as stigma transformation in contemporary white supremacist discourse. *Sociological Quarterly* 40 (3): 411–33.

Berlet, Chip, ed. 1995. *Eyes right! Challenging the right wing backlash.* Somerville, Mass.: Political Research Associates.

————. 2006. *White supremacist, anti-Semitic, and race hate groups in the U.S.: A geneology.* Political Research Associates 2004. http://publiceye.org/racism/white-supremacy.html (accessed April 24, 2006).

Bernal, Victoria. 2006. Diaspora, cyberspace and political imagination: The Eritrean diaspora online. *Global Networks* 6 (2): 161–79.

Berners-Lee, Tim. 2000. *Weaving the Web: The original design and ultimate destiny of the World Wide Web.* With Mark Fischetti. New York: HarperCollins.

Best, Michael R. 2004. Can the Internet be a human right? *Human Rights & Human Welfare* 4:23–31.

Best, Steven, and Douglas Kellner. 1991. *Postmodern theory: Critical interrogations.* New York: The Guilford Press.

————. 1997. *The postmodern turn.* New York: The Guilford Press.

Bianco, Anthony. 2006. *The bully of Bentonville: How the high cost of Wal-Mart's everyday low prices is hurting America.* New York: Doubleday.

Billing, Michael. 2001. Humour and hatred: The racist jokes of the Ku Klux Klan. *Discourse & Society* 12 (3): 267–89.

Bimber, Bruce. 2000. Measuring the gender gap on the Internet. *Social Science Quarterly* 81 (3): 868–76.

Binder, Amy. 1993. Constructing racial rhetoric: Media depictions of harm in heavy metal and rap music. *American Sociological Review* 58:753–67.

Bissonette, Susan Travis. 2003. Smothering free speech: Filtering the World Wide Web. *Journal of Library Administration* 39 (2–3): 87–100.

Blau, Judith, and Elizabeth Stearns. 2003. *Race in the schools: Perpetuating white dominance?* Boulder, Colo.: Lynne Rienner Publishers.

Blazak, Randy. 2001. White boys to terrorist men: Target recruitment of Nazi skinheads. *American Behavioral Scientist* 44 (6): 982–1000.

Blee, Kathleen. 1991. *Women of the Klan: Racism and gender in the 1920s.* Berkeley: University of California Press.

————. 1996. Becoming a racist: Women in contemporary Ku Klux Klan and neo-Nazi groups. *Gender & Society* 10 (6): 680–702.

————. 1998. White-knuckle research: Emotional dynamics in fieldwork with racist activists. *Qualitative Sociology* 21 (4): 381–99.

————. 2003. *Inside organized racism: Women in the hate movement.* Berkeley: University of California Press.

Bocij, Paul, and Leroy McFarlane. 2003. Cyberstalking: The technology of hate. *International Journal of Police Science and Management* 76 (3): 204–21.

Boczkowski, Pablo J. 2004. Books to think with. *New Media and Society* 6 (1): 144–50.

Boeckmann, Robert J., and Carolyn Turpin-Petrosino. 2002. Understanding the harm of hate crime. *Journal of Social Issues* 58 (2): 207–25.

Bonilla-Silva, Eduardo. 1999. The essential social fact of race. *American Sociological Review* 64 (6): 899–906.

———. 2001. *White supremacy and racism in the post–civil rights era*. New York: Lynne Rienner Publishers.

———. 2004. Race in the world system. *Du Bois Review* 1 (1): 189–94.

Booth, Austin, and Mary Flanagan, eds. 2002. *Reload: Rethinking women and cyberculture*. Boston: MIT Press.

Born in slavery: Slave narratives from the federal writers' project, 1936–1938. 2001. Manuscript Division, Library of Congress, and Prints and Photographs Division, Library of Congress. http://memory.loc.gov/ammem/snhtml/snhome.html (accessed July 28, 2007).

Bortree, Denise. 2006. Book review: Girl Wide Web. *New Media and Society* 8 (5): 851–56.

Borzekowski, Dina L. G. 2006. Adolescents' use of the Internet: A controversial, coming-of-age resource. *Adolescent Medicine Clinics* 17 (1): 205–16.

———. and Vaughn I. Rickert. 2001a. Adolescents, the Internet, and health: Issues of access and content. *Journal of Applied Developmental Psychology* 22 (1): 49–59.

———. 2001b. Adolescent cybersurfing for health information. *Archives of Pediatrics & Adolescent Medicine* 155 (7): 813–17.

Bostdorff, Denise M. 2004. The Internet rhetoric of the Ku Klux Klan: A case study in Web site community building run amok. *Communication Studies* 55 (Summer): 340–61.

Brail, Stephanie. 1996. The price of admission: Harassment and free speech in the wild, wild West. In *Wired_Women: Gender and New Realities in Cyberspace*, eds. Lynn Cherny and Elizabeth Reba Weise, 141–57. Seattle: Seal Press.

Breckheimer, Peter J., II. 2002. A haven for hate: The foreign and domestic implications of protecting Internet hate speech under the First Amendment. *Southern California Law Review* 75 S.Cal.L.Rev. 75 (2): 1493–1528.

Brenner, Neil. 1999. Beyond state-centrism? Space, territoriality, and geographical scale in globalization studies. *Theory and Society* 28 (1): 39–78.

Brilmayer, Lea. 1994. *American hegemony: Political morality in a one-superpower world*. New Haven, Conn.: Yale University Press.

Brown, John S., and Paul Duguid. 2000. *The social life of information*. Cambridge, Mass.: Harvard Business School Press.

Bruce, Bertram C. 2000. Credibility of the Web: Why we need dialectical reading. *Journal of Philosophy of Education* 34 (1): 97–109.

Brunsting, Suzanne, and Tom Postmes. 2002. Social movement participation in the digital age: Predicting offline and online collective action. *Small Group Research* 33 (5): 525–54.

Bryson, Mary. 2004. When Jill jacks in: Queer women and the Net. *Feminist Media Studies* 4 (3): 239–54.

Burbules, Nicholas C. 1997. Rhetorics of the Web: Hyperreading and critical literacy. In *Page to screen: Taking literacy into the electronic era*, ed. Ilana Snyder. Sydney, New South Wales, Australia: Allen and Unwin.

———. 2000. *Watch it: The risks and promises of information technologies in education.* Boulder, Colo.: Westview Press.

———. 2001. Paradoxes of the Web: The ethical dimensions of credibility. *Library Trends* 49 (3): 441–53.

Burlein, Ann. 2003. *Lift high the cross: Where white supremacy and the Christian right converge.* Durham, N.C.: Duke University Press.

Burris, Val, Emery Smith, and Ann Strahm. 2000. White supremacist networks on the Internet. *Sociological Focus* 33 (2): 215–34.

Bury, Rhiannon. 2005. *Cyberspaces of their own: Female fandoms online.* New York: Peter Lang.

Bushart, Howard L., John R. Craig, and Myra Edward Barnes. 2000. *Soldiers of God.* New York: Kensington Publishing Corporation.

Butler, Don. 2007. One man's war on Internet hate. *The Ottawa Citizen*, July 11, 2007. http://canada.com/ottawacitizen/news/story.html?id=7704be24-8e3a-4090-b4f3-a5a4909e1d54&k=8944.

Butler, Judith. 1997. *Excitable speech: A politics of the performative.* New York: Routledge.

Byrne, Dara N. 2007. The future of (the) "race": Identity, discourse, and the rise of computer-mediated public spheres. In *Learning race and ethnicity: Youth and digital media*, ed. Anna Everett. Cambridge, Mass.: MIT Press.

Byrne, Paul. 1997. *Social movements in Britain.* London: Routledge.

Byrne, Séamus. 2004. Stop worrying and love the Google-bomb. Review of Reviewed Item. *Fibreculture Journal* 3 (2004). http://journal.fibreculture.org/issue3/issue3_byrne.html (accessed February 28, 2007).

Calabrese, Andrew. 2004. Stealth regulation: Moral meltdown and political radicalism at the Federal Communications Commission. *New Media and Society* 6 (1): 106–113.

Calhoun, Craig. 1998. Community without propinquity revisited: Communication technology and the transformation of the urban public sphere. *Sociological Inquiry* 68 (3): 373–97.

Cameron, Gavin. 2000. Freedom, hate, and violence on the American right. *Studies in Conflict and Terrorism* 23 (3): 197–204.

Camp, L. Jean. 1996. We are geeks, and we are not guys: The systers mailing list." In L. Cherny and E. R. Weise (eds.), *Wired_Women: Gender and new realities in cyberspace*, 114–25. Seattle: Seal Press.

Campbell, Alex. 2006. The search for authenticity: An exploration of an online skinhead newsgroup. *New Media and Society* 8 (2): 269–94.

Capitanchik, David, and Michael Whine. 1996. The governance of cyberspace: The far right on the Internet. London: Institute for Jewish Policy Research.

Card, Stuart K., Peter Pirolli, Mija Van Der Wege, Julie B. Morrison, Robert W. Reeder, Pamela K. Schraedley, and Jenea Boshart. 2001. Information scent as a driver of Web behavior graphs: Results of a protocol analysis method for Web usability. *CHI* 3 (1): 456–505.

Carvin, Andy. 2000. Mind the Gap: The Digital Divide as the Civil Rights Issue of the New Millennium. *MultiMedia Schools* 7 (1): 56–58.

Case, Sue-Ellen. 1996. *The domain-matrix: Performing lesbian at the end of print.* Bloomington: Indiana University Press.

Cassell, Justine, and Henry Jenkins. 2000. *From Barbie to Mortal Kombat: Gender and computer games.* Boston: MIT Press.

Castells, Manuel. 1996. *The rise of the network society.* Vol. 1 of *The information age: Economy, society and culture.* Oxford: Blackwell.

———. 1997. *The power of identity.* Vol. 2 of *The information age: Economy, society and culture.* Oxford: Blackwell.

———. 1998. *End of millennium.* Vol. 3 in *The information age: Economy, society and culture.* Oxford: Blackwell.

———. 2001. *Internet galaxy: Reflections on the Internet, business, society.* New York: Oxford University Press.

Chatterjee, Bela Bonita. 2002. Razorgirls and cyberdykes: Tracing cyberfeminism and thoughts on its use in a legal context. *International Journal of Sexuality and Gender Studies* 7 (2–3): 197–213.

Chaudry, Lakshmi. 1999. AOL struggles with hate speech. *Wired*, October 25, 1999. http://www.wired.com/culture/lifestyle/news/1999/10/32081.

Cherny, Lynn, and Elizabeth Reba Weise, eds. 1996. *Wired_Women: Gender and new realities in cyberspace.* Seattle: Seal Press.

Chilcoat, Michelle. 2004. Brain sex, cyberpunk cinema, feminism, and the dis/location of heterosexuality. *NWSA Journal* 16 (2): 156–76.

Chou, Rosalind S., and Joe R. Feagin. 2008. *The myth of the model minority: Asian Americans facing racism.* Boulder, Colo.: Paradigm Books.

Chow-White, Peter A. 2006. Race, gender and sex on the Net: Semantic networks of selling and storytelling sex tourism. *Media, Culture & Society* 28 (6): 883–905.

Christensen, Loren. 1994. *Skinhead street gangs.* Boulder, Colo.: Paladin Press.

Cleary, Edward J. 1994. *Beyond the burning cross: A landmark case of race, censorship, and the First Amendment.* New York: Vintage.

Clegg, Sue. 2001. Theorising the machine: Gender, education and computing. *Gender and Education* 13 (3): 307–24.

Cleveland Leader. 2007. Conservapedia: Like Wikipedia, but rooted in Christianity. June 8, 2007. http://clevelandleader.com/node/2235 (accessed July 26, 2007).

CNNMoney.com. 2006. PR firm admits it's behind Wal-Mart blogs: Sites that appeared to be grass-roots support for retailer revealed to be backed by Edelman employees. October 20, 2006. http://money.cnn.com/2006/10/20/news/companies/walmart_blogs/index.htm (accessed July 24, 2007).

Collins, Patricia Hill. 1990. *Black feminist thought: Knowledge, consciousness, and the politics of empowerment.* New York: Routledge.

———. 1998. *Fighting words: Black women and the search for justice.* Minneapolis: University of Minnesota Press.

———. 2000. Gender, black feminism, and black political economy. *The Annals of the American Academy of Political and Social Science* 568: 41–53.

———. 2004. *Black sexual politics: African Americans, gender and the new racism.* New York: Routledge.

Collins, Randall. 1979. *The credential society.* New York: Academic.

Conason, Joe. 2003. *Big lies: The right-wing propaganda machine and how it distorts the truth.* New York: Thomas Dunne Books.

Cooter, Amy Beth. 2006. Neo-Nazi normalization: The skinhead movement and integration into normative structures. *Sociological Inquiry* 76 (2): 145–65.

Cope, B., and M. Kalantzis, eds. 2000. *Multiliteracies: Literacy, learning and social futures.* South Yarra, Victoria, Australia: Macmillan.

Corn, D. 2003. *The lies of George W. Bush: Mastering the politics of deception.* New York: Crown Publishers.

Council of Europe, Additional protocol to the convention on cybercrime, concerning the criminalisation of acts of a racist and xenophobic nature committed through computer systems, 28 January 2003 <http://conventions.coe.int/Treaty/en/Treaties/Word/189.doc> (accessed June 28, 2006)

———. 2001. Committee on Legal Affairs and Human Rights. *Racism and xenophobia in cyberspace.* Doc. 9263. October 12, 2001. http://assembly.coe.int/Documents/WorkingDocs/doc01/EDOC9263.htm.

———. 2003. Additional protocol to the convention on cybercrime, concerning the criminalisation of acts of a racist and xenophobic nature committed through computer systems, Strasbourg, 28.I.2003. http://conventions.coe.int/Treaty/en/Treaties/Html/189.htm.

Cowan, Gloria, and Désirée Khatchadourian. 2003. Empathy, ways of knowing, and interdependence as mediators of gender differences in attitudes toward hate speech and freedom of speech. *Pyschology of Women Quarterly* 27 (4): 300–308.

Cowen, Tyler. 1998. *In praise of commercial culture.* Cambridge, Mass.: Harvard University Press.

Cox, Oliver Cromwell. 1948. *Caste, class, and race: A study in social dynamics.* New York: Doubleday & Co.

Craig, Kellina M. 1999. Retaliation, fear, or rage: An investigation of African American and white reactions to racist hate crimes. *Journal of Interpersonal Violence* 14 (2): 128–51.

Crawford, Beverly, and Ronnie D. Lipshutz, eds. 1998. *The myth of 'ethnic conflict': Politics, economics, and 'cultural' violence.* Berkeley: University of California Press.

Cronin, Blaise, and Elisabeth Davenport. 2001. E-rogenous zones: Positioning pornography in the digital economy. *The Information Society* 17 (1): 33–48.

Cull, Nicholas J., David Culbert, and David Welch, eds. 2003. *Propaganda and mass persuasion: A historical encyclopedia, 1500 to the present.* Santa Barbara, Calif.: ABC-CLIO.

Daniels, Jessie. 1997. *White lies: Race, class, gender and sexuality in white supremacist discourse.* New York: Routledge.

———. 2005. Hate online and global responses. Paper presented at Cyberspace, Brno, Czech Republic.

———. 2006. Finding civil rights in cyberspace: A study of adolescents' Internet use. Paper presented at the Eastern Sociological Association Meetings, Boston, Mass.

———. 2008a. Race, civil rights and hate speech in the digital era. In *Learning race and ethnicity: Youth and digital media,* ed. Anna Everett. Cambridge, Mass.: MIT Press.

———. 2008b. Searching for Dr. King: Teens, race, and cloaked websites. In *Electronic techtonics: Thinking at the interface,* ed. Erin Ennis, Harry Halpin, Paolo Mangiafico, Jennifer Rhee, et al. Durham, N.C.: Lulu Press.

———. 2009a. Rethinking Cyberfeminism(s): Race, Gender, and Embodiment. *Women's Studies Quarterly* (June) in press.

———. 2009b. Cloaked Websites: Propaganda, cyber racism and epistemology in the digital era. *New Media & Society,* 11 (4): *in press.*

Darling-Wolf, Fabienne. 2004. Virtually multicultural: Trans-Asian identity and gender in an international fan community of a Japanese star. *New Media and Society* 6 (4): 507–28.

Davis, Angela. 2000. *The prison industrial complex and the global economy.* Oakland, Calif.: AK Press.

Davis, Steve, Larry Elin, and Grant Reeher. 2002. *Click on democracy: The Internet's power to change political apathy into civic action.* Boulder, Colo.: Westview Press.

de Jong, Wima, Martin Shaw, and Neil Stammers, eds. 2005. *Global activism, global media.* London and Ann Arbor, Mich.: Pluto Press.

Dean, Jodi. 2003. Why the Net is not a public sphere. *Constellations* 10 (1): 85–112.

Decker, Edwin. 2007. Sickopedia: Displaying an agenda in online encyclopedias. *San Diego City Beat,* July 25, 2007. http://sdcitybeat.com/article.php?id=6018 (accessed July 26, 2007).

Deegan, Mary Jo. 2006. Online forum sponsored by the MacArthur Foundation in November 2006. http://www.macfound.org.

———, ed. 1998. *American ritual tapestry: Social rules and cultural meanings, Contributions in Sociology.* Westport, Conn.: Greenwood Publishing Group.

Dees, Morris, and Steve Fiffer. 1993. *Hate on trial: The case against America's most dangerous neo-Nazi.* New York: Villard Books.

Delgado, Richard, and Jean Stefancic. 2004. *Understanding words that wound.* Boulder, Colo.: Westview Press.

Delwiche, Aaron. 2005. Agenda-setting, opinion leadership, and the world of Web logs. *First Monday* 10 (12) (December).

———. 2007. Propaganda Critic, July 8, 2007. http://propagandacritic.org.

Denzin, Norman K. 2003. Prologue: Online environments and interpretive social research. In *Online social research: Methods, issues, and ethics*, eds. Mark D. Johns, Shing-Ling Sarina Chen, and G. Jon Hall. New York: Peter Lang.

DeVoss, Danielle Nichole. 2000. Rereading cyborg(?) women: The visual rhetoric of images of cyborg (and cyber) bodies on the World Wide Web. *CyberPsychology & Behavior* 3 (5): 835–45.

Dias, Karen. 2003. The ana sanctuary: Women's pro-anorexia narratives in cyberspace. *Journal of International Women's Studies* 4 (2): 31–45.

DiMaggio, Paul, Eszter Hargittai, W. Russell Neuman, and John P. Robinson. 2001. Social implications of the Internet. *Annual Review of Sociology* 27: 307–36.

Dixit, Jay. 2001. A banner day for neo-Nazis. *Salon.com*, May 9, 2001. http://archive.salon.com/tech/feature/2001/05/09/hatewatch/.

Dobratz, Betty A. 2001. The role of religion in the collective identity of the white racialist movement. *Journal for the Scientific Study of Religion* 40 (2): 287–302.

Dobratz, Betty A., and Stephanie L. Shanks-Meile. 1995. Conflict in the white supremacist/racialist movement in the U.S. *International Journal of Group Tensions* 25 (1): 57–75.

———. 1997. *White power, white pride: The white separatist movement in the United States*. Baltimore: Johns Hopkins University Press.

Doherty, Martin. 1994. Black propaganda by radio: the German Concordia broadcasts to Britain, 1940–1941. *Historical Journal of Film, Radio, and Television* 14 (2): 167–97.

Doob, L. W. 1950. Goebbels' principles of propaganda. *Public Opinion Quarterly* 14 (3): 419–42.

Doring, Nicola. 2000. Feminist views of cybersex: Victimization, liberation, and empowerment. *CyberPsychology & Behavior* 3 (5): 863–84.

Douglas, Karen M., Craig McGarty, Ana-Maria Bliuc, and Girish Lala. 2005. Understanding cyberhate: Social competition and social creativity in online white supremacist groups. *Social Science Computer Review* 23 (1): 68–76.

Douglass, John Aubrey. 2005. How all globalization is local: Countervailing forces and their influence on higher education markets. *Higher Education Policy* 18 (4): 445–73.

D'Souza, Dinesh. 1995. *The end of racism: Principles for a multiracial society*. New York: Free Press.

Du Bois, W. E .B. 1903/1989. *The souls of black folk: Essays and sketches*. New York: Bantam.

Duke, David. 2002. Behind the mask of respectability: The truth about the Anti-Defamation League of B'nai B'rith. *DavidDuke.com*, November 19, 2002. http://www.davidduke.com/date/2002/11/19.

———. 2007. The coming white revolution: Born on the Internet. July 17, 2007. http://duke.org/writings/internet.html.

Duster, Troy. 2003. *Backdoor to eugenics*. 2nd ed. Berkeley: University of California Press.

Dyer, Richard. 1997. *White*. New York: Routledge.

Earl, Jennifer, and Alan Schussman. 2003. The new site of activism: On-line organizations, movement entrepreneurs, and the changing location of social movement decision making. Vol. 24 in *Consensus Decision Making, Northern Ireland and Indigenous Movements*, ed. Patrick G. Coy. Research in Social Movements, Conflicts and Change. Boston: JAI Press.

Ebo, Bosah, ed. 1998. *Cyberghetto or cybertopia: Race, class, and gender on the Internet*. Westport, Conn.: Praeger Publishers.

Edwards, Arthur. 2004. The Dutch women's movement online: Internet and the organizational infrastructure of a social movement. In *Cyberprotest: New media, citizens and social movements*, eds. Wim van De Donk, Brian D. Loader, Paul G. Nixon, and Dieter Rucht. London and New York: Routledge.

Eglash, Ron. 2001. The race for cyberspace: Information technology in the black diaspora. *Science as Culture* 10 (3): 353–74.

———. 2002. Race, sex and nerds: From black geeks to Asian American hipsters. *Social Text* 20 (2): 49–64.

Eisenstein, Zillah. 1998. *Global obscenities: Patriarchy, capitalism, and the lure of cyberfantasy*. New York: NYU Press.

Endeshaw, Assafa. 2004. Internet regulation in China: The never-ending cat and mouse game. *Information & Communications Technology Law* 13 (1): 41–57.

Enteen, Jilliana B. 2005. Siam remapped: Cyber-interventions by Thai women. *New Media and Society* 7 (4): 457–82.

Erel, Umut. 2007. Racism and anti-racism in Europe: a critical analysis of concepts and frameworks. *Transfer* 13 (3) (Autumn): 359–75.

Ervin, Kelly S., and Geoff Gilmore. 1999. Traveling the superinformation highway: African Americans' perceptions and use of cyberspace technology. *Journal of Black Studies* 29 (3): 398–407.

Escobar, Arturo. 2004. Beyond the Third World: Imperial globality, global coloniality and anti-globalization social movement. *Third World Quarterly* 25 (1): 207–30.

Esteban, Maria Luisa Fernandez. 2001. The Internet: A new horizon for hatred? In *Discrimination and human rights: The case of racism*, ed. Sandra Fredman. Cambridge: Oxford University Press.

Everett, Anna. 2002. The revolution will be digitized: Afrocentricity and the digital public sphere. *Social Text* 20 (2): 125–46.

———. 2004. On cyberfeminism and cyberwomanism: High-tech mediations of feminism's discontents. *Signs* 30 (1): 1278–86.

———, ed. 2008. *Learning Race and Ethnicity: Youth and digital media*. Cambridge, Mass.: MIT Press.

Ezekiel, Raphael S. 1995. *The racist mind: Portrait of American neo-Nazis and Klansmen*. New York: Viking.

———. 2002. An ethnographer looks at neo-Nazi and Klan groups: The racist mind revisited. *American Behavioral Scientist* 2002 46 (1): 51–71.

Facing History and Ourselves. Raphael Lemkin: International law in the age of genocide. http://www2.facinghistory.org/Campus/reslib.nsf/sub/onlinecampus/publications/readings/lemkin_international_law.

Feagin, Joe R. 2006a. Online forum sponsored by MacArthur Foundation.

———. 2006b. *Systemic racism: A theory of oppression.* New York: Routledge.

Feagin, Joe R., Anthony Orum, and Gideon Sjoberg, eds. 1991. *The case for the case study.* Chapel Hill, N.C.: University of North Carolina Press.

Feagin, Joe R., and Melvin P. Sykes. 1993. *Living with racism: Experiences of middle-class black Americans.* New York: Beacon Press.

Feagin, Joe R., and Hernan Vera. 1996. *White racism.* New York: Routledge.

Feagin, Joe R., Hernan Vera, and Nikitah Imani. 1996. *The agony of education.* New York: Routledge.

Featherstone, Mike. 1995. *Undoing culture: Globalization, postmodernism, and identity.* Thousand Oaks, Calif.: Sage Publications.

Featherstone, Mike, and Scott Lash. 1999. *Spaces of culture: City, nation, world.* Thousand Oaks, Calif.: Sage.

Ferber, Abby. 1998. *White man falling: Race, gender and white supremacy.* Lanham, Md.: Rowman & Littlefield.

———. 2000. Racial warriors and weekend warriors: The construction of masculinity in mythopoetic and white supremacist discourse. *Men and Masculinities* 3 (1): 30–56.

———, ed. 2003. *Home grown hate: Gender and organized racism.* New York: Routledge.

Fernandez, Maria, Faith Wilding, and Michelle M. Wright, eds. 2003. *Domain errors! Cyberfeminist practices.* Brooklyn, N.Y.: Autonomedia.

Ferrigno-Stack, Josephine, John Robinson, Meyer Kestnbaum, Alan Neustadtl, and Anthony Alvarez. 2003. Internet and society: A summary of research reported at Webshop 2001. *Social Science Computer Review* 21 (1): 73–117.

Festa, Paul. 2002. Controversial domains go to civil rights groups. *c|net News.* http://news.com.com/Controversial+domains+go+to+civil+rights+groups/2100-1023_3-210803.html (accessed June 18, 2007).

Finn, Jerry, and Mary Banach. 2000. Victimization online: The downside of seeking human services for women on the Internet. *CyberPsychology & Behavior* 3 (5): 785–96.

Flanagan, Mary. 2002. Hyperbodies, hyperknowledge: Women in games, women in cyberpunk, and strategies of resistance. In *Reload: Rethinking women + cyberculture,* eds. Mary Flanagan and Austin Booth. Cambridge, Mass.: MIT Press.

———. 2003. Next Level: Women's digital activism through gaming. In *Digital media revisited,* eds. Gunnar Liestøl, Andrew Morrison, and Terje Rasmussen. Cambridge, Mass.: MIT Press.

Flanagan, Mary, and Austin Booth, eds. 2002. *Reload: Rethinking women + cyberculture.* Cambridge, Mass.: MIT Press.

Flanders, Vince. 1998. *Web pages that suck: Learn good design by looking at bad design*, with Michael Willis. Hoboken, N.J.: Sybex.

———. 2001. *Web pages that suck: Learn good design by looking at bad design* with Dean Peters. Hoboken, N.J.: Sybex.

———. 2002. *Son of Web pages that suck: Learn good design by looking at bad design*, with Dean Peters. San Francisco: Sybex.

Flax, Jane. 1987. Postmodernism and gender relations in feminist theory. *Signs* 12 (4): 621–43.

Flint, Colin. 2004a. United States hegemony and the construction of racial hatreds: The agency of hate groups and the changing world political map. In *Spaces of hate: Geographies of discrimination and intolerance in the U.S.A.*, ed. Colin Flint. New York: Routledge.

———, ed. 2004b. *Spaces of hate: Geographies of discrimination and intolerance in the U.S.A.* New York: Routledge.

Fogg, B. J. 2003. *Persuasive technology: Using computers to change what we think and do.* Palo Alto, Calif.: Morgan Kaufman.

Fogg, B. J., T. Kameda, J. Boyd, J. Marshall, R. Sethi, M. Sockol, and T. Trowbridge. 2002. *Stanford-Makovsky Web credibility study 2002: Investigating what makes Web sites credible today.* Palo Alto, Calif.: Stanford University.

Fraser, Nancy. 1989. *Unruly practices: Power, discourse and gender in contemporary social theory.* Minneapolis: University of Minnesota Press.

Frederick, Howard. 1986. *Cuban-American radio wars: Ideology in international telecommunications.* Norwood, N.J.: Ablex Publishing Corporation.

Freeman, Peter, and William Aspray. 1999. *The supply of information technology workers in the United States.* Washington, D.C.: CRA. http://cra.org/reports/wits/it_worker_shortage_book.pdf (accessed December 1, 2008).

Futrell, Robert, and Pete Simi. 2004. Free spaces, collective identity, and the persistence of U.S. white power activism. *Social Problems* 51 (1): 16–42.

Futrell, Robert, Pete Simi, and Simon Gottschalk. 2006. Understanding music in movements: The white power music scene. *Sociological Quarterly* 47 (2): 275–304.

Gabriel, John. 1998. *Whitewash: Racialized politics and the media.* London: Routledge.

Gaine, Chris. 2000. Stereotypes in cyberspace: Writing an anti-racist website. *Curriculum Journal* 11: 87–99.

Gajjala, Radhika. 1999. Cyberfeminism, technology and international "development." *Gender & Development* 7 (2): 8–16.

———. 2002. An interrupted postcolonial/feminist cyberethnography: Complicity and tesistance in the "Cyberfield." *Feminist Media Studies* 2 (2): 177–93.

———. 2003. South Asian digital diasporas and cyberfeminist Webs: Negotiating globalization, nation, gender and information technology design. *Contemporary South Asia* 12 (1): 41–56.

———. 2004. *Cyber selves: Feminist ethnographies of South Asian women.* Walnut Creek, Calif.: AltaMira Press.

Gallaher, Carolyn, and Oliver Froehling. 2002. New world warriors: "Nation" and "state" in the politics of the Zapatista and U.S. Patriot Movements. *Social & Cultural Geography* 3 (1): 81–102.

Garlick, Steve. 2003. What is a man? Heterosexuality and the technology of masculinity. *Men and Masculinities* 6 (2): 156–72.

Gelber, Katharine. 2002. *Speaking back: The free speech versus hate speech debate.* Amsterdam: John Benjamins Publishing.

George, Alexander L. 1959. *Propaganda analysis: A study of the inferences made from Nazi propaganda in World War II.* Evanston, Ill.: Row, Peterson.

Gerstenfeld, Phyllis B., Diana R. Grant, and Chau-Pu Chiang. 2003. Hate online: A content analysis of extremist Internet sites. *Analyses of Social Issues and Public Policy* 3 (1): 29–44.

Gibson, Rachel K., Paul Nixon, and Stepehn Ward. 2003. *Political parties and the Internet.* New York: Routledge.

Gillies, James, and Roberts Cailliau. 2000. *How the Web was born: The story of the World Wide Web.* New York: Oxford University Press.

Gilster, Paul. 1997. *Digital literacy.* New York: John Wiley & Sons.

Ginsburg, Faye D. 1998. *Contested lives: The abortion debate in an American community.* Berkeley: University of California Press.

Giroux, Henry A. 2006a. Reading Hurricane Katrina: Race, class, and the biopolitics of disposability. *College Literature* 33 (3): 171–96.

———. 2006b. *Theory and resistance in education: Towards a pedagogy for the opposition.* Englewood Cliffs, N.J.: Praeger/Greenwood.

Glaser, Jack, Jay Dixit, and Donald P. Green. 2002. Studying hate crime with the Internet: What makes racists advocate racial violence? *Journal of Social Issues* 58 (1): 177–93.

Godoy, Julio. 2004. This fight is not virtual any more. *Inter Press Service News Agency,* June 18, 2004. http://www.ipsnews.net/new_nota.asp?idnews=24265 (accessed July 15, 2006). Archived at http://www.inach.net/content/osce-paris-pressarticles.html (accessed April 18, 2008).

Godwin, Mike. 1994. Nine principles for making virtual communities work. *Wired* 2 (6) (June): 72–73.

———. 1998. *Cyber rights: Defending free speech in the digital age.* Cambridge, Mass.: MIT Press.

Goffman, Erving. 1974. *Frame analysis: An essay on the organization of experience.* Cambridge, Mass.: Harvard University Press.

Goldberg, David Theo. 1990a. The social formation of racist discourse. In *Anatomy of racism,* ed. D. T. Goldberg. Minneapolis: University of Minnesota Press.

———, ed. 1990b. *Anatomy of racism.* Minneapolis: University of Minnesota Press.

———. 1993. *Racist culture: Philosophy and the politics of meaning.* Oxford: Blackwell.

———. 2002. *The racial state.* London: Blackwell.

Goldberg, Michelle. 2006. *Kingdom coming: The rise of Christian nationalism.* New York: Norton.

Goldsmith, Jack, and Tim Wu. 2006. *Who controls the Internet? Illusions of a borderless world*. New York: Oxford University Press.

Google. *An explanation of our search results*. http://www.google.com/explanation .html.

Gore, Al. 1998. Remarks by Vice President Al Gore to the DLC 1998 Annual Conference. December 2, 1998. http://dlc.org/ndol_ci.cfm?kaid=127&subid= 173&contentid=2716.

Green, Donald P., Laurence H. McFalls, and Jennifer K. Smith. 2001. Hate crime: An emergent research agenda. *Annual Review of Sociology* 27: 479–504.

Green, R. Michelle. 2005. Predictors of digital fluency. PhD diss., Northwestern University.

———. 2006. Personality, race, age and the development of digital fluency. Paper presented at the meeting of the American Educational Researchers Association. San Francisco, Calif.

Green, Venus. 2001. *Race on the line: Gender, labor & technology in the Bell System, 1880–1980*. Durham, N.C.: Duke University Press.

Greenfield, P. M., and K. Subrahmanyam. 2003. Online discourse in a teen chat room: New codes and new modes of coherence in a visual medium. *Journal of Applied Developmental Psychology* 24: 713–38.

Griffiths, M. D., Mark N. O. Davies, and Darren Chappell. 2004. Online computer gaming: A comparison of adolescent and adult gamers. *Journal of Adolescence* 27: 87–96.

Griswold, Wendy. 1987. A methodological framework for the sociology of culture. *Sociological Methodology* 17: 1–35.

———. 1994. *Cultures and societies in a changing world*. 2nd ed. Thousand Oaks, Calif.: Pine Forge Press.

Guba, E. G., and Y. S. Lincoln. 1994. Competing paradigms in qualitative research. In *Handbook of qualitative research*, Norman K. Denzin and Y. S. Lincoln, eds. Thousand Oaks, Calif.: Sage.

Grumke, Thomas. 2003. The transatlantic dimension of right-wing extremism. *Human Rights Review* 4 (4): 56–72.

Guillen, Mauro F. 2001. Is globalization civilizing, destructive or feeble? A critique of five key debates in the social science literature. *Annual Review of Sociology* 27: 235–60.

Gunkel, David J. 2003. Second thoughts: Toward a critique of the digital divide. *New Media and Society* 5 (4): 499–522.

Habermas, Jurgen. 1981. *The structural transformation of the public sphere*. Cambridge, Mass.: MIT Press.

Hafner-Burton, Emilie M., and Kiyoteru Tsutsui. 2005. Human rights in a globalizing world: The paradox of empty promises. *American Journal of Sociology* 110 (5): 1373–1411.

Hage, Ghassan. 2000. *White nation: Fantasies of white supremacy in a multicultural society*. New York: Routledge.

Hagel, John III, and Arthur G. Armstrong. 1997. Net gain: Expanding markets through virtual communities. *The McKinsey Quarterly* (1): 55–65.

Hamm, Mark. 1994. *Hate crime: International perspective on causes and control.* Cincinnati, Ohio: Anderson.

Hampton, Keith, and Barry Wellman. 2003. Neighboring in Netville: How the Internet Supports Community and Social Capital in a Wired Suburb. *City and Community* 2 (4): 277–311.

Hansen, Mark B. N. 2006. *Bodies in code: Interfaces with digital media.* New York: Routledge.

Hara, Noriko, and Zilia Estrada. 2003. Hate and peace in a connected world: Comparing MoveOn and Stormfront. *First Monday* 8 (12), December 1, 2003. http://firstmonday.org/htbin/cgiwrap/bin/ojs/index.php/fm/article/view/1104/1024 (accessed June 18, 2007).

———. 2005. Analyzing the mobilization of grassroots activities via the Internet: A case study. *Journal of Information Science* 31 (6): 503–14.

Harcourt, Wendy. 1999. Conclusion: Local/global encounters. In *Women@Internet: Creating new cultures in cyberspace*, ed. Wendy Harcourt. New York: Zed Books.

———, ed. 1999. *Women@Internet: Creating new cultures in cyberspace.* New York: Zed Books.

———. 2000. The personal and the political: Women using the Internet. *CyberPsychology & Behavior* 3 (5): 693–97.

Harding, Sandra. 1986. *The science question in feminism.* Ithaca, N.Y.: Cornell University Press.

———. 1991. *Whose science? Whose knowledge? Thinking from women's lives.* Ithaca, N.Y.: Cornell University Press.

Hargittai, Eszter. 2002. Second-level digital divide: Differences in people's online skills. *First Monday* 7 (4).

———. 2004a. Internet access and use in context. *New Media and Society* 6: 137–43.

———. 2004b. The changing online landscape: From free-for-all to commercial gatekeeping. In *Community practice in the network society: Local actions/global interaction*, eds. Peter Day and Doug Schuler. New York: Routledge.

Harmon, Amy. 2004. Internet gives teenage bullies weapons to wound from afar. *New York Times*, Education, August 26, 2004. http://nytimes.com/2004/08/26/education/26bully.html (accessed March 28, 2006).

Harris, Cheryl I. 1998. Whiteness as property. *Harvard Law Review* 106 (1993): 1709–95.

Harris, Frances Jacobson. 2005. *I found it on the Internet: Coming of age online.* Chicago: American Library Association.

———. 2007. Challenges to teaching credibility assessment in contemporary schooling. In *Digital media, youth and credibility*, eds. Miriam J. Metzger and Andrew J. Flanagin. Cambridge, Mass.: MIT Press.

Heintze, Hans-Joachim. 2007, 51–63. The prohibition of propaganda advocating war, racism and hatred under international law: Inter-state obligations with far reaching consequences. In *The emotion and the truth: Studies in mass communication and conflict*, Mariano Aguirre and Francisco Fernándiz, eds. Bilbao: Humanitarian-Net.

Heinz, Bettina, Li Gu, Ako Inuzuka, and Roger Zender. 2002. Under the rainbow flag: Webbing global gay identities. *International Journal of Sexuality and Gender Studies* 7 (2–3): 107–24.

Herman, Andrew, and Thomas Swiss, eds. 2000. *The World Wide Web and contemporary cultural theory*. New York: Routledge.

Herrnstein, Richard J., and Charles Murray. 1994. *The bell curve: Intelligence and class structure in American life*. New York: Free Press.

Herring, Susan C. 1994, 278–94. Politeness in computer culture: Why women thank and men flame. In *Cultural performances: Proceedings of the third Berkeley Women and Language Conference*, eds. M. Bucholtz, A. Liang, and L. Sutton. Berkeley: Berkeley Women and Language Group, 1994.

———. 1996, 115–45. Posting in a different voice: Gender and ethics in computer-mediated communication. In *Philosophical perspectives on computer-mediated communication*, ed. Charles Ess. Albany: SUNY Press.

———. 2004. Slouching toward the ordinary: Current trends in computer-mediated communication. *New Media and Society* 6: 26–36.

Herring, Susan, Deborah Johnson, and Tamra DiBenedetto. 1992. Participation in electronic discourse in a "feminist" field. In K. Hall, M. Bucholtz, and B. Moonwomon (eds.), *Locating power: The proceedings of the second Berkeley Women and Language Conference*, 250–62. Berkeley, Calif.: Berkeley Women and Language Group. Reprinted (1998) in J. Coates (ed.), *Language and gender: A reader*. Oxford: Blackwell.

———. 1995. "This discussion is going too far!" Male resistance to female participation on the Internet. In M. Bucholtz and K. Hall (eds.), *Gender articulated: Language and the socially constructed self*, 67–96. New York: Routledge.

Hess, Jim, Karen L. Nero, and Michael L. Burton. 2001. Creating options: Forming a Marshallese community in Orange County, California. *The Contemporary Pacific* 13 (1): 89–121.

Hessler, Richard M., Jane Downing, Cathleen Beltz, Angela Pelliccio, Mark Powell, and Whitney Vale. 2003. Qualitative research on adolescent risk using e-mail: A methodological assessment. *Qualitative Sociology* 26 (1): 111–24.

Hewitt, Christopher. 2003. *Understanding terrorism in America: From the Klan to al Qaeda*. New York: Routledge.

Hewson, Claire, Carl Vogel, Peter Yule, and Dianna Laurent. 2003. *Internet research methods (A practical guide for the social and behavioral sciences)*. London: Sage.

Hicks, Steven, Edward F. Halpin, and Eric Hoskins, eds. 2000. *Human rights and the Internet*. New York: Palgrave Macmillan.

Higgins, Rosie, E. Rushaija, and A. Medhurst. 1999. Technowhores. In *Desire by design: Body, territories and the new technologies.*, edited by T. W. s. R. Group: Tauris, I.B.

Hine, Christine. 2000. *Virtual ethnography*. Thousand Oaks, Calif.: Sage.

——, ed. 2005. *Virtual methods: Issues in social research on the Internet/*. Oxford, UK: Berg Publishers.

Hockenos, Paul. 1993. *Free to hate: The rise of the right in post-Communist Eastern Europe*. New York: Routledge.

Hoffer, Eric. 1951. *The true believer: Thoughts on the nature of mass movements*. New York: Harper and Row.

Hoffman, David S. 1995. *Hate group recruitment on the Internet*. New York: Anti-Defamation League.

——. 1996. *Web of hate: Extremists exploit the Internet*. New York: Anti-Defamation League.

Hoffman, Donna L., and Thomas P. Novak. 1998. Bridging the digital divide: The impact of race on computer access and Internet use. *Science* 280 (April 17): 390–91.

Holmes, Steven A. 2000. White supremacist agrees to make a public apology to victim. *New York Times*, May 12, 2000. http://query.nytimes.com/gst/fullpage.html?res= 980DE3DC143BF931A (accessed June 28, 2002).

Hondageu-Sotelo, Pierrette. 1994. *Gendered transitions: Mexican experiences of immigration*. Berkeley: University of California Press.

Hossfeld, Karen J. 2001. Their logic against them: Contradictions in sex, race and class on the Silicon Valley shop floor. In *Technicolor: Race, technology and everyday life*, eds. Alondra Nelson, Thuy Linh N. Tu, and Alicia Headlam Hines. New York: New York University Press.

Houston, Douglas A. 2003. Can the Internet promote open global societies? *The Independent Review* 7 (3): 353–69.

Hull, Gordon. 2003. Thoughts on the fetishization of cyberspeech and the turn from "public" to "private" law. *Constellations* 10 (1): 113–34.

Human Rights and Equal Opportunity Commission. 1991. *Racist violence: Report of the national inquiry into racist violence in Australia*. Canberra: AGPS.

Hunt, Darnell M. 1999. *O. J. Simpson facts and fictions: News rituals in the construction of reality*. Cambridge, UK, and New York: Cambridge University Press.

Hunter, Richard. 2002. *World without secrets: Business, crime and privacy in the age of ubiquitous computing*. Hoboken, N.J.: John Wiley & Sons.

Ignacio, Emily Noelle. 2005. *Building diaspora: Filipino community formation on the Internet*. New Brunswick, N.J.: Rutgers University Press.

——. 2006. E-scaping Boundaries: Bridging Cyberspace and Diaspora Studies through Nethnography, Pp.181–93, in *Critical cyberculture studies*, edited by David Silver Adrienne Massanari, and Steve Jones. New York: New York University.

International Network Against Cyberhate. 2008. Craigslist not liable for its users' racism. March 27, 2008. http://www.inach.net/index.php/article/13/Craigslist-not-liable-for-its-user-s-racism(USA).

Jackson, Linda A., Kelly S. Ervin, Phillip D. Gardner, and Neal Schmitt. 2001. Gender and the Internet: Women communicating and men searching. *Sex Roles* 44 (5–6): 363–79.

Jacobs, James B., and Kimberly Potter. 1998. *Hate crimes: Criminal law and identity politics*. New York: Oxford University Press.

Jacobs, David. 2005. Internet activism and the democratic emergency in the U.S. *Ephemera, Theory & Politics in Organization*, 5(1): 68–77.

Jameson, Fredric. 2002. *A singular modernity: An essay on the ontology of the present*. London: Verso.

Jameson, Fredric, and Masao Miyoshi, eds. 1998. *The cultures of globalization*. Durham, N.C.: Duke University Press.

Jayakar, Roshni. 2000. "What stops free flow of information is dangerous": Interview: John Perry Barlow. *Business Today*, December 6, Living Media India, at india-today.com/btoday/20001206/interview.html.

Jefferson, Thomas. 1787/1853. *Notes on the state of Virginia*. Richmond, Va.: J.W. Randolph.

———. 1914. *Autobiography of Thomas Jefferson, 1743-1790*. New York and London: The Knickerbocker Press.

Jenkins, Henry. 2004. Media literacy goes to school. *Technology Review*, January 2, 2004, at http://technologyreview.com/biomedicine/13429/ (accessed November 12, 2006).

———. 2006a. Confronting the challenges of participatory culture: Media education for the 21st century. In *An occasional paper on digital media and learning*. Chicago, Ill.: MacArthur Foundation.

———. 2006b. *Convergence culture: Where old and new media collide*. New York: New York University Press.

Jenkins, Henry, and David Thorburn, eds. 2003. *Democracy and new media*. Cambridge, Mass.: MIT Press.

Jhally, Sut, and Justin Lewis. 1992. *Enlightened racism: The Cosby Show, audiences, and the myth of the American dream*. Boulder, Colo.: Westview Press.

John S. and James L. Knight Foundation. 2005. The Future of the First Amendment. Report, January 31, 2005. http://firstamendment.jideas.org/findings/findings.php.

Johns, Mark D., Shing-Ling Sarina Chen, and G. Jon Hall. 2004. *Online social research: Methods, issues and ethics*. New York: Peter Lang Publishers.

Jones, Steve. 2003. Introduction: Ethics and Internet studies. In *Online social research*, eds. Mark D. Johns, Shing-Ling Sarina Chen, and G. Jon Hall. New York: Peter Lang.

———, ed. 1999. *Doing Internet research: Critical issues and methods for examining the Net*. Thousand Oaks, Calif.: Sage.

Jones, Steven G., ed. 1997. *Virtual culture: Identity and communication in cybersociety*. Thousand Oaks, Calif.: Sage.

Jowett, Garth S., and Victoria O'Donnell. 2006. *Propaganda and persuasion*. 4th ed. Thousand Oaks, Calif.: Sage.

Kahn, Richard, and Douglas Kellner. 2003. Internet subcultures and oppositional Politics. In *The post-subcultures reader*, eds. David Muggleton and Rupert Weinzierl. London: Berg Publishers.

———. 2004. New media and Internet activism: From the "Battle of Seattle" to blogging. *New Media and Society* 6 (1): 87–95.

———. 2005. Reconstructing technoliteracy: A multiple literacies approach. *E-Learning* 2 (3): 238–51.

Kallen, Evelyn. 1998. Hate on the net: A question of rights/a question of power. *Electronic Journal of Sociology.* www.sociology.org/content/vol003.002/kallen.html.

Kaplan, Carl S. 1998. Children's First Amendment rights lost in the filtering debate. *New York Times*, March 6, 1998. http://partners.nytimes.com/library/tech/98/03/cyber/cyberlaw/06law.html.

Kaplan, Jeffery. 1998. Religiosity and the radical right: Toward the creation of a new ethnic identity. In *Nation and race: The developing Euro-American racist subculture*, eds. Jeffrey Kaplan and Tore Bjørgo. Boston: Northeastern University Press.

———, ed. 2000. *Encyclopedia of white power: A sourcebook on the radical racist right.* Lanham, Md.: Rowman & Littlefield Publishers.

Kaplan, Jeffery, and Tore Bjørgo, eds. 1998. *Nation and race: The developing Euro-American racist subculture.* Boston: Northeastern University Press.

Kaplan, Jeffery, Leonard Weinberg, and Ted Oleson. 2003. Dreams and realities in cyberspace: White Aryan resistance and the World Church of the Creator. *Patterns of Prejudice* 37 (2): 139–55.

Kaplan, Nancy. 2000. Literacy beyond books: Reading when all the world's a Web. In *The World Wide Web and contemporary cultural theory*, eds. Andrew Herman and Thomas Swiss. New York: Routledge.

Kellner, Douglas. 1998. Multiple literacies and critical pedagogy in a multicultural society. *Educational Theory* 48 (1): 103–22.

———. 2002. Theorizing globalization. *Sociological Theory* 20 (3): 285–305.

———. 2004. Technological transformation, multiple literacies, and the re-visioning of Education. *E-Learning* 1 (1): 9–37.

Kellner, Douglas, and Jeff Share. 2005. Toward critical media literacy: Concepts, debates, organizations, and policy. *Discourse: Studies in the Cultural Politics of Education* 26 (3): 369–86.

Kendall, Lori. 1996. MUDder? I hardly knew 'er! Adventures of a feminist MUDder. In *Wired_women: Gender and new realities in cyberspace*, eds. Lynn Cherny and Elizabeth Reba Weise. Seattle: Seal Press.

———. 1998. Meaning and identity in "cyberspace": The performance of gender, class and race online. *Symbolic Interaction* 21 (2): 129–54.

———. 2000. "Oh no! I'm a nerd!" Hegemonic masculinity in an online forum. *Gender & Society* 14 (2): 256–74.

———. 2002. *Hanging out in the virtual pub: Masculinities and relationships online.* Berkeley: University of California Press.

Kennedy, Tracy L. 2000. An exploratory study of feminist experiences in cyberspace. *CyberPsychology & Behavior* 3 (5): 707–19.

Kennedy, Tracy L., Barry Wellman, and Kristine Klement. 2003. Gendering the digital divide. *IT & Society* 1 (5): 72–96.

Kensinger, Loretta. 2003. Plugged in praxis: Critical reflections on U.S. feminism, Internet activism, and solidarity with women in Afghanistan. *Journal of International Women's Studies* 5 (1): 1–28.

Kim, Amy Jo. 2000. *Community building on the Web: Secret strategies for successful online communities.* Berkeley, Calif.: Peachpit Press.

Kim, T. K. 2005. Electronic storm: Stormfront grows into thriving neo-Nazi community. *Southern Poverty Law Center*, Summer 2005. http://splcenter.org/intel/intel report/article.jsp?pid=908 (accessed June 28, 2005).

King, Rawlson O'Neil. 2004. Solutions and policy combat spreading hate. *The Whir*, May 21, 2004. http://thewhir.com/features/hate-sites.cfm (accessed June 9, 2005).

Kinsell, Warren. 1996. *Web of hate: Inside Canada's far right network.* New York: HarperCollins.

Kirby, Andrew. 2004. When extreme political ideas move into the mainstream. In *Spaces of hate*, ed. Colin Flint. New York: Routledge.

Klein, Hans K. 1999. Tocqueville in cyberspace: Using the Internet for citizens' associations. *The Information Society* 15 (4): 213–20.

Klein, Renate 1999. If I'm a cyborg rather than a goddess will patriarchy go away? In *Cyberfeminism: Connectivity, critique and creativity*, eds. Susan Hawthorne and Renate Klein. Melbourne: Spinifex.

Kling, Rob, Spencer C. Olin, and Mark Poster. 1991. *Postsuburban California: The transformation of Orange County since World War II.* Berkeley: University of California.

Knessel, Neil J. 1996. *Mass hate: The global rise of genocide and terror.* New York: Plenum Press.

Kolbert, Kathryn, and Zak Mettger. 2002. *Justice Talking from NPR (National Public Radio): Censoring the Web: Leading advocates debate today's most controversial issues.* New York: The New Press.

Kolko, Beth, Lisa Nakamura, and Gilbert B. Rodman, eds. 2000. *Race in cyberspace.* New York: Routledge.

Koopmans, Ruud, and Susan Olzak. 2004. Discursive opportunities and the evolution of right-wing violence in Germany. *American Journal of Sociology* 110 (1): 198–230.

Korenman, Joan. 2000. Women, women, everywhere: Looking for a link. *CyberPsychology & Behavior* 3 (5): 721–29.

Korgen, Kathleen, Patricia M. Odell, and Phyllis Schumacher. 2001. Internet use among college students: Are there differences by race/ethniciy? *Electronic Journal of Sociology* 5 (3).

Krigman, Eliza. 2007. The activists of Jena six. *The Nation*, October 11, 2007. http://www.thenation.com/doc/20071029/jena6activists (accessed December 12, 2007).

Kronenwetter, Michael. 1992. *United they hate.* New York: Walker and Company.

Krysan, Maria. 1998. Privacy and the expression of white racial attitudes: A comparison across three contexts. *Public Opinion Quarterly* 62 (4): 506–44.

Kuipers, Giselinde. 2006. The social construction of digital danger: Debating, defusing and inflating the moral dangers of online humor and pornography in the Netherlands and the United States. *New Media and Society* 8 (3): 379–400.

Kvasny, Lynnette. 2006. Cultural (re)production of digital inequality in a U.S. community technology initiative. *Information, Communication & Society* 9 (2): 160–81.

Ladd, Donna. 2000. "Don't link to hate sites!" *Salon.com*, April 14, 2000. http://archive.salon.com/tech/log/2000/04/14/hate_sites/.

Lamberg, Lynne. 2001. Hate-group Web sites target children, teens. *Psychiatric News* 36 (3): 26.

Lambrianidou, Kyriaki. 2001. Hate sites on the Internet: Their calls for violence and their targets, criminal justice. Unpublished master's thesis, City University of New York, John Jay College, New York.

Langer, Elinor. 1990. The American neo-Nazi movement today. *The Nation*, July 16–23: 82–107.

———. 2003. *A hundred little Hitlers: The death of a black man, the trial of a white racist, and the rise of the neo-Nazi movement in America*. New York: Henry Holt and Company.

Langman, Lauren. 2005. From virtual public spheres to global justice: A critical theory of internetworked social movements. *Sociological Theory* 23 (1): 42–74.

Langman, Lauren, and Douglas Morris. 2003. Globalization, alienation and identity: A critical approach. Paper read at American Sociological Association, August, Atlanta, Ga.

Lavelle, K., and Joe R. Feagin. 2006. Hurricane Katrina: The race and class debate. *Monthly Review* (July–August). www.monthlyreview.org/0706lavelle.htm (accessed August 28, 2006).

Lawrence, Frederick M. 2003. Enforcing bias-crime laws without bias: Evaluating the disproportionate-enforcement critique. *Law and Contemporary Problems* 66 (3): 49–70.

LeBesco, K. 2003. Online critical ethnography. In *Online social research*, eds. Mark D. Johns, Shing-Ling Sarina Chen, and G. Jon Hall. New York: Peter Lang.

Lederer, Laura, and Richard Delgado, eds. 1995. *The price we pay: The case against racist speech, hate propaganda, and pornography*. New York: Hill and Wang.

Lee, Elissa, and Laura Leets. 2002. Persuasive storytelling by hate groups online: Examining its effects on adolescents. *American Behavioral Scientist* 45 (6): 927–57.

Lee, Heejin, and Jonathan Liebenau. 2000. Time and the Internet at the turn of the millennium. *Time and Society* 9 (1): 43–56.

Lee, Rachel C., and Sau-ling Cynthia Wong, eds. 2003. *Asian America.net: Ethnicity, nationalism and cyberspace*. London and New York: Routledge.

Leets, Laura. 2001. Responses to Internet hate sites: Is speech too free in cyberspace? *Law & Policy* 6 (2): 287–318.

Leggon, Cheryl B. 2006. Gender, race/ethnicity and the digital divide. In *Women, gender and technology*, eds. Mary Frank Fox, Deborah G. Johnson, and Sue V. Rosser. Urbana: University of Illinois.

Lenhart, Amanda, Mary Madden, and Paul Hitlin. 2005. *Teens and technology: Youth are leading the transition to a fully wired and mobile nation*. Washington, D.C.: Pew Internet & American Life Project.

Lennie, June. 2002. Care and connection in online groups linking rural and urban women in Australia: Some contradictory effects. *Feminist Media Studies* 2 (3): 289–306.

Lennon, Kathleen, and Margaret Whtiford. 1994. *Knowing the difference: Feminist perspectives in epistemology*. New York: Routledge.

Lessig, Lawrence. 1999. *Code: And other laws of cyberspace*. New York: Basic Books.

Leung, Linda. 2005. *Virtual ethnicity: Race, resistance and the World Wide Web*. Burlington, Vt.: Ashgate Publishing, Ltd.

Levin, Brian. 1999. Hate crimes: Worse by definition. *Journal of Contemporary Criminal Justice* 15 (1): 6–21.

———. 2001. History as a weapon: How extremists deny the Holocaust in North America. *American Behavioral Scientist* 44 (6): 1001–1031.

———. 2002. Cyberhate: A legal and historical analysis of extremists' use of computer networks in America. *American Behavioral Scientist* 45 (6): 958–88.

Levin, Jack, and Jack McDevitt. 1993. *Hate crimes: The rising tide of bigotry and bloodshed*. New York: Plenum Press.

Levin, Jack, and Gordana Rabrenovic. 2004. *Why we hate*. Amherst, N.Y.: Prometheus Books.

Levitas, Daniel. 2002. *The terrorist next door: The militia movement and the radical right*. New York: Thomas Dunne Books/St. Martin's Press.

Lewis, Michael, and Jacqueline Serbu. 1999. Kommemorating the Ku Klux Klan. *Sociological Quarterly* 40 (1): 139–57.

Li, Qing. 2005. Gender and CMC: A review on conflict and harassment. *Australasian Journal of Educational Technology* 21 (3): 382–406.

Liestøl, Gunnar, Andrew Morrison, and Terje Rasmussen, eds. 2003. *Digital media revisited: Theoretical and conceptual innovation in digital domains*. Cambridge, Mass.: MIT Press.

Lievrouw, Leah A. 2004. What's changed about new media? Introduction to the fifth anniversary issue of *New Media and Society*. *New Media and Society* 6 (1): 9–15.

Lipsitz, George. 1998. *The possessive investment in whiteness: How white people profit from identity politics*. Philadelphia: Temple University Press.

Livingstone, Sonia. 2004a. Media literacy and the challenge of new information and communication technologies. *The Communication Review* 7 (1): 2–14.

———. 2004b. The challenge of changing audiences: Or, what is the audience researcher to do in the age of the Internet? *European Journal of Communication* 19 (1): 75–86.

Lohan, Maria, and Wendy Faulkner. 2004. Masculinities and technologies: Some introductory remarks. *Men and Masculinities* 6 (4): 319–29.

Lovink, Geert. 2005. Talking race and cyberspace: An interview with Lisa Nakamura. *Frontiers* 26 (1): 60–65.

Lubman, Sarah. 1998. Good grades are just part of the story for Asians at UC. *San Jose Mercury News*, February 21, 1998. http://modelminority.com/modules .php?name=News&file=article&sid=89.

Luke, Carmen. 2000. Cyber-schooling and technology change: Multiliteracies for new times. In *Multiliteracies:Literacy, learning and the design of social futures*, eds. Bill Cope and Marey Kalantzis. South Yarra, Victoria, Australia: Macmillan.

Luke, Timothy. 2003. Cybercritique: A social theory of online agency and virtual structures. *Current Perspectives in Social Theory* 22: 133–59.

Lunenfeld, Peter. 2004. Media design: New and improved without the new. *New Media and Society* 6 (1): 65–70.

Lynch, Michael. 1998. The Discursive Production of Uncertainty: the OJ Simpson "Dream Team" and the Sociology of Knowledge Machine. *Social Studies of Science* 28 (5–6): 829–68.

Macek, Steve. 2006. Divergent critical approaches to new media. *New Media and Society* 8 (6): 1031–1038.

Machado Case Materials. 2007. ComputingCases.org, July 17, 2007. http://computing cases.org/case_materials/machado/machado_case_intro.html (accessed August 26, 2007).

MacKinnon, Catherine. 1993. *Only words*. Cambridge, Mass.: Harvard University Press.

Mansell, Robin. 2004. Political economy, power and new media. *New Media and Society* 6 (1): 96–105.

Marcus, Brian. 2000. *Hacking and hate: Virtual attacks with real consequences.* Boston, Mass.: HateWatch.org.

———. 2006. INACH: A model for international cooperation in the fight against cyber hate. Speech delivered to the October 9 Implementation Meeting of the Organization for Security and Cooperation in Europe (OSCE), Human Dimension Implementation Meeting, Warsaw, Poland. Posted October 11, 2006. http://adl .org/main_internet/INACH_1.htm.

Marcus, Laurence. 1996. *Fighting words: The politics of hateful speech.* Westport, Conn.: Praeger Publishers.

Markham, Annette. 1998. *Life online: Researching real experience in virtual space.* Walnut Creek, Calif.: AltaMira Press.

Marks, Kathy. 1996. *Faces of right-wing extremism.* Boston: Branden Pub. Co.

Martinez-Torres, Maria Elena. 2001. Civil society, the Internet and the Zapatistas. *Peace Review: A Journal of Social Justice* 13 (3): 347–55.

Marton, Christine. 2000. Evaluating the Women's Health Matters website. *CyberPsychology & Behavior* 3 (5): 747–60.

Marx, Karl. 1845. Thesis on Feuerbach:13. Pp.171–74 in *Karl Marx Selected Writings*, 2nd ed., David McLellan (ed.). New York: Oxford University Press (2002).

Maschke, Karen J. 1997. *Pornography, sex work and hate speech*. New York: Garland Publishing.

Matthews, Glenna. 2003. *Silicon valley, women, and the California dream: Gender, class, and opportunity in the twentieth century*. Stanford: Stanford University Press.

Matsuda, Mari J., Charles R. Lawrence III, Richard Delgado, and Kimberle Williams Crenshaw, eds. 1993. *Words that wound: Critical race theory, assaultive speech, and the First Amendment*. Boulder, Colo.: Westview Press.

Maxwell, Christopher, and Shelia Royo Maxwell. 1995. Youth participation in hate-motivated crimes: Research and policy implication. Boulder, Colo.: Center for the Study and Prevention of Violence.

Mayer, Robert N. 2007. Winning the war of words: The "front group" label in contemporary consumer politics. *The Journal of American Culture* 30 (1): 96–109.

Mazzarella, Sharon A., ed. 2005. *Girl Wide Web: Girls, the Internet and the negotiation of identity*. New York: Peter Lang Publishing.

McCarthy, John D., and Mayer N. Zald. 1977. Resource mobilization and social movements: A partial theory. *American Journal of Sociology* 82 (6): 1212–41.

McCaughey, Martha, and Michael D. Ayers, eds. 2003. *Cyberactivism: Online activism in theory and practice*. New York: Routledge.

McDevitt, Jack, Jack Levin, and Susan Bennett. 2002. Hate crime offenders: An expanded typology. *Journal of Social Issues* 58 (22): 303–17.

McGerty, Lisa-Jane. 2000. "Nobody lives only in cyberspace": Gendered subjectivities and domestic use of the Internet. *CyberPsychology & Behavior* 3 (5): 895–99.

McMichael, Philip, and David Mhyre. 1991. Global regulation vs. the nation-state: Agro-food systems and the new politics of capital. *Capital and Class* 43 (Spring): 83–106.

McPherson, Tara. 2000. I'll take my stand in Dixie-net: White guys, the South, and cyberspace. In *Race in cyberspace*, eds. Beth Kolko, Lisa Nakamura, and Gilbert Rodman. New York: Routledge.

———, ed. Forthcoming. In *Interactive fictions*, T. McPherson and M. Kinder (eds.). Berkeley: University of California Press.

McVeigh, Rory. 1999. Structural incentives for conservative mobilization: Power devaluation and the rise of the Ku Klux Klan, 1915–1925. *Social Forces* 77 (4): 1461–96.

———. 2004. Structured ignorance and organized racism in the United States. *Social Forces* 82 (3) 895–936.

McVeigh, Rory, Daniel J. Myers, and David Sikkink. 2004. Corn, Klansmen, and Coolidge: Structure and framing in social movements. *Social Forces* 83 (2): 653–90.

Mehta, Michael. 2002. Censoring cyberspace. *Asian Journal of Social Science* 30 (2): 319–38.

Meikle, Graham. 2002. *Future activism: Media activism and the Internet*. New York: Routledge.

Mellstrom, Ulf. 2004. Machines and masculinities: Technology as an integral part of men's life experiences. *Men and Masculinities* 6 (4): 368–82.

Merithew, Charlene. 2004. Women of the (Cyber) World: The Case of Mexican Feminist NGOs. *Journal of Interdisciplinary Gender Studies: JIGS* Volume 8, Issue 1/2, (June): 87–102. Available at <http://search.informit.com.au/document Summary;dn=929268635526589;res=IELHSS> (accessed June 9, 2007).

Mernissi, Fatima. 2005. The satellite, the prince and Scheherazade: Women as communicators in digital Islam. In *On shifting Ground: Muslim women in the global era*, ed. Fereshteh Nouraie-Simone. New York: The Feminist Press.

Metzger, Miriam J., and Andrew J. Flanagin, eds. 2007. *Digital media, youth, and credibility*. The John D. and Catherine T. MacArthur Foundation series on digital media and learning. Cambridge, Mass.: MIT Press.

Metzger, Miriam J., Andrew J. Flanagin, K. Eyal, D. R. Lemus, and R. M. McCann. 2003. Credibility for the 21st century: Integrating perspectives on source, message, and media credibility in the contemporary media environment. *Communication Yearbook* 27: 293–336.

Michael, George. 2006. *The enemy of my enemy: The alarming convergence of militant Islam and the extreme right*. Lawrence, Kans.: University Press of Kansas.

Mills, C. Wright. 1958. *The causes of World War Three*. New York: Simon & Schuster.

Mills, Charles W. 1997. *The racial contract*. Ithaca, N.Y.: Cornell University Press.

———. 1959. *The Sociological Imagination*. New York: Oxford University Press.

Mitchell, William J. 1992. *The reconfigured eye: Visual truth in the post-photographic era*. Cambridge, Mass.: MIT Press.

Mock, Karen. 2000. Hate on the Internet. In *Human rights and the Internet*, eds. Steven Hicks, Edward F. Halpin, and Eric Hoskins. New York: Palgrave Macmillan.

Morahan-Martin, Janet. 2000. Women and the Internet: Promises and perils. *CyberPsychology & Behavior* 3 (5): 683–91.

Moss, Donald. 2002. Internalized homophobia in men: Wanting in the singular, hating in the first person plural. *Psychoanalytic Quarterly* 71 (1): 21–50.

———, ed. 2003. *Hating in the first person plural: Psychoanalytic essays on racism, homophobia, misogyny and terror*. New York: Other Press.

Mossberger, Karen, Caroline J. Tolbert, and Mary Stansbury. 2003. *Virtual inequality: Beyond the digital divide*. American Governance and Public Policy series. Washington, D.C.: Georgetown University Press.

Mowery, David C., and Timothy Simcoe. 2002. Is the Internet a U.S. invention? An economic and technological history of computer networking. *Research Policy* 31 (8–9) (December): 1369–87.

Mullings, Leith, and Amy J. Schulz, eds. 2006. *Gender, race, class and health: Intersectional approaches*. San Francisco, Calif.: Josey-Bass.

Mulveen, Ruaidhri, and Julie Hepworth. 2006. An interpretative phenomenological analysis of participation in a pro-anorexia Internet site and its relationship with disordered eating. *Journal of Health Psychology* 11 (2): 283–96.

Na, Misu. 2001. The home computer in Korea: Gender, technology and the family. *Feminist Media Studies* 1 (3): 291–306.

Nakamura, Lisa. 2002. *Cybertypes: Race, ethnicity, and identity on the Internet*. New York: Routledge.

Nielsen, Jakob. 2006. Participation inequality: Encouraging more users to contribute. UseIt.com, October 6, at useit.com/alertbox/participation_inequality.html (accessed June 18, 2007).

Nip, Joyce Y. M. 2004a. The Queer Sisters and its electronic bulletin board: A study of the Internet for social movement mobilization. In *Cyberprotest: New media, citizens and social movements*, eds. Wim van de Donk, Brian D. Loader, Paul G. Nixon, and Dieter Rucht. London and New York: Routledge.

———. 2004b. The relationship between online and offline communities: The case of the Queer Sisters. *Media, Culture & Society* 26 (3): 409–28.

Nissenbaum, Helen. 2004. Hackers and the ontology of contested cyberspace. *New Media and Society* 6 (2): 195–217.

Nonnecke, Blair, and Jenny Preece. 2000. Lurker demographics: Counting the silent. Paper read at Proceedings of the Conference on Human Factors 2000, The Hague.

Norman, Al. 2004. *The case against Wal-Mart*. New York: Raphael Publishing.

Norris, Pippa. 2001. *Digital divide: Civic engagement, information poverty, and the Internet worldwide*. Cambridge, UK: Cambridge University Press.

Nouraie-Simone, Fereshteh. 2005a. Wings of freedom: Iranian women, identity and cyberspace. In *On shifting ground: Muslim women in the global era*, ed. Fereshteh Nouraie-Simone. New York: The Feminist Press.

———, ed. 2005b. *On shifting ground: Muslim women in the global era*. New York: The Feminist Press.

O'Brien, Jodi. 1999. Writing in the body: Gender (re)production in online interaction. In *Communities in cyberspace*, eds. Marc Smith and Peter Kollock. New York: Routledge.

O'Hara, Kieron. 2002. The Internet: A tool for democratic pluralism? *Science as Culture* 11 (2): 287–98.

Olesen, Thomas. 2004. Globalizing the Zapatistas: From Third World solidarity to global solidarity? *Third World Quarterly* 25 (1): 255–67.

———. 2005. Transnational publics: New spaces of social movement activism and the problem of global long-sightedness. *Current Sociology* 53 (3): 419–40.

Olin, Spencer C. 1991. Globalization and the politics of locality: Orange County, California, in the Cold War era. *The Western Historical Quarterly* 22 (2): 143–61.

Ono, Hiroshi, and Madeline Zavodny. 2003. Gender and the Internet. *Social Science Quarterly* 84 (1): 111–21.

O'Neill, Edward T., Brian F. Lavoie, and Rick Bennett. 2003. Trends in the evolution of the public Web, 1998–2002. *D-Lib Magazine* 9 (4). http://dlib.org/dlib/april03/lavoie/04lavoie.html.

O'Neill, Edward T., Patrick D. McClain, and Brian F. Lavoie. A methodology for sampling the World Wide Web. *Journal of Library Administration* 34 (3–4): 279–91.

O'Reilly, Tim. 2005. What is Web 2.0? Design patterns and business models for the next generation of software. *O'Reilly*, September 30, 2005. http://oreillynet.com/

pub/a/oreilly/tim/news/2005/09/30/what-is-web-20.html?page=1 (accessed November 1, 2006).

Orgad, Shani. 2005. The transformative potential of online communication: The case of breast cancer patients' Internet spaces. *Feminist Media Studies* 5 (2): 141–61.

Paap, Kris, and Douglas Raybeck. 2005. A differently gendered landscape. *Electronic Journal of Sociology.*

Pan, Bing, Helene Hembrooke, Thorsten Joachims, Lori Lorigo, Geri Gay, and Laura Granka. 2007. In Google we trust: Users' decisions on rank, position and relevance. *Journal of Computer-Mediated Communication* 12 (3): 801–23.

Park, Edward J. W. 1999. Racial ideology and hiring decisions in Silicon Valley. *Qualitative Sociology* 22 (3): 223–33.

Park, Han Woo. 2003. Hyperlink network analysis: A new method for the study of social structure on the Web. *Connections* 25 (1): 49–61.

Park, Han Woo, and Mike Thelwall. 2003. Hyperlink analyses of the World Wide Web: A review. *Journal of Computer-Mediated Communication* 8 (4).

Patchin, Justin W., and Sameer Hinduja. 2006. Bullies move beyond the schoolyard: A preliminary look at cyberbullying. *Youth Violence and Juvenile Justice* 4 (2): 148–69.

Patel, Rajeev, and Philip McMichael. 2004. Third Worldism and the lineages of global facism: The regrouping of the global south in the neoliberal era. *Third World Quarterly* 25 (1): 231–54.

Perera, Suvendrini. 2006. Race terror, Sydney, December 2005. *borderlands e-journal* 5 (1). http://borderlands.net.au/vol5no1_2006/perera_raceterror.htm (accessed April 18, 2008).

Perry, Barbara. 2002. Defending the color lLine: Racially and ethnically motivated hate crime. *American Behavioral Scientist* 46 (1): 72–92.

Picca, Leslie and Joe R. Feagin. 2007. *Two-Faced Racism*: Whites in the Backstage and Frontstage. New York: Routledge.

Pini, Barbara, Kerry Brown, and Josephine Previte. 2004. Politics and identity in cyberspace: A case study of Australian women in agriculture online. In *Cyberprotest: New media, citizens and social movements*, eds. Wim van de Donk, Brian D. Loader, Paul G. Nixon, and Dieter Rucht. London and New York: Routledge.

Piper, Paul S. 2000. Better read that again: Web hoaxes and misinformation. *Searcher* 8 (8). http://infotoday.com/searcher/sep00/piper.htm.

Pitti, Stephen J. 2003. *The devil in Silicon Valley: Northern California, race, and Mexican Americans.* Princeton: Princeton University Press.

Pitts, Victoria. 2004. Illness and Internet empowerment: Writing and reading breast cancer in cyberspace. *Health: An Interdisciplinary Journal for the Social Study of Health, Illness and Medicine* 8 (1): 53–54.

Pizarro, M. 1988. Chicana/o power! Epistemology and methodology for social justice and empowerment in Chicana/o communities. *Qualitative Studies in Education* 11 (1): 57–80.

Polletta, Francesca, and James Jasper. 2001. Collective identity and social movements. *Annual Review of Sociology* 27 (August): 283–305.

Prensky, Marc. 2001. Digital natives, digital immigrants. *On the Horizon*, NCB University Press 9 (5) (October). http://pre2005.flexiblelearning.net.au/projects/resources/Digital_Natives_Digital_Immigrants.pdf.

Purewal, Navtej. 2004. Sex Selection and Feminist "Internet-works." *Journal of Interdisciplinary Gender Studies: JIGS* 8 (1/2): 103–19. Available at <http://search.informit.com.au/documentSummary;dn=929287268497847;res=IELHSS> (accessed June 9, 2007).

Quinby, Lee. 1999. Virile-reality: From Armageddon to Viagra. *Signs* 24 (4): 1079–87.

Quinn, B. 2000. *How Wal-Mart is destroying the world and what you can do about it.* San Francisco: Ten Speed Press.

Rainie, Lee, and Peter Bell. 2004. The numbers that count. *New Media and Society* 6 (1): 44–54.

Rajagopal, Indhu. 2002. Digital representation: Racism on the World Wide Web. With Nis Bojin. *First Monday* 7 (10). http://firstmonday.org/htbin/cgiwrap/bin/ojs/index.php/fm/article/view/995/916 (accessed November 10, 2002).

Ramasastry, Anita. 2003. Can Europe block racist websites from its borders? *Writ*, February 5, 2003. http://writ.news.findlaw.com/ramasastry/20030205.html (accessed June 10, 2005).

Rebecca Fairley. 1998. Man in hate-mail case given probation and fine. *New York Times*, Technology, Cybercrimes, May 8.

Rasmussen, Terje. 2003. On distributed society: The Internet as a guide to a sociological understanding of communication. In *Digital media revisited*, eds. Gunnar Liestøl, Andrew Morrison, and Terje Rasmussen. Cambridge, Mass.: MIT Press.

Ray, Beverly. 2006. November. Online forum sponsored by MacArthur Foundation.

Ray, Beverly, and George E. Marsh. 2001. Recruitment by extremist groups on the Internet. *First Monday* 6 (2), February 5, 2001. http://firstmonday.org/htbin/cgiwrap/bin/ojs/index.php/fm/article/view/834/743 (accessed June 18, 2007).

Resnick, Michael. 2002. Rethinking learning in the digital age. In *The global information technology report: Readiness for the networked world*, ed. Geoffrey Kirkham. Oxford, UK: Oxford University Press.

Reuters. 2008. German police raid homes in far-right Internet probe. February 28, 2008. http://reuters.com/article/rbssConsumerGoodsAndRetailNews/idUSL2817646220080228.

Rheingold, Howard. 1993. *The virtual community: Homesteading on the electronic frontier.* Reading, Penn..: Addison-Wesley.

———. 2002. *Smart mobs: The next social revolution.* New York: Perseus Book Group.

———. 2003. From the screen to the streets. *In These Times* 27(26), October 28, 2003. http://inthesetimes.com/article/641/from_the_screen_to_the_streets/.

———. 2006. Keynote speech. Paper read at NMC Online Conference, October 24–25, 2006, http://archive.nmc.org/events/2006fall_online_conf/.

Ribak, Rivka. 2001. "Like immigrants": Negotiating power in the face of the home computer. *New Media and Society* 3 (2): 220–38.

Rich, Frank. 2006. *The greatest story ever sold: The decline and fall of truth from 9/11 to Katrina.* New York: Penguin.

Richardson, Harry W., and Peter Gordon. 2005a. Globalization and Los Angeles. In *Globalization and urban development.* Berlin: Springer.

———. 2005b. *Globalization and urban development.* Berlin: Springer.

Richardson, Tim. 2005. AOL subscribers go AWOL: 2.3m disappear in a year. *The Register*, May 5, 2005. http://www.theregister.co.uk/2005/05/05/aol_q1_2005_earnings/.

Ridley, Matt. 1997. *The origins of virtue.* New York: Viking Press.

Roberts, Donald F., Ulla G. Foehr, and Victoria Rideout. 2005. Generation M: Media in the lives of 8–18 year-olds. In *A Kaiser Family Foundation study.* Menlo Park, Calif.: Kaiser Family Foundation.

Robins, Kevin, and Frank Webster. 2002. Prospects of virtual culture. *Science as Culture* 11 (2): 235–56.

Robison, Kristopher Kyle, and Edward M. Crenshaw. 2002. Post-industrial transformations and cyber-space: A cross-national analysis of Internet development. *Social Science Research* 21:334–63.

Rogers, Everett M. 1995. *Diffusion of innovations.* 4th ed. New York: The Free Press.

Rogers, Richard. 2002. Operating issue networks on the Web. *Science as Culture* 11: 192–213.

Ronkin, Maggie, and Helen E. Karn. 1999. Mock Ebonics: Linguistic racism in parodies of Ebonics on the Internet. *Journal of Sociolinguistics* 3 (3): 360–80.

Rosenberg, David. 2000. Combating extremism in cyberspace: The legal issues affecting Internet hate speech. New York: Anti-Defamation League.

Ross. Loretta. 1995. *White supremacy in the 1990s.* Political Research Associates http://publiceye.org/eyes/whitsup.html.

Rosser, Sue V. 2005. Through the lenses of feminist theory: Focus on women and information technology. *Frontiers* 26 (1): 1–23.

———. 2006. Using the lenses of feminist theories to focus on women and technology. In *Women, gender and technology*, eds. Mary Frank Fox, Deborah G. Johnson, and Sue V. Rosser. Urbana: University of Illinois.

Rossler, P. 2002. Content analysis in online communication: A challenge for traditional methodology. In *Online social sciences*, eds. Bernard Batinic, Ulf-Dietrich Reips, and Michael Bosnjak. Seattle: Hogrefe & Huber.

Roth, Lorna. 2000. Reflections on the colour of the Internet. In *Human rights and the Internet*, eds. Steven Hick, Edward F. Halpin, and Eric Hoskins. New York: Palgrave Macmillan.

Rothkopf, David. 1997. Globalization: The debate—In praise of cultural imperialism? *Foreign Policy* (Summer): 38–53.

Rothman, Barbara Katz. 2006. Genetic technology and women. In *Women, gender and technology*, eds. Mary Frank Fox, Deborah G. Johnson, and Sue V. Rosser. Urbana: University of Illinois.

Royal, Cindy. 2003. Representations of race and sexuality on feminist Web sites. Paper presented at the annual meeting of the International Communications Association, San Diego, Calif.

———. 2005. Gendered spaces and digital discourse: Framing women's relationship with the Internet. PhD diss., University of Texas, Austin.

Ryan, Nick. 2004. *Into a world of hate: A journey among the extreme right.* New York: Routledge.

Salazar, Juan Francisco. 2003. Articulating an activist imaginary: Internet as counter public sphere in the Mapuche movement, 1997/2002. *Media International Australia Incorporating Culture and Policy* 2003 (107): 19–30.

Salen, Katie, and Eric Zimmerman. 2004. *Rules of play: Game design fundamentals.* Boston, Mass.: MIT Press.

Sandoval, Chela. 2000. New sciences: Cyborg feminism and the methodology of the oppressed. In *The cybercultures reader*, eds. David Bell and Barbara M. Kennedy. London and New York: Routledge.

Sassen, Saskia. 1996. *Losing control? Sovereignty in an age of globalization.* New York: Columbia University Press.

———. 1998. *Globalization and its discontents: Essays on the new mobility of people and money.* New York: The New Press.

———. 2001. *The global city: New York, London, Tokyo.* 2nd ed. Princeton, N.J.: Princeton University Press.

———. 2002. Towards a sociology of information technology. *Current Sociology* 50 (3): 365–88.

Savelsberg, Joachim J., and Ryan D. King. 2005. Institutionalizing collective memories of hate: Law and law enforcement in Germany and the United States. *American Journal of Sociology* 111 (2): 579–616.

Savicki, Victor, and Merle Kelley. 2000. Computer mediated communication: Gender and group composition. *CyberPsychology & Behavior* 3 (5): 817–26.

Schafer, Joseph A. 2002. Spinning the web of hate: Web-based hate propagation by extremist organizations. *Journal of Criminal Justice and Popular Culture* 9 (2): 69–88.

Scheurich, J. J., and M. D. Young. 1997. Coloring epistemologies: Are our research epistemologies racially biased? *Educational Researcher* 26 (4): 4–16.

Schiller, Herbert I. 1989. *Culture, Inc.: The corporate takeover of public expression.* New York: Oxford University Press.

Schneider, Steven M., and Kirsten A. Foot. 2004. The Web as an object of study. *New Media and Society* 6 (1): 114–22.

Schroer, Todd J. 1998. White nationalists' media-constructed rituals. In *American ritual tapestry*, ed. Mary Jo Deegan. Westport, Conn.: Greenwood.

Scott-Dixon, Krista. 2004. *Doing IT: Women working in information technology.* Toronto: Sumach Press.

———. 2005. From digital binary to analog continuum: Measuring gendered IT labor: Notes toward multidimensional methodologies. *Frontiers* 26 (1): 24–42.

Sharpe, Christina Elizabeth. 1999. Racialized fantasies on the Internet. *Signs* 24 (4): 1089–96.

Shenk, David. 1997. *Data smog: Surviving the information glut.* New York: HarperEdge.

Sherman, Chris, and Gary Price. 2001. *The invisible Web: Uncovering information sources search engines can't see.* Toronto: CyberAge Books.

Sherman, Richard C., Christian End, Egon Kraan, Alison Cole, Jamonn Campbell, Zachary Birchmeier, and Jaime Klausner. 2000. The Internet gender gap among college students: Forgotten but not gone? *CyberPsychology & Behavior* 3 (5): 885–94.

Shih, Johanna. 2006. Circumventing discrimination: Gender and ethnic strategies in Silicon Valley. *Gender & Society* 20 (2): 177–206.

Siegel, Michael L. 1999. Comment: Hate speech, civil rights, and the Internet: The jurisdictional and human rights nightmare. 9 *Alb. L.J. Sci. & Tech.* 375.

Silver, David. 2004. Internet/cyberculture/digital culture/new media/fill-in-the-blank studies. *New Media and Society* 6 (1): 55–64.

Sinclair, Carla. 1996. *Net chick: A smart-girl guide to the wired world.* New York: Henry Holt and Company.

Singel, Ryan, and Kevin Poulsen. 2006. Your own personal Internet. Wired.com, June 29, 2006. http://blog.wired.com/27bstroke6/2006/06/your_own_person.html (accessed August 24, 2006).

Singh, Supriya. 2003. Gender and the use of the Internet at home. *New Media and Society* 3 (4): 395–416.

Skinner, David, and Paul Rosen. 2001. Opening the white box: The politics of racialised science and technology. *Science as Culture* 10 (3): 285–300.

Skitka, Linda J., and Edward G. Sargis. 2006. Social psychological research and the Internet: The promise and peril of a new methodological frontier. In *The social net: Human behavior in cyberspace* ed. Yair Amichai-Hamburger. New York: Oxford University Press.

Slater, Don. 2002. Social relationships and identity on/off-line. In *Handbook of new media: Social shaping and consequences of ICTs*, eds. Leah A. Lievrouw and S. Livingstone. London: Sage.

Smith, Catherine E. 2002. Intentional infliction of emotional distress: An old arrow targets the new head of the hate hydra. *Denver University Law Review* 80 (Denv. U. L. Rev. 1).

Smith, John R., and Shih-Fu Chang. 1997. Visually searching the Web for content. *IEEE Multimedia* 4 (3): 12–20.

Smith, Marc, and Peter Kollock, eds. 1999. *Communities in cyberspace.* New York: Routledge.

Snow, David A., Louis A. Zurcher, and Sheldon Ekland-Olson. 1980. Social networks and social movements: A microstructural approach to differential recruitment. *American Sociological Review* 45:787–801.

Snowden, Frank M. 1983. *Before color prejudice: The ancient view of blacks.* Cambridge, Mass.: Harvard University Press.

Sobel, David, ed. 2001. *Filters and freedom 2.0: Free speech perspectives on Internet content controls/Electronic Privacy Information Center*. Washington, D.C.: The Center.

Sofaer, Abraham, and Seymour E. Goodman, eds. 2001. *Transnational dimension of cyber crime and terrorism*. United States: Hoover Press.

Soley, Lawrence C., and John C. Nichols. 1986. *Clandestine radio broadcasting: A study of revolutionary and counterrevolutionary electronic communication*. Englewood Cliffs, N.J.: Praeger Press.

Southern Poverty Law Center. 1998. The year in hate. *Intelligence Report*. http://splcenter.org/intel/intelreport/article.jsp?aid=356.

———. 2002. "Patriot" free fall. *Intelligence Report* (Summer). http://splcenter.org/intel/intelreport/article.jsp?aid=90.

———. 2008. The year in hate. *Intelligence Report* (129). http://splcenter.org/intel/intelreport/intrep.jsp?iid=44 (accessed April 18, 2008).

Sowell, Thomas. 1984. *Civil rights: Rhetoric or reality?* New York: Morrow.

Spender, Dale. 1995. *Nattering on the Net: Women, power and cyberspace*. Melbourne: Spinifex Press.

Sperling, Valerie, Myra Marx Ferree, and Barbara Risman. 2001. Constructing global feminism: Transnational advocacy networks and Russian women's activism. *Signs* 26 (4): 1155–86.

Spiegel Online. 2007. EU agrees on watered-down anti-racism law. April 20, 2007. http://spiegel.de/international/europe/0,1518,478526,00.html.

Spilker, Hendrik, and Knut H. Sorensen. 2000. A ROM of one's own or a home for sharing? Designing the inclusion of women in multimedia. *New Media and Society* 2 (3): 268–85.

Spotts, Greg. 2005. *Wal-Mart: The high price of low cost*. New York: The Disinformation Company.

Starr, Sandy. 2004. Understanding Hate Speech. In *The media freedom internet cookbook*, pp. 125–41. Amsterdam: OSCE. <http://www.osce.org/item/13570.html> (accessed June 28, 2006).

Statzel, R. Sophie. 2006. The Apartheid Conscience: Gender, race and re-magining the white nation in cyberspace. *Ethnic Studies Review* 29(2): 20–45.

Stauber, John C., and Sheldon Rampton. 1995. *Toxic sludge is good for you: Lies, damn lies and the public relations industry*. Monroe, Maine: Common Courage Press.

Steinberg, Annie, Jane Brooks, and Tariq Remtulla. 2003. Youth hate crimes: Identification, prevention, and intervention. *American Journal of Psychiatry* 160 (5): 979–89.

Stern, Kenneth S. 1996. *A force upon the plain: The American militia movement and the politics of hate*. New York: Simon & Schuster.

———. 2002. *Hate and the Internet*. Report. New York: American Jewish Committee. www.ajc.org/atf/cf/%7B42D75369-D582-4380-8395-D25925B85EAF%7D/Hate_and_%20the%20Internet.pdf (accessed February 8, 2009).

Stoecker, Randy. 2002. Cyberspace vs. face-to-face: Community organizing in the new millennium. *Perspectives on Global Development and Technology* 1:143–64.

Sudbury, Julia, and Julia Chinyere Oparah, eds. 2005. *Global lockdown: Race, gender and the prison-industrial complex.* London and New York: Routledge.

Sunden, Jenny. 2001. What happened to difference in cyberspace? The (re)turn of the she-cyborg. *Feminist Media Studies* 1 (2): 216–32.

Sunstein, Cass R. 2001. *Republic.com.* Princeton, N.J.: Princeton University Press.

Sutton, Jo, and Scarlet Pollock. 2000. Online activism for women's rights. *Cyber Psychology & Behavior* 3 (5): 699–706.

Swain, Carol M. 2002. *The new white nationalism in America: Its challenge to integration.* New York: Cambridge University Press.

Szalai, George. 2005. Jonathan Miller, AOL. *THR.com,* June 21, 2005. http://www.hollywoodreporter.com/hr/search/article_display.jsp?vnu_content_id=1000965503.

Taft, Jessica K. 2006. "I'm not a politics person": Teenage girls, oppositional consciousness, and the meaning of politics. *Politics and Gender* 2 (3): 329–52.

Tal, Kalí. 1996. The unbearable whiteness of being: African American critical theory and cyberculture. *Wired,* October 1996. http://gse.buffalo.edu/FAS/Bromley/classes/socprac/readings/Kali-Tal-unbearable.htm (accessed January 19, 1998).

———. 2001. Lisa Nakamura, *Cybertypes*: Race, ethnicity, and identity on the Internet (New York: Routledge) 2002. *Kali Tal*, at kalital.com/Text/Reviews/Nakamura.html.

Tateo, Luca. 2005. The Italian extreme right on-line network: An exploratory study using an integrated social network analysis and content analysis approach. *Journal of Computer-Mediated Communication* 10 (2), January 2005. http://jcmc.indiana.edu/vol10/issue2/tateo.html (accessed June 28, 2006).

Thiel, Shayla. 2004. Shifting identities, creating new paradigms: Analyzing the narratives of women online journalists. *Feminist Media Studies* 4 (1): 21–36.

Thiesmeyer, Lynn. 1999. Racism on the Web: Its rhetoric and marketing. *Ethics and Information Technology* 1 (2): 117–25.

Thomas-Lester, Avis. 2007. Neo-Nazi Web site probed in Jena case. *Washington Post,* September 22, A08. http://washingtonpost.com/wp-dyn/content/article/2007/09/22/AR2007092200105.html (accessed September 23, 2007).

Thompson, Denise. 2000. Pure tolerance revisited. *Feminist Theory* 1 (3): 371–74.

Thompson, Margaret E., Katerina Anfossi Gomez, and Maria Suarez Toro. 2005. Women's alternative Internet radio and feminist interactive communications: Internet audience perceptions of Feminist International Radio Endeavour (FIRE). *Feminist Media Studies* 5 (2): 215–36.

Tierney, John. 1997. What technology is doing to us: It's making us faster. Richer. Smarter. Also alienated. Materialistic. And a little crazy. *New York Times Magazine,* September 28.

Tillberg, Heather K., and J. McGrath Cohoon. 2005. Attracting women to the CS major. *Frontiers* 26 (1): 126–40.

Traub, James. 2007. Does Abe Foxman have an anti-anti-Semite problem? *New York Times Magazine*, January 14, 2007. http://www.nytimes.com/2007/01/14/magazine/14foxman.t.html?partner=rssnyt&emc=rss.

Tsesis, Alexander. 2002. *Destructive messages: How hate speech paves the way for harmful social movements.* New York: NYU Press.

Tsikalas, Kallen E. 2004. Differential effects of home computing on the academic engagement of low- and high-performing middle-school students in low-income communities. Paper read at the annual meeting of the American Educational Research Association, April 12–16, San Diego, Calif.

Turkle, Sherry. 1997. *Life on the screen: Identity in the age of the Internet.* New York: Simon & Schuster.

Turner, Wallace. 1986. Extremist finds cable TV is forum for right-wing views. *The New York Times*, National Desk, October 7, Tuesday, Late City Final Edition, Section A, Page 23.

Turpin-Petrosino, Carolyn. 2002. Hateful sirens: Who hears their song? An examination of student attitudes toward hate groups and affiliation potential. *Journal of Social Issues* 58 (2): 281–301.

Tynes, Brendesha, Lindsay Reynolds, and Patricia M. Greenfield. 2004. Adolescence, race, and ethnicity on the Internet: A comparison of discourse in monitored vs. unmonitored chat rooms. *Applied Developmental Psychology* 25:667–84.

UNDP Regional Centre for Europe and the Commonwealth of Independent States and UNIFEM Central and Eastern Europe. 2004. Bridging the gender digital divide: A report on gender and ICT in Central and Eastern Europe and the Commonwealth of Independent States.

U.S. Census Bureau. 2007. State and county quickfacts, July 11, 2007. http://quickfacts.census.gov/.

U.S. Congress. Senate. Committee on the Judiciary. 1999, 2. *Hate crime on the Internet: Hearing before the Committee on the Judiciary, United States Senate.* 106th Cong., 1st sess., 14 September 1999. Washington, D.C.: GPO. http://purl.access.gpo.gov/GPO/LPS12394.

U.S. Departrment of State. 2008. Contemporary global anti-Semitism report: A report provided to the United States Congress. http://state.gov/g/drl/rls/102406.htm.

van Dijk, Jan A. G. M. 1999. The one-dimensional network society of Manuel Castells. *New Media and Society* 1 (1): 127–38.

van Dijk, Teun A. 1988. Mediating racism: The role of the media in the reproduction of racism. In *Language, power and ideology: Studies in political discourse*, ed. Ruth Wodak. Philadelphia: John Benjamins Publishing Company.

van Someren, Maarten W., Yvonne F. Barnard, and Jacobijn A. C. Sandberg. 1994. *The think aloud method: A practical guide to modelling cognitive processes.* London: Academic Press.

van Zoonen, Liesbet. 2002. Gendering the Internet: Claims, controversies and cultures. *European Journal of Communication* 17 (1): 5–23.

Verton, Dan. 2003. *Black ice: The invisible threat of cyber-terrorism*. Emeryville, Calif.: McGraw-Hill.

Vise, David A., and Mark Malseed. 2006. *The Google story: Inside the hottest business, media and technology success of our time*. New York: Bantam Dell.

Wajcman, Judy. 2002. Addressing technological change: The challenge to social theory. *Current Sociology* 50 (3): 347–63.

———. 2004. *Technofeminism*. Cambridge: Polity Press.

———. 2006. The feminization of work in the information age. In *Women, gender and technology*, eds. Mary Frank Fox, Deborah G. Johnson, and Sue V. Rosser. Urbana: University of Illinois.

Wakeford, Nina. 2000. New media, new methodologies: Studying the Web. In *Web studies: Rewiring media studies for the digital age*, ed. David Gauntlett. New York: Oxford University Press.

———. 2004. Pushing at the boundaries of new media studies. *New Media and Society* 6 (1): 130–36.

Walker, Samuel. 1994. *Hate speech: The history of an American controversy*. Lincoln: University of Nebraska Press.

Walsh, Peter. 2003. The withered paradigm: The Web, the expert and the information highway. In *Democracy and new media*, eds. Henry Jenkins and David Thorburn. Cambridge, Mass.: MIT Press.

Ware, Vron, and Les Back. 2001. *Out of whiteness: Color, politics, and culture*. Chicago: University of Chicago Press.

Warf, Barney, and John Grimes. 1997. Counterhegemonic discourses and the Internet. *Geographical Review* 87 (2): 259–74.

Warnick, Barbara. 2002. *Critical literacy in a digital era*. New York: Lawrence Erlbaum.

———. 2004. Online ethos: Source credibility in an "authorless" environment. *American Behavioral Scientist* 48 (2): 256–65.

Wasserman, Ira M., and Marie Richmond-Abbott. 2005. Gender and the Internet: Causes of variation in access, level, and scope of use. *Social Science Quarterly* 86 (1): 252–70.

Waters, Malcolm. 2001. *Globalization*. 2nd ed. New York: Routledge.

Weare, Christopher, and Wan-Ying Lin. 2000. Content analysis of the World Wide Web: Opportunities and challenges. *Social Science Computer Review* 18 (3): 272–93.

Weber, Terry. 2007. Volpe to return some contributions. *The Globe and Mail*, January 6, 2007. http://theglobeandmail.com (accessed July 28, 2007).

Weimann, Gabriel. 1986. *Hate on trial: The Zundel affair*. Oakville, ON.: Mosaic Press.

Weitzman, Mark, and Steven Leonard Jacobs. 2003. *Dismantling the big lie: The protocols of the elders of Zion*. Los Angeles: KTAV Publishing House.

Wellman, Barry. 2001. Computer networks as social networks. *Science* 293 (5537): 2031–34.

———. 2004. The three ages of Internet studies: Ten, five and zero years ago. *New Media and Society* 6 (1): 108–14.

Wellman, Barry, and Carolyn Haythornthwaite, eds. 2002. *The Internet in everyday life*. Malden, Mass.: Blackwell.

Wellman, Barry, Janet Salaff, Dimitrina Dimitrova, Laura Garton, and Carolyn Haythornthwaite. 1996. Computer networks as social networks: Collaborative work, telework and virtual community. *Annual Review of Sociology* 22:213–38.

West, Cornell. 1993. *Race matters*. New York: Vintage Books.

Westfall, Joseph. 2000. What is cyberwoman? The second sex in cyberspace. *Ethics and Information Technology* 2 (3): 159–66.

Whillok, Rita, K., and David Slayden, eds. 1995. *Hate speech*. Thousand Oaks, Calif.: Sage Press.

Whine, Michael. 1999. Cyberspace: A new medium for communication, command and control by extremists. *Studies in Conflict and Terrorism* 22 (3): 231–45.

———. 2000. Far right extremists on the Internet. In *Cybercrime: Law enforcement, security and surveillance in the information age*, eds. Douglas Thomas and Brian D. Loader. New York: Routledge.

White, Michele. 2003. Too close to see: Men, women and webcams. *New Media and Society* 5 (1): 7–28.

Whitley, Edgar A. 1997. In cyberspace all they see is your words: A review of the relationship between body, behavior and identity drawn from the sociology of knowledge. *Information Technology & People* 10 (2): 147–63.

Widmer, Rolf, Heidi Oswald-Krapf, Deepali Sinha-Khetriwal, Max Schnellmann, and Heinz Böni. 2005. Global perspectives on e-waste. *Environmental Impact Assessment Review* 25 (5): 436–58.

Wiesenthal Center. 2005. *Digital terrorism and hate*. New York: Simon Wiesenthal Center.

Wilding, Faith. 1998. Where is the Feminism in Cyberfeminism? *n.paradoxa* 1 (2): 6–13.

Williams, Patricia. 1991. *Alchemy of race and rights*. Cambridge, Mass.: Harvard University Press.

Williamson, Larry, and Eric Pierson. 2003. The rhetoric of hate on the Internet: Hateporn's challenge to modern media ethics. *Journal of Mass Media Ethics* 18 (3–4): 250–67.

Wilson, Brian. 2006. Ethnography, the Internet, and youth culture: Strategies for examining social resistance and "online-offline" relationships. *Canadian Journal of Education* 29 (1): 307–28.

Winant, Howard. 2001. *The world is a ghetto: Race and democracy since World War II*. New York: Basic Books.

Winter, Debra and Chuck Huff. 1996. Adapting the Internet: Comments from a women-only electronic forum. *The American Sociologist* 27 (1): 30–54.

Wired News Report. 2005. The right to sell hate. *Wired*, February 11, 2005. http://wired.com/techbiz/media/news/2005/02/66573 (accessed April 12, 2005).

Wiesenthal, Center. 2005. *Digital terrorism and hate*. New York: Simon Wiesenthal Center.

Wise, Tim. 2000. Everyday racism, white liberals & the limits of tolerance. Review of reviewed item. *Race and history*, December 4, 2000. http://raceandhistory.com/historicalviews/18062001.htm (accessed June 18, 2007).

Wodak, Ruth, ed. 1988. *Language, power and ideology: Studies in political discourse*. Philadelphia: John Benjamins Publishing Company.

Wolf, Alecia. 2000. Emotional expression online: Gender differences in emoticon use. *CyberPsychology & Behavior* 3 (5): 827–33.

Worotynec, Z. Sonia. 2000. The good, the bad and the ugly: Listserv as support. *CyberPsychology & Behavior* 3 (5): 797–810.

Wright, Michelle M. 2005. Finding a place in cyberspace: Black women, technology and identity. *Frontiers* 26 (1): 48–59.

Yin, Robert K. 2003. *Case study research design: Design and methods*. 3rd ed. Thousand Oaks, Calif.: Sage.

Young, Robert M. 2002. Sexuality and the Internet. *Science as Culture* 11 (2): 215–33.

Yousman, Bill. 2003. White youth, the consumption of rap music, and white supremacy. *Communication Theory* 13 (4): 366–91.

Zanini, Michele, and Sean J. A. Edwards. 2001. The networking of terror in the information age. In *Networks and netwars: The future of terror, crime and militancy*, eds. J. Arquilla and D. Ronfeldt. Arlington, Va.: Rand Corporation.

Zeller, Tom. 2005. After the storm, the swindlers. *New York Times*, Technology Section, September 8.

Zhou, Yilou, Edna Reid, Jialun Qin, Hsinchun Chen, and Guanpi Lai. 2005. U.S. domestic extremist groups on the Web: Link and content analysis. *Intelligent Systems* 20 (5): 44–51.

Zickmund, Susan. 1997. Approaching the radical other: The discursive culture of cyberhate. In *Virtual culture: Identity and communication in cyberspace*, ed. Steven G. Jones. Thousand Oaks, Calif.: Sage Publishers.

Index

~

About the Author

Jessie Daniels holds an M.A. and Ph.D. in sociology from the University of Texas at Austin. She teaches at Hunter College, at City University of New York. She is the author of *White Lies* (1997), which examines the connections among race, class, gender, and sexuality in white supremacist discourse in print. She is a cofounder (with Joe R. Feagin) and regular contributor to the blog RacismReview.com.

Recognized as a national expert on white racism, Daniels was featured in Elizabeth Thompson's Emmy award-winning documentary *"Blink"* (2000) about Gregory Withrow, a supposedly reformed white supremacist. Daniels was selected as scholar-in-residence at the International Center for Tolerance Education (2005–2006), where she worked on the development of a video competition about tolerance in conjunction with Current TV, which aired as the "Seeds of Tolerance Competition." In 2007, Daniels received partial support for the research in this book from the John D. and Catherine T. MacArthur Foundation.

Currently, Daniels is at work on a number of research projects including a study of feminist bloggers and an exploration of the ways mobile digital technologies shape the lives of lesbian, gay, bisexual, transgender, and queer homeless teens in New York City.